Philosophy of Law and Jurisprudence

By

Mortimer J. Adler
and
Peter Wolff

Preface by

Edward H. Levi, Professor of Law and Dean
The University of Chicago Law School

ENCYCLOPÆDIA BRITANNICA, INC.

Chicago • London • Toronto • Geneva • Sydney

PRINTED IN THE U.S.A.

PREFACE

The readings in philosophy of law and jurisprudence raise questions about, and attempt to secure answers for, problems which are central to the relationship among individuals in an organized society. Many of these relationships, legal in nature, are taken for granted when no unusual strain is placed upon them; yet these relationships, even for the situations of the everyday, may be quite complicated and may involve justifying or explanatory concepts which are most intricate. Important questions are inherent in any situation where the coercive power of the state is brought to bear to confirm a transaction, to settle a dispute, to punish or condemn, or to redistribute the wealth of the community in terms of an evaluation of the worth of men. Extreme situations are useful in revealing these questions and in indicating the difficulty of applying some of the concepts which are often accepted without thought. Two examples—in some sense they are the same example—may serve to illustrate.

The first example is the American case of *United States* v. *Holmes,* decided in 1842. Holmes was a seaman who was indicted for manslaughter upon the high seas. He was a member of the crew of the U.S. ship "William Brown," which left Liverpool on March 13, 1841, bound for Philadelphia. On the night of April 19, the vessel struck an iceberg and sank. The longboat and jolly boat were lowered. The first mate, eight seamen (Holmes among them), and thirty-two passengers got into the longboat. The captain, the second mate, seven of the crew, and one passenger went in the jolly boat. The next morning the two lifeboats parted company. At that time the longboat was leaking. In parting, the captain advised the crew on the longboat to obey all the orders of the first mate. The first mate told the captain that the longboat was unmanageable, and that unless the captain could take some of the longboat's passengers, it would be necessary to cast lots and to throw some people overboard. It was later reported that the captain replied, "I know what you'll have to do. Don't speak of that now. Let it be the last resort." That night the sea grew heavier; waves splashed over the bow. There were pieces of ice floating about. It was thought that if the boat struck ice she would inevitably go down. There was a hole in the boat which had been plugged. The plug apparently came out. The first mate, who had been bailing for some time, stopped bailing and cried out, "This work won't do. Help me, God. Men, go to work." After a while the mate again exclaimed, "Men, you must go to work, or we shall all perish." The mate directed the crew "Not to part man and wife, and not to throw over any woman." No lots were cast. The crew, including Holmes, threw into the water fourteen male passengers and two women. No member of the crew was thrown into the water. The next afternoon the longboat was picked up by the ship "Crescent," and all remaining persons were saved. Holmes was convicted.

The second example is the English case of *The Queen* v. *Dudley and Stephens,* decided in 1884. Three able-bodied English seamen and a seventeen-year-old English boy were in a shipwreck 1,600 miles from the Cape of Good Hope. They were compelled to put out in the open seas in a lifeboat. They had no water and no food except two tins of turnips. On the fourth day they caught a small turtle. This was the only food they had for twenty days. On the eighteenth day, when they had been seven days without food and five without water, two of the seamen (Dudley and Stephens) suggested to the third—who, however, did not agree—that someone should be sacrificed to save the rest. On the nineteenth day, seaman Dudley proposed that lots should be drawn to determine who should be put to death. Finally, on the twentieth day, without drawing lots, Dudley, with the assent of Stephens, went to the boy, told him that his time had come, put a knife into his throat, and killed him. The boy had been lying at the bottom of the boat, quite helpless, extremely weakened by famine and by drinking sea water, and was unable to make any resistance. The three men fed upon the body and blood of the boy for four days. On the fourth day after the act was committed, the three seamen were picked up by a passing vessel. Dudley and Stephens were indicted for murder. The jury found that if the men had not fed upon the body of the boy, they probably would not have survived, and that the boy, being in a much weaker condition, was likely to have died before them. Dudley and Stephens were convicted. Sentence of death was passed upon them, but was later commuted by the Crown to six months' imprisonment.

These two cases raise interesting problems of philosophy of law and jurisprudence. The crimes were committed on the high seas and perhaps were crimes of necessity. Possibly the participants had returned to a state of nature. Holmes, in any event, was a seaman carrying out orders. Surely some killing is against the natural law, but these were acts of self-defense. Possibly sailors who get paid are in a less privileged position than are paying passengers who therefore have the right to be saved. But seamen are needed to navigate the boat. The U.S. court thought that the law of necessity could not justify a supernumerary sailor sacrificing the life of a passenger. It thought also that when possible the selection in such circumstances should be by lot "in some sort, as an appeal to God." The English court, while agreeing that sailors had no right to throw passengers overboard to save themselves, thought that the idea of determining who was to be sacrificed by ballot was "somewhat strange." So far as Dudley and Stephens were concerned, the Lord Chief Justice of England declared: "We are often compelled to set up standards we cannot reach ourselves, and to lay down rules which we could not ourselves satisfy. But a man has no right to declare temptation to be an excuse, though he might himself have yielded to it, nor allow compassion for the criminal to change or weaken in any manner the legal definition of the crime."

In times of stress the hierarchical structure of law is likely to become an issue with an appeal from the positive law to some higher law or with an emphasis on the elements of freedom and discretion in the application or enforcement of law. The nature of this asserted hierarchy both within and outside the formal mechanism of law is in itself a characterization of the nature of law; that is, law may be seen as based upon the nature of man with a consequent right to override positive law when it outrages reason or some moral sense, or law may be seen—as another possibility among many—as rules which must be obeyed by subordinate officials and citizens because the rules were promulgated by higher appropriate governmental authority. Both the Holmes case and Stephens and Dudley involve the question of the extent to which individuals might take the law into their own hands, going against what was perhaps the positive law because of some overriding human need. They involve also the question as to how far judges might go in remaking or in refusing to apply the positive law. On a larger scale, revolutions frequently justify themselves as appeals to some higher law; at the minimum, they characterize the existing order as so unjust as not to be binding. Both sides in such a violent controversy can appeal in different ways to the rule of law.

The complicated institutions of the modern democratic state reflect a continuing dialogue upon the nature of law. Law is not regarded as unchangeable or merely customary. The legislature exists to change the law. But in some way or other conditions are imposed to limit the magnitude or speed of the change. The community itself is frequently involved in a discussion of the wisdom of the laws and participates through elected or appointed legislators, enforcement officials, and judges in the making and interpretations of the laws. The separateness of the institutions of justice and the clarity with which different functions are designated reflect distinctions between legislative and judicial justice.

In times of less stress, in stable periods, it is easier to distinguish the formal or procedural aspects of law from questions of general policy or determinations of fact. The question of a fair hearing for a defendant need not be confused with the question of his guilt. The question of constitutionality—that is, the question of the formal power to promulgate—can be seen as different from the question of the wisdom of the legislation. Law, while it covers a vast array of human activity, is thus seen as distinguishable from the value judgments which it implements. In times of stress, however, the very appeal to higher law is likely to blur these distinctions, and it is of course true that the concepts with which law operates, such as property or individual responsibility, to some degree make law the equivalent of what our society has to say about the nature of man. It is true also that in times of stress the institutions of law may become the guardians of basic values of the society, the means for the expression of the sober second thought of the community.

It hardly needs emphasis that these are times of stress and change which make urgent a renewed understanding of our basic jurisprudence and philosophy of law, and which invite us to consider whether those concepts so powerful and important for domestic tranquillity can be used in some measure to aid in the accomplishment of an international order. These readings bring to us for this task the best of our heritage.

EDWARD H. LEVI

FOREWORD

I

This Reading Plan considers problems in the philosophy of law and in the field of jurisprudence. Like all the reading plans in this series, it is designed to be used independently of the others. Nevertheless, the reader will be well advised to start his exploration of *Great Books of the Western World* with the first Reading Plan, *A General Introduction to the Great Books and to a Liberal Education* before tackling the Reading Plan on law.

How to use the Reading Plan. The Reading Plan contains three major parts: (1) A list of readings; (2) Guides to each of the readings; and (3) Suggestions for additional readings.

1. *The Reading List.* There are fifteen readings. You should take about two weeks for each reading. The length and difficulty of each reading are designed for that period.

2. *The Guides.* These should prove most helpful to the reader of *Great Books of the Western World* who is going it alone, without teacher, discussion leader, or other study aids. The purpose of the guide is to help you get started on an assignment and to make your reading more meaningful to you. Here you will find the highlights of the reading assignment pointed out, often by quotation. Difficult passages are discussed and explained. The structure of the whole book is considered and the individual parts related to it. There is usually some comment on the form and style of the book being studied.

Wherever it is relevant, attention is paid to the background or historical circumstances under which the book was written.

Special problems are presented to you, the critical reader, to think about. These problems are not questions that can be answered by repeating what the text has said. The statement of a problem is followed by a brief discussion which illuminates the problem, indicates some of the possible answers, and emphasizes the importance of the question. Some readers will be satisfied simply to read the problems, and to give them some thought. Others may want to write out answers to them. The questions cannot be answered by a mere "yes" or "no," or "true" or "false." Each problem requires real analysis, and several paragraphs or even an essay may be required for the answer. Since there is no "right" answer to these questions, and since their main purpose is to stimulate some thought about the reading matter, you alone will be able to check and judge your answer.

Each guide concludes with a section entitled SELF-TESTING QUESTIONS. This section gives you an opportunity to check the thoroughness of your reading. Here you will find a series of questions about the reading. The questions are factual; the information asked for is found in the reading. The right answer can, therefore, be simply indicated by reference to a page or pages from the reading assignment. In order to give you an opportunity to check yourself, the correct references are given on pages 238-239.

3. *The Additional Readings.* These give you an opportunity to delve more deeply into the subjects treated in this Reading Plan. We have tried especially to recommend works or parts of works that, in importance and in difficulty, are on a level with those in the Reading Plan, as well as contemporary works that will give you some notion of important current problems in the field of law and how they are being treated.

II

Before starting on the assignments in this Reading Plan, the reader may find it useful to survey the Reading List. The readings represent a considerable variety; this is due to the fact that they are from different kinds of books. Some of the assignments are from the field of literature; this includes the readings from Aeschylus, Shakespeare, and Dostoevsky. Other assignments are predominantly historical in character; this group includes Plutarch, Aristotle's *The Athenian Constitution,* and Montesquieu. The Bible readings and the *American State Papers* can, perhaps, be placed in this group, each being an example of a famous set of laws. The majority of the readings, however, are from the works of writers who consider law philosophically, such as Plato, Aristotle, Aquinas, Hobbes, Rousseau, Kant, and Hegel.

What are some of the questions asked in this Reading Plan? The variety of the problems considered reflects the variety of the books read. In the works of literature, the authors' concern is broad and ranges beyond the mere legal aspects of a situation. Aeschylus, Shakespeare, and Dostoevsky are all concerned with guilt in the largest sense and with the problems of revenge and expiation that follow from a crime. Who is guilty? Are legal guilt and moral guilt the same? Is revenge a proper way of dealing with an unjust act? What sort of punishment cleanses a man's guilt?

The historical writers ask quite different questions. What is the origin of law? Who was responsible for making the first laws? From the evidence of history, should laws be changed? How do laws vary from time to time and from place to place? Does the variety of laws indicate something about the nature of law as such? Are the old laws better than the new laws or vice versa?

The philosophers of law ask typically philosophical questions. They begin, of course, with the most basic problem of all—"What is a law?" From this, other questions follow. Who is entitled to make a law? What are the effects of law on the people for whom it is made? Can a law be changed? Should it be changed?

After these basic considerations, most writers turn to questions such as these: Are there different kinds of law? If so, what are they? Is natural law or divine law the same kind of law as human positive law? Are all laws just? If not, what determines the justice of a law? If there can be unjust laws, are there any remedies to which the just man may have recourse?

This is only a sampling of the questions which the reader will encounter. Other topics are touched on—natural rights and civil rights, laws pertaining to property, the manner in which laws are made, the manner in which laws are applied, and many more. Layman and expert alike will find that in the field of law—as in most other fields—*Great Books of the Western World* offer a wealth of provocative reading.

CONTENTS

A NOTE ON REFERENCE STYLE

In referring to *Great Books of the Western World,* the same style is used as in the *Syntopicon.* Pages are cited by number and section. In books that are printed in single column, "a" and "b" refer to the upper and lower halves of the page. In books that are printed in double column, "a" and "b" refer to the upper and lower halves of the left column, "c" and "d" to the upper and lower halves of the right column. For example, "Vol. 53, p. 210b" refers to the lower half of page 210, since Vol. 53, James's *Principles of Psychology,* is printed in single column. But "Vol. 7, p. 202b" refers to the lower left quarter of page 202, since Vol. 7, Plato's *Dialogues,* is printed in double column.

In Bible references, if there is a difference between the King James and the Douay version, the King James reference is given first, followed by (D) and the Douay reference.

THE READING LIST

1 Aeschylus, *Agamemnon, Choephoroe, Eumenides.* Vol. 5, pp. 52-91.

2 Plato, *Euthyphro.* Vol. 7, pp. 191-199. *Laws,* Selections from Books I and IV, pp. 643c-644a, 683a-686b. (Also, *Apology* and *Crito.*)

3 Aristotle, *Nicomachean Ethics,* Book V. Vol. 9, pp. 376-387.

4 Old Testament, *Exodus,* 19-20; *Deuteronomy,* 5-6.
New Testament, *Matthew,* 15:1-20, 22:15-40; *Romans,* 7-8.

5 Aristotle, *The Athenian Constitution.* Vol. 9, pp. 553-584.
Plutarch, *Lives of the Noble Grecians and Romans,* "Solon." Vol. 14, pp. 64-77.

6 Aquinas, *Summa Theologica,* Part I-II, QQ. 90, 91. Vol. 20, pp. 205-208, 220-226.

7 Aquinas, *Summa Theologica,* Part I-II, QQ. 95-97. Vol. 20, pp. 226-239.

8 Hobbes, *Leviathan,* Ch. 14-15, 26-28. Vol. 23, pp. 86-96, 130-148.

9 Shakespeare, *The Merchant of Venice.* Vol. 26, pp. 406-433.

10 MONTESQUIEU, *The Spirit of Laws,* Books I, XIV-XVII, XXIX. Vol. 38, pp. 1-3, 102-125, 262-269.

11 ROUSSEAU, *A Discourse on Political Economy, The Social Contract,* Book II. Vol. 38, pp. 367-385, 395-406.

12 KANT, *The Science of Right,* Part I. Vol. 42, pp. 403-434.

13 *Articles of Confederation.* Vol. 43, pp. 5-9.
The Constitution of the United States of America. Vol. 43, pp. 11-20.

14 HEGEL, *Philosophy of Right,* Third Part, Subsection II, B (The Administration of Justice). Vol. 46, pp. 69d-75b.

15 DOSTOEVSKY, *The Brothers Karamazov,* Book XII, "A Judicial Error." Vol. 52, pp. 348-401.

AESCHYLUS

Agamemnon

Choephoroe

Eumenides

Vol. 5, pp. 52-91

The fascination of men of all ages with the Trojan War and with the Homeric heroes is apparently inexhaustible. The events of the war and the men who participated in it are familiar to all of us. "Homeric" is an adjective that is still used to designate something grand; and an "odyssey" is a long drawn out journey in quest of something. Nor are these poems and the people that we meet in them the rediscovery of recent ages; they have always been a basic part of the mythology and culture of the Western world.

In Aeschylus' time, there was no subject considered more fit for tragedy than the Trojan War and the men who fought in it. The conflict was supposed to right a wrong—the abduction of Helen by Paris. Primitive justice, in the absence of any legal machinery, could only be served by Menelaus, Helen's husband, and his brother Agamemnon waging war against Paris and the city of Troy.

If the figure of Helen is central to the legal question of right and wrong in the Trojan War, her sister Clytaemnestra, who is Agamemnon's wife, is central to another legal question in these plays.

Who is right? the poet asks, but he is only repeating a question that must have been asked ever since the story of the Trojan War and Agamemnon has been told. Was Agamemnon right, who sacrificed his daughter Iphigenia in order that the Achaean fleet might sail on its errand of vengeance against Troy? Was Clytaemnestra right, who revenged her daughter by killing Agamemnon? Or was Iphigenia's death merely a pretext for Clytaemnestra to excuse the murder of Agamemnon? Was Orestes, the son of Agamemnon and Clytaemnestra, justified in killing his mother to revenge his father?

Passions and moral indignation run high in these plays. Through them all runs the dark curse that haunts Agamemnon and all his forbears and descendants, a curse that makes parents and children die by each other's swords. The goddess Athena finally is able to break the curse. The solution lies in the institution which is the subject of our Reading Plan: law.

GUIDE TO

First Reading

I

The three plays which are included in this reading are often grouped together under the name of the *Oresteia.* They are named after Orestes, the son of Agamemnon, who has the leading part in the last two plays. These three plays were written by Aeschylus, the earliest of the Greek tragedians whose plays have survived. But the story of Agamemnon's death and the revenge which his son Orestes took with the help of his sister Electra fascinated the other tragedians also. Sophocles wrote a play called *Electra,* while from Euripides' hand there survives another *Electra,* as well as an *Orestes.* Euripides also wrote two plays dealing with the fate of Iphigenia, the sister of Orestes and Electra (*Iphigenia at Aulis* and *Iphigenia Among the Tauri*).

Only seven of Aeschylus' plays survive, out of a total of more than ninety. He won prizes for his plays at least twelve times. Aeschylus reached maturity during the golden age of Athens, after the defeat of the Persians and before the Peloponnesian War toppled Athens from her place of power and glory. Aeschylus himself fought at the decisive battle of Marathon in 490 B.C. (and possibly also at other battles against the Persians), as his epitaph attests:

> This memorial stone covers Aeschylus the Athenian,
> Euphorion's son, who died in wheat-bearing Gela.
> His famed valor the precinct of Marathon could tell
> and the long-haired Mede, who knows it well.

Aeschylus died and was buried at Gela in 456.

II

There are many ways of considering these three plays. We could discuss them as literature; or we might be interested in them from the dramatic point of view, since they have been performed on the stage for over two thousand years. Again, a consideration of their content could well lead one to develop a theory of tragedy; perhaps it would be different from Aristotle's (as set forth in the *Poetics*). From still another point of view these plays are instructive concerning Greek mythology and religion.

In this Reading Plan, however, we shall examine Aeschylus' plays in order to discover what they can teach us about the problems of law. Let the reader not forget, however, that the *Oresteia* also has something to say to him in all the other respects we have mentioned.

There is probably no better way of seeing how important law and lawbreaking are in the *Oresteia* than by summarizing the events of the plays, as well as those parts of the legend of the house of Atreus that precede the events dramatized by Aeschylus. As is the case with most legends, there is more than one version. This is partly accounted for by the fact that the story is pieced together from different authors, such as Homer, Pindar, and Ovid. The main events, substantially agreed upon in all versions, are as follows.

The genealogy of the house of Atreus begins with Tantalus. He was a descendant of Zeus and therefore almost a god himself. Tantalus had a son named Pelops. In order to test whether the gods were all-knowing, Tantalus killed Pelops and served his dead son to the gods in a banquet. The gods, however, discovered the horrible deed and restored Pelops to life. Tantalus was condemned to a punishment from which we derive the word "tantalize." He stood in water up to his neck; however, whenever he bent down to drink, the waters receded. Similarly, a branch with fruits dangled before him; but whenever he reached up to pluck a fruit, the wind wafted the fruit away. Among Pelops' sons were Atreus and Thyestes. The two brothers quarreled because Thyestes seduced Atreus' wife. Atreus defeated Thyestes, and drove him out. Thyestes then sent Pleisthenes, Atreus' son whom Thyestes had brought up, to kill Atreus. Instead, however, Atreus killed Pleisthenes, not realizing he was killing his own son. When Atreus found out whom he had killed, he pretended to consent to reconciliation with Thyestes. Thereupon Thyestes came to Atreus' house, and Atreus served a meal containing the flesh of Thyestes' children, all except one of whom (Aegisthus) Atreus had slaughtered. Atreus thus repeated the sin of his grandfather Tantalus. Thyestes unknowingly ate of the flesh of his own children, but when he discovered his deed, he cursed Atreus and his entire house and fled with his surviving son, Aegisthus.

Agamemnon and Menelaus were the sons of Atreus. Agamemnon married Clytaemnestra, and Menelaus, Helen. Agamemmon and Menelaus made war against Troy seeking to revenge the abduction of Helen. In order to obtain favorable winds to sail to Troy, Agamemnon was required to sacrifice his daughter, Iphigenia, to the goddess Artemis. Thus, like Tantalus and Atreus before him, Agamemnon put to death his own flesh and blood. While Agamemnon was away at Troy, Aegisthus seduced Clytaemnestra.

The play *Agamemnon* begins at the point where Agamemnon, unaware of his wife's infidelity, returns victorious from Troy. Citing the death of her daughter Iphigenia as justification, Clytaemnestra traps Agamemnon in his bath. She and Aegisthus kill him.

In the *Choephoroe* we see how Agamemnon's son, Orestes, is urged by the god Apollo to revenge his father. With the help of his sister Electra, Orestes kills his mother Clytaemnestra, as well as her lover Aegisthus.

Immediately Orestes is persecuted by the avenging Furies for his matricide. In the *Eumenides* we read of his escape and how the curse that turned members of the family against one another is finally lifted from the house of Atreus. Seeking refuge from the Furies and to be purified from his sin, Orestes comes to the city of Athens and throws himself under the protection of her guardian goddess, Athena. To decide his fate, Athena convenes the first court in the history of Athens, a group of citizens. The Furies argue for Orestes' death, while Apollo defends Orestes. The jury is unable to come to a decision, since their vote results in a tie. Athena then casts the deciding vote in favor of Orestes, thus freeing him. The Furies,

GENEALOGY OF THE HOUSE OF ATREUS

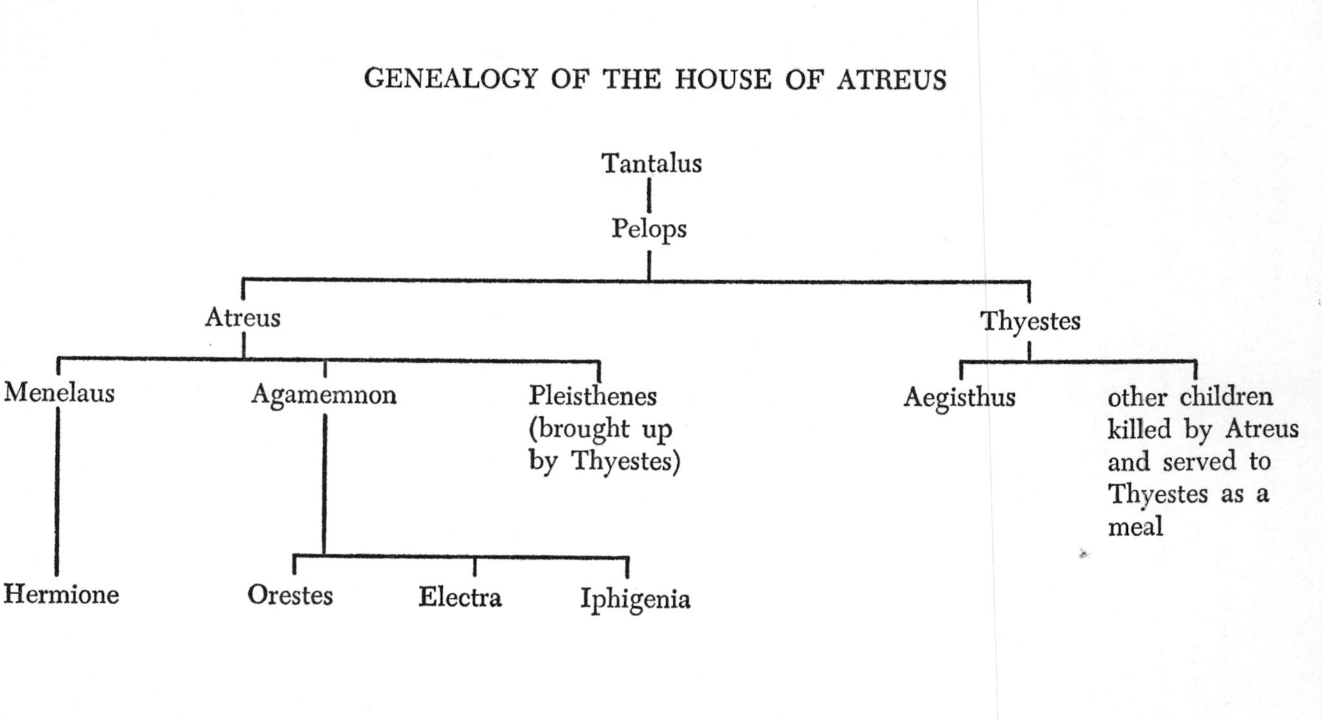

Note: Agamemnon and Menelaus married sisters, Clytaemnestra and Helen. These were the daughters of Tyndareus.

however, promise to avenge themselves on all of Athens. Finally, Athena manages to pacify them by promising them a special place of honor in the hearts and worship of the Athenians.

Even in this sketchy retelling, the legend contains an appalling amount of bloodshed. In each generation, the intra-family strife is renewed. Parents, children, siblings, husbands, and wives are at each other's throats. There seems to be no possible end to it, until divine intervention stops the cycle of murder and revenge. The curse of the house of Atreus lies precisely in the inability of the conflicts to be resolved on the human level. Without the gods, generation after generation would have to go on killing and being killed.

III

The situation in which the descendants of Atreus find themselves, as we see them in these plays, is a hopeless moral tangle. There is no solution possible that does not lead to doom.

Agamemnon has slain his daughter Iphigenia. Clytaemnestra takes this as the excuse for killing Agamemnon. Thus she in turn is guilty of murdering her husband. This is taken by Orestes as requiring him to kill Clytaemnestra, making him guilty of matricide. Clytaemnestra herself recognizes that this continuous killing is a curse, when she tells the chorus:

> Now is thy judgment just, when thou dost cry
> To that cursed Spirit, that thrice-fatted Doom,
> A Lust Incarnate, Death that cannot die,
> That makes all Tantalids murderers in the womb,
> Athirst for fresh blood ere the old be dry. (p. 67d)

A little later the chorus agrees with Clytaemnestra that it is still the curse of Tantalus which is at work:

> This bloody deluge, like an on-coming sea
> That may not halt until it makes the flood,
> Rolls its rough waves, with kindred-murder red,
> Till Justice lave the rank corruption bred
> Of that foul, cannibal roast of childish flesh. (p. 68a)

The curse manifests itself in the inability of any person involved in the cycle of murder to stop it and is due to the fact that there is no civil law to govern the actions of men. The only standard they have to guide themselves is the *lex talionis,* thc law of revenge and retribution, which we also find in the Old Testament. There we read

> ... thou shalt give life for life,
>
> Eye for eye, tooth for tooth, hand for hand, foot for foot,
>
> Burning for burning, wound for wound, stripe for stripe. (Exodus, 21:23-25)

In both the *Choephoroe* and the *Eumenides* we find the law of retribution referred to again and again. Near the beginning of the former play, Orestes' sister Electra appeals to the dead Agamemnon:

> ... on our enemies
> I pray Avenging Justice may rise up
> And hew them down, even as they hewed thee. (p. 71c)

A little later the chorus, too, refers to the time-honored law.

> "To tongue of gall the bitter word,"
> Loud is the voice of Vengeance heard,
> When she exacts the debt.
> "To dagger-hand the dagger-law,"
> "The doer quit"—'tis an old saw
> Whose salt hath savour yet. (p. 73a-b)

And the same thought is repeated again:

> It is the Law; when man's blood falls
> Man's blood shall pay full cess:
> With "Haro! Haro!" Murder calls
> God's fell Erinyes,
> And in some late succeeding age
> For souls slain long ago
> Fresh horrors mount the bloody stage
> For blacker deeds of woe. (p. 74a)

All of these appeals to the law of vengeance are to encourage Orestes to avenge his father by killing his mother. But after he has done so, the tables are turned. Now it is his turn to be killed in retribution for matricide. The Furies or Erinyes take over the task of exacting the vengeance for the dead mother. In the *Eumenides*, the Furies state their intention plainly:

> The mother-blood those murderous hands have shed
> Is irrevocably fled!
> The swallowing earth shall yield it nevermore!
> Thy life for hers; thou shalt fill me a cup
> Drawn from those veins of thine;
> Deep draughts of jellied blood I will sip and sup,
> Though bitter be the wine.
> And then, when I have sucked thy life-blood dry,
> I'll drag thee down below!
> There mother's son shall mother's agony
> Expiate, throe for throe! (pp. 83d-84a)

Aeschylus is emphatic about the curse on the house of Atreus, and repeatedly points to the seemingly endless chain of killings. There is no indication that Orestes could have acted otherwise than he did. Apollo commanded him to kill his mother; and yet the Furies, also divine, and older than Apollo or Athena, are perfectly right in pursuing him.

About 100 years after this trilogy had been written, Euripides presented his play *Orestes*. The facts concerning the descendants of Atreus are, of course, unchanged. But Euripides, living in a later and more sophisticated time, had definite ideas about the crime of Orestes and what could have been done to avoid it. Unlike the older poet, Euripides does not seem to think that the path of doom was inevitable. He puts the following words in the mouth of Tyndareus (the father of Clytaemnestra and Helen). They are addressed to Menelaus:

> If right and wrong are clear to all, who was ever more senseless than this man, seeing that he never weighed the justice of the case, nor yet appealed to the universal law of Hellas? For instance, when Agamemnon breathed his last beneath the blow my daughter dealt upon his head—a deed most foul, which I will never defend—he should have brought a charge against his mother and inflicted the penalty allowed by law for bloodshed, banishing her from his house; thus would he have gained the credit of forbearance from the calamity, keeping strictly to the law and showing his piety as well. As it is, he is come into the same misfortune as his mother; for though he had just cause for thinking her a wicked woman, he has surpassed her himself by murdering her. (p. 399a-b)

Unless this is done, Tyndareus continues, "where, pray, will the chain of horrors end?" For this reason, the proper punishment would have been exile, "but no retaliation!" Otherwise, Tyndareus goes on,

> there must always have been one who, by taking the pollution last upon his hands, would be liable to have his own blood shed. (p. 399b)

No doubt, Euripides in these words has put his finger on the difficulty and also on the only solution. Let the law punish the guilty persons and let the law do it in such a fashion that no guilt is transmitted to those who execute the laws. However, we must quickly add that it is completely unhistorical for Euripides to have put these words into the mouth of Tyndareus. Orestes was not negligent and headstrong because he did not appeal to legal processes instead of taking the revenge into his own hands. The facts are that there was no law or civil authority at the time in which Orestes is supposed to have lived, *i.e.*, at the very beginning of Hellenic culture, around 1000 B.C. The Athens of Aeschylus' time and of Euripides' time did, of course, have courts of law, but it is a deliberate anachronism on Euripides' part to transfer these legal institutions to the time of the Trojan War. Aeschylus, instead, takes the occasion of the Oresteian legend in order to tell a fable concerning the origin of the Athenian courts.

IV

That fable is related in the *Eumenides*. Orestes, pursued by the Furies, takes refuge first in Apollo's temple at Delphi, and then, at Apollo's bidding, at Athena's temple in Attica. He is followed by the Furies, and when Athena appears, both Orestes and the Furies appeal to her for justice.

But even Athena finds the case too difficult for her, and seems to put herself almost on a human level.

> If any man think he can judge herein,
> 'Tis much too weighty; neither were it lawful
> That I try murder, wreaked in bitter wrath.
> ....
> . . . whether they [the Furies] stay or I bid them hence
> I shall find trouble and perplexity. (p. 86b)

Consequently she puts the matter into the hands of a court which she proposes to establish:

> But, since . . . the business comes this way,
> I will appoint a court for murder sworn
> And make it a perpetual ordinance. (p. 86b)

Soon the Furies begin to plead the case for the prosecution, while Orestes and Apollo speak for the defense. Orestes admits that he has killed his mother, at the behest of Apollo. He then asks what seems like a logical question. Why did the Furies not persecute Clytaemnestra for her crime, as they now persecute Orestes? The answer he receives is that husband and wife are not related, so that the husband-killer does not spill her own blood, while the matricide does. Then follows an argument that borders on the sophistical, revolving around the question: are child and mother really related? Orestes and Apollo both favor the proposition that it is really only the father who is the parent of the child; the mother is merely the host for the developing seed. Whether or not this argument has any plausibility, Athena announces that she will cast her vote for the male (*i.e.*, for Orestes) in case of a tie, since she came into being without any mother, springing directly from Zeus' head. And the vote of the court does end in a tie; Athena casts her vote as announced, and Orestes goes free.

The Furies, as might be expected, are full of rage at the verdict. They threaten dire consequences to Athens. It takes all of Athena's patience and wisdom to calm them. She promises them that they will be specially honored in Athens, and that, if they consent, they will be known no longer as Furies, but as "Eumenides" or "the kindly ones." Thus finally the goddesses are appeased, and the play ends with a grand procession of Eumenides, Athenian Women, and Pallas Athena herself.

V

Was justice done to Orestes?

This question is related to the question, Did Orestes act justly? The last two plays of the trilogy certainly revolve around these two questions. We can perhaps answer them best by resolving them into a series of subsidiary questions having to do with particular actions rather than general conduct.

Concerning Orestes himself we must ask: In killing his mother, did he act justly? In avenging his father, did he act justly? In obeying the command of Apollo, did he act justly? In killing Aegisthus, did he act justly?

Concerning Clytaemnestra we must ask: In killing her husband, Agamemnon, did she act justly? In revenging the death of her daughter Iphigenia, did she act justly? In being unfaithful to her husband during his absence, did she act justly?

Concerning the god Apollo we must ask: In urging Orestes (and even commanding him) to kill Clytaemnestra, did he act justly?

Concerning the goddess Athena we must ask: In casting her vote for Orestes, did she act justly?

Concerning the Furies we must ask: In pursuing Orestes, did they act justly? In not pursuing Electra, did they act justly? In not pursuing Clytaemnestra after she had killed her husband, did they act justly? In resting satisfied with the judgment of the Athenian court, as the result of Athena's persuasion and flattery, did they act justly?

This whole series of questions is difficult to answer. Part of the difficulty lies in the fact that we have not said what we mean by "justice." Suppose that we were to rephrase all the questions above, substituting the word "lawful" for "just." Could we then answer the questions?

Let us try the substitution. The questions concerning Orestes now become: In killing his mother, did he act lawfully? In avenging his father, did he act lawfuly? In obeying the command of Apollo, did he act lawfully? In killing Aegisthus, did he act lawfully?

We have already pointed out earlier that (contrary to the treatment in Euripides) there was no civil law to guide Orestes' conduct. If Orestes' actions are to meet the standards of lawfulness, therefore, there must be something other than civil law to which they conform. We have mentioned the *lex talionis,* the law of retribution and revenge. But is this really a law? In the Old Testament, it certainly is a law, because it is given by

God to Moses, together with various other laws and ordinances. But is there some law of Zeus, or of some other god, which commands Orestes to act as he does? Orestes tells us that Loxias (*i.e.*, Apollo) commanded him to avenge his father, and predicted terrible consequences if he did not follow this command. Being pursued by the Furies was one of the threatened dire results if Orestes failed in his filial duty. (See pp. 72d-73a.)

Hence, with respect to the questions raised above, we can answer that Orestes acted in accord with Apollo's law or command, in avenging his father and killing Aegisthus. This also answers the question whether his matricide was lawful. If there was no other way to avenge his father than to kill his mother, Orestes acted in accord with the law laid down by Apollo.

On some interpretations of justice, therefore, Orestes acted justly. On other interpretations, however, he did not. For Thomas Hobbes, whom we shall read later in this Reading Plan, justice and injustice come into being only with civil society and its laws.

> . . . before the names of *just* and *unjust* can have place, there must be some coercive power to compel men equally to the performance of their covenants, by the terror of some punishment greater than the benefit they expect by the breach of their covenant . . . (*Leviathan,* Vol. 23, p. 91b)

And a little later he continues,

> . . . where there is no *own,* that is, no propriety, there is no injustice; and where there is no coercive power erected, that is, where there is no Commonwealth, there is no propriety, all men having right to all things: therefor where there is no Commonwealth, there nothing is unjust. (*Ibid.*)

According to the Hobbesian view, then, Orestes' acts can be called neither just nor unjust, for there was no civil law to deal with the situation which confronted Orestes. Consequently he neither broke a law nor obeyed one. This view, though it has something to recommend it, seems somewhat strange in that it deprives Orestes' acts (and indeed all the acts described in these plays) of any moral quality whatsoever. Yet, quite obviously, these plays are concerned with nothing so much as the morality or immorality of matricide, revenge, and punishment.

Quite probably the answer is that the justice and injustice of these acts are to be measured in terms of some law, but not civil law. We may guess that the standard is divine law. Apollo's command to Orestes is perhaps in the nature of a particular decree, but the Furies, in making their case against Orestes, quite clearly seem to be appealing to a divinely made law (namely, that matricide is a crime). Orestes, in defending himself, tries to argue that it is also a divine law that faithless and murderous wives should be killed.

Thus we see that even the divine laws are so tangled and mixed up that no clear decision of right and wrong, just and unjust, can be made. Hence it makes sense for Athena to try to solve the puzzle by inventing a new institution, namely, a court.

Does the solution to the tangle—the institution of a court and its verdict—seem satisfactory to you? Is human law placed above divine law? Is the verdict just? In terms of what law are you judging the justice of the verdict? Do the Furies act justly, in yielding to Athena's entreaties?

What do you think of the court procedure?

Does the court follow the rules and customs that are used in British or American courts? First of all, is the court duly constituted? This question seems difficult to answer, because without either a written constitution or a body of precedents, how can one decide what "duly constituted" would mean?

Nothing is said about how "the jurors" are selected, except that Athena chooses them. None of them is excused because of prejudice in the case or for other reasons. Is there any assurance that this is a fair jury?

In a modern court of law, what happens when a jury is split evenly, six for a verdict of acquittal and six for a verdict of guilty? Is a majority vote, such as 8 to 4, sufficient to find a defendant guilty?

Is the existence of law a good or an evil?

It is often claimed that laws coerce men, and that this coercion diminishes their freedom. No doubt, the fear of law and of its sanctions prevents men from doing many things which they would otherwise do. But is this evil?

Agamemnon, Clytaemnestra, and Orestes live in a lawless condition, or anarchy. Are they better off because of this? They are free to kill, in the sense that there are no laws against it; on the other hand, they have no legal protection against being killed in turn. Is there a sense in which men are freer in a civil society, with laws, than they are in a lawless condition?

It seems in any case that life in a civil society is more secure than life in an unregulated state of nature. Is that society best which has the most laws? Or is the best society halfway between the extremes of having no laws (anarchy) and regulating everything by laws?

SELF-TESTING QUESTIONS

The following questions are designed to help you test the thoroughness of your reading. Each question is to be answered by giving a page or pages of the reading assignment. Answers will be found on page 238 of this Reading Plan.

1 Who predicts Agamemnon's fate?

2 What are Agamemnon's arguments against walking on the purple carpet?

3 What is Cassandra's fate?

4 What proof of his identity does Orestes offer to Electra when he returns from his exile to avenge his father Agamemnon?

5 Does Orestes show any hesitation about killing his mother Clytaemnestra?

6 When do the Furies first appear to Orestes?

7 Apollo puts the Furies to sleep to let Orestes escape to Athens; who wakes them up?

8 The action of the *Eumenides* occurs in two different places; what are they?

9 What do the Furies—now Eumenides—promise Athena in return for their being worshiped and honored?

Second Reading

PLATO

Euthyphro

Vol. 7, pp. 191-199

Laws

Selections from Books I and IV

Vol. 7, pp. 643c-644a, 683a-686b

Also, PLATO

Apology

Crito

For a discussion of this assignment,
see the First Reading in
A General Introduction to the Great Books

Most of us tend to take the law pretty much for granted. As law-abiding citizens, we are hardly aware of the laws, except on special occasions; for instance, when the income tax has to be paid. Sometimes, when the law unexpectedly comes into our lives, it annoys us; for example, when we receive a traffic ticket.

When we vote for representatives or senators in the United States Congress, or for members of the legislative assemblies of the various states, we are, of course, participating in the lawmaking process, though indirectly. Yet for the most part, we do not think of ourselves as participating in lawmaking. "They" ought to make a law, we think and say, when confronted with a situation that needs governmental remedy.

Stop and think for a moment how much of our daily activity is subject to legal regulation. Taxes are perhaps the most obvious example of law entering our private lives. But beyond that, think of traffic laws, of the laws governing compulsory education, of zoning laws, of ordinances licensing businesses—we hardly can make a move without being circumscribed by laws.

It is surprising, therefore, that few of us are very passionate about, or even interested in, laws. Occasionally, there will be a Thoreau writing on civil disobedience, a Gandhi using passive resistance to call attention to what he conceives to be excesses of the law, or a Euthyphro who is willing to put the law ahead of family and piety. Whether these men are right may well be questioned; but it is clear that they are interested in the law, in what it says, and in the purpose it serves. We would do well to emulate their interest in the law.

GUIDE TO

Second Reading

I

Few authors in the history of philosophy have been as concerned with laws and their importance as Plato. Not only did he write a dialogue called *Laws,* but the theme of good laws and good lawmaking is also discussed in the *Republic,* in the *Gorgias,* the *Apology,* the *Crito,* and the *Euthyphro,* to name only some of the more obvious examples. It is not difficult to see why Plato is so concerned with laws. The entire subject of jurisprudence and lawmaking is intimately connected with questions of right and wrong, of justice and injustice. Now Plato specialized in writing about moral questions (such as the nature of justice); hence it is not surprising that he should be frequently led to discuss matters having to do with laws.

What is surprising, however, is that there is no formal, unified discussion of the problems of law anywhere in Plato. A lot of attention is paid to the content of laws; we are told what are good laws, what are bad ones, what are the laws of an ideal community. Furthermore, Plato describes in detail many laws concerned with many different subjects: laws concerning education, concerning marriage, concerning drinking, concerning warfare, and many others.

But we do not find in Plato a sustained discussion that answers questions such as the following: What is a law? How does a law differ from a decree? Who is empowered to make a law? What is the purpose of a law? What is the standard of justice by which just and unjust laws are measured? How is a law to be applied in a particular case? The answers to these and similar questions must be gathered from several Platonic dialogues and put together by us in order to have the equivalent of a Platonic "Treatise on Law."

II

In *A General Introduction to the Great Books,* the First Reading consists of the *Apology* and the *Crito.* Both of these dialogues make important points concerning law. From the *Apology* we can get an idea of the Athenian procedure in a trial court. Evidently the accused (in this case, Socrates) had the right to cross-examine his accusers, and, having been convicted, he had the right to suggest an appropriate penalty. The *Crito* is almost wholly devoted to an investigation of the question, Should a law be obeyed, even though it is unjust or at least unjustly applied?

The present reading also presents two questions, the first one having to do with an actual trial, the second one with the general theory of law. In the *Euthyphro* we see a man, Euthyphro, who proudly announces that he is preferring charges of murder against his father. Socrates is astonished at this, especially when he finds out that the man whom Euthyphro's father has killed was a laborer who worked for Euthyphro.

Euthyphro maintains that his father is guilty of murder and must be brought to justice. The father and the rest of the family deny this, in a triple argument. *First,* the father did not kill the servant; he simply happened to die while word from Athens was being awaited. *Second,* even if Euthyphro's father contributed to the death, the dead man was himself a murderer and so met his deserved fate. *Third,* no matter what the finding with respect to the father might be, Euthyphro has no business accusing him, since a son ought to honor his father and to do otherwise is impious.

Euthyphro denies that it makes any difference to the case whether the accused murderer is his father or not.

> The real question is whether the murdered man has been justly slain. If justly, then your duty is to let the matter alone; but if unjustly, then even if the murderer lives under the same roof with you and eats at the same table, proceed against him. (p. 192b)

Those who think that one ought not to proceed against one's father, even if he is a murderer, show "how little they know what the gods think about piety and impiety" (p. 192c).

This dialogue, therefore, considers the conflicting demands

of justice and piety. Justice demands prosecution of the father; piety demands that a son honor his father. This kind of conflict is not a rare occurrence; in fact, we have met it in the three Aeschylean tragedies of the First Reading.

The plight of Orestes, in the *Choephoroe*, is similar to that of Euthyphro. Justice demands that he kill his mother, piety demands that he honor her. In the *Eumenides* justice is represented by the Furies who demand Orestes' life. Here there is no conflict between piety and justice. Rather, the opposition is between the *old* justice (vengeance and retaliation represented by the Furies) and the *new* justice (the rule of civil law represented by Athena). In the *Euthyphro* the *new* justice is in conflict with piety.

In other words, though the *Oresteia* shows us how civil law supersedes the law of retaliation, this by no means eliminates the conflict between the demands of justice and piety. Justice is giving every man his due (as Plato tells us in the *Republic*) and that is how Euthyphro claims he treats his father. Piety is giving to the gods their due. It is part of man's duty to the gods to honor his parents; in so doing he is giving their due to the gods, not to the parents.

There are many problems here from the religious point of view; but we are interested in looking at the matter from the legal point of view. If religious observances are not written into the civil law, how can the law take account of them? There is no civil law that says parents should be honored. If a man commits a crime and claims he did it in order to honor his parents (suppose that he steals in order to support them comfortably in old age), will the civil law allow such a claim? The answer is that it will not, for at least two reasons. First, stealing is prohibited by law; and second, even if it is acknowledged that it is good for children to support their parents, how do we know that the son stole for that reason? Acts of piety, in other words, often differ from ordinary or even criminal acts only in the intention of the doer. But how is the law to judge such an intention? It seems that the law has to go by the overt act.

The matter would be different, of course, in a society where there is an official state religion. In that case, all or some of the observances of piety would also be matters of civil law and a transgression against piety would also be a civil crime. But the civil punishment would always be for the act insofar as it is a civil crime. Only the gods can punish impiety.

III

The other two selections in this reading assignment are from the *Laws*. This is Plato's longest dialogue and the last one he wrote. It is in fact hardly a dialogue, except in superficial form; for the most part it consists of long speeches by an Athenian Stranger. The other persons of the dialogue are Cleinias, a Cretan, and Megillus, a Lacedaemonian (Spartan). The Athenian Stranger discusses the laws of their countries with these two men and soon the conversation gets around to what the laws ought to be in a perfect state. Thus, the *Laws* is much like the *Republic* in subject matter; yet the tone of the later dialogue is quite different. The *Laws* is less extravagant, less utopian, and more realistic than the *Republic*.

Both of our short selections have to do with the purpose of laws. The Athenian Stranger praises the Cretan laws, for, he says,

> they fulfil the object of laws, which is to make those who use them happy . . . (p. 643c)

There is a slight variation on this in the second selection where we find the Athenian Stranger saying that he

> should wish the citizens to be as readily persuaded to virtue as possible; this will surely be the aim of the legislator in all his laws. (p. 684a)

The purpose of law, then, is happiness or virtue or both. How is the law, or perhaps more correctly, the legislator, going to accomplish this object? There are, says Plato, two means to this end. Every law should use both of them. They are coercion and persuasion. Most laws and legislators ignore the latter; the law simply states a command together with a penalty for disobedience. Plato compares this procedure to that of a doctor who simply prescribes certain medication and regimen without telling the patient why these things are to be done. Both doctor and legislator would be well advised to tell patient or citizen the reason for their prescription. This explanation belongs in a preamble to the law:

> The arbitrary command, which was compared to the commands of doctors, whom we described as of the meaner sort, was the law pure and simple; and that which preceded, and was described by our friend here as being hortatory only, was, although in fact, an exhortation, likewise analogous to the preamble of a discourse. For I imagine that all this language of conciliation, which the legislator has been uttering in the preface of the law, was intended to create good-will in the person whom he addressed, in order that, by reason of this good-will, he might more intelligently receive his command, that is to say, the law. And therefore, in my way of speaking, this is more rightly described as the preamble than as the matter of the law. And I must further proceed to observe, that to all his laws, and to each separately, the legislator should prefix a preamble; he should remember how great will be the difference between them, according as they have, or have not, such preambles, as in the case already given. (p. 686a-b)

IV

What are the subjects concerning which laws can or should be made?

Before considering the answer which Plato gives to this question, we can see that theoretically three different answers are possible. One answer is that nothing is properly the subject of legal regulation. This is what is said by anarchists. They usually give as their reason that greater happiness results without the coercions and restrictions of law and that tyrannical oppressions are avoided. They are opposed, of course, by all those who point out that anarchists envisage an unreal utopia. Society without laws would, in fact, degenerate into a condition of war of everyone against everyone. In any case, anarchism is clearly not advocated by Plato.

A second answer is that everything comes properly under the purview of law. This would be the answer of totalitarianism. Every action of every citizen, public or private, is the business of the state and so must be subject to state regulation. A few insignificant sorts of action may actually be left to private discretion simply because the state does not wish to bother with them, but in theory—on this view— even such actions could be subject to legislation.

The third view holds that there may properly be legislation about some, but not all, actions. Here there is wide divergence on all the kinds of actions that may or may not be regulated by law. One version of this view has it that "that government is best which governs least." (This is the motto which Thoreau quotes, with approval, at the beginning of *On Civil Disobedience.*) This view favors the minimum number of regulations, while agreeing that some regulation is necessary. A socialistic state would presumably find many more areas of human activity within its legislative purview than a state run on the principles of "rugged individualism." The philosophy of government in the United States has always tended in the direction of few laws, but more and more areas of conduct are gradually being encompassed. Only some very few subjects are definitely and forever excluded from legislation. The first amendment to the Constitution tells what some of them are.

> Congress shall make no law respecting an establishment of religion, or prohibiting the free exercise thereof; or abridging the freedom of speech, or of the press; or the right of the people peaceably to assemble, and to petition the Government for a redress of grievances. (Vol. 43, p. 17a)

Certain other matters about which legislation is proscribed are mentioned in the body of the Constitution. (See, for instance, Vol. 43, p. 13d.)

Which is Plato's position? He is sometimes accused of being a totalitarian, of believing in a "closed society," *i.e.*, one in which everything is subject to state control and nothing is left open to the individual's discretion. There is some evidence for this view in the *Republic,* where the minutest matters are subject to laws.

Even if this is an exaggeration of Plato's position, and if Plato is one of those who believe that some things are outside the sphere of law, it is still true that for Plato many actions are subject to legal regulation that we would think are purely private.

Thus Plato tells us (p. 685b) that a man should marry between the ages of thirty and thirty-five, and that if he does not do so, he should pay a fine. We customarily consider whether and when a man gets married a thoroughly private matter. As a matter of fact, in the *Republic* Plato goes much further. The state rules when children should be conceived, and the education of the children is thoroughly controlled by the state to the exclusion of the natural parents.

Again, in both the *Republic* and the *Laws* Plato lays down rules concerning the writings of the poets—what they are to write about and what subjects they are prohibited from considering.

What do you think is the reason for Plato's attitude toward laws? Is there any connection between the statement that the end of law is virtue and happiness and the view that law must be all-embracing? Is it possible for the law to make men happy unless it directs their private actions? Does this indicate that there is something strange about saying that the object of law is happiness?

Is it true that law in the United States does not invade the privacy of citizens? For instance, we do not fine men who do not marry between thirty and thirty-five; but we do levy a higher income tax on bachelors of all ages than on married men. Is this the equivalent of a fine? Again, could the very high taxes on whisky be interpreted as laws designed to prevent and diminish the consumption of hard liquor? If so, is this legislating about private matters?

Does every law need a preamble stating the reason for the law?

Plato tells us that the preamble will persuade the citizens to obey the law, because they will recognize its reasonableness. Thus, there will be less need for coercion to enforce the law. This, however, assumes that every law is reasonable. Is this a warranted assumption?

Are there not some laws, especially those made about indifferent matters, which are such that the only reason to obey them is that they are *laws*? For example, reason can hardly muster any arguments in favor of driving on the right-hand side of the road, beyond saying that all cars should drive on one side only and that it is the law of the land (in the U.S.A.) that this should be the right side.

In other cases, the reasonableness of the law in general may be apparent, but its particular pronouncement may not be so persuasive. For example, we may agree in general that an excise tax on automobiles is necessary, without being able to demonstrate that the exact amount of the tax is right.

Suppose that a man is not persuaded by the preamble to a law that it is reasonable. Should he obey the law anyhow? Does it make any difference whether he is mistaken or correct?

Do the laws now made in the United States and Great Britain have preambles? Does the Constitution of the United States, often referred to as the supreme law of the land, have a preamble? If so, does it serve the purpose that Plato says it should?

Do you think that Euthyphro acted correctly in bringing charges against his father?

We purposely avoid asking whether he acted justly. There is a sense in which everyone would agree that his action is in the interest of justice. The question is whether this just action is compatible with piety.

There seems to be little doubt that Euthyphro's father was responsible for the servant's death. Does the contention that the dead man was himself a murderer have any value as a defense? It would seem not. First of all, the dead man had not yet been found guilty in any court; and secondly, even if he were guilty, the punishment should be administered by the state, not by a single man.

Does law, or justice, require Euthyphro to proceed against his father? What is the law, in this respect, in the contemporary United States? Would a son be expected to prefer charges against a father whom he suspected of murder? The law recognizes that a husband cannot testify against his wife, and vice versa. Actually, in the United States, no private person prosecutes another for a crime. The people of the United States, or the people of one of the 50 states, prosecute crimes through the office of Attorney General or district attorney. A private person can make a complaint to the district attorney, who then may or may not prosecute. Does this arrangement make any difference to the case? Should a son bring a complaint to the district attorney in order that the latter may prosecute his father?

This question is a special instance of a more general one. Laws are made for the common good. This includes the laws about murder. Must a private citizen always endeavor to promote the common good, or is it enough if he promotes his private good? The common good of the state certainly will be served if Euthyphro's father is prosecuted; but Euthyphro's private good will be served if he is enabled to honor his father (which involves being quiet about the murder). Which is the moral course of action? We shall encounter this question again.

SELF-TESTING QUESTIONS

The following questions are designed to help you test the thoroughness of your reading. Each question is to be answered by giving a page or pages of the reading assignment. Answers will be found on page 238 of this Reading Plan.

1 Do the gods love that which is holy, or does their love make something holy?

2 In defending himself against the charge of impiety, to which action of the gods does Euthyphro refer?

3 Do the gods benefit from the sacrifices of men?

4 What are the eight goods which the Athenian Stranger enumerates as conferred on men by laws?

5 Does the Athenian Stranger think it important to honor one's parents?

6 What are the two kinds of physicians, according to the Athenian Stranger?

Third Reading

ARISTOTLE

Nicomachean Ethics

Book V

Vol. 9, pp. 376-387

Sometimes a subject is so well treated in one place by an author that it never needs to be treated again. No geometer has really been able to excel Euclid's treatment of plane geometry in Book I of the *Elements;* no poet would think of competing with Dante in a detailed description of the sufferings of the damned in Hell. The discussion of justice in the fifth book of the *Nicomachean Ethics* is similarly unrivalled; moral philosophers have for the most part been content to begin where Aristotle left off.

In his customary fashion, Aristotle combines keen theoretical insight with great down-to-earth practicality. He not only discusses justice as a moral virtue and analyzes its place among the other virtues: he also deals with the daily problems of justice in the ordinary dealings that men have with one another—in selling and buying, for example.

Justice is often represented as a blind figure. Certainly Aristotle would agree that justice must be meted out equally to all, to rich and poor alike. But the blindness of justice does not mean that the circumstances of actions must be disregarded. On the contrary, in the search for justice we must take into account a great many circumstances.

Only then will we be able to answer the questions that recur again and again in connection with justice. Was this action performed voluntarily or not? If it was performed voluntarily, was it done after full deliberation, and what was its purpose? Was this man just because he obeyed the law of the land? Can it ever be just to trespass against a law? Does a human law ever need to be corrected by reference to higher standards, such as the principles of natural law?

GUIDE TO

Third Reading

I

The fifth book of the *Nicomachean Ethics* might be called a "Treatise on Justice." For justice is its subject matter, and it is considered in a very orderly and systematic fashion.

Let us begin by putting Book V of the *Ethics* in its proper context. Book I of the *Ethics* deals with the question, What is happiness? (Cf. the Fourth Reading in *A General Introduction to the Great Books*.) Happiness, the reader may remember, is there defined as "activity of the soul in accordance with virtue" (Vol. 9, p. 343c). This definition leads Aristotle to consider the nature of virtue. He divides virtues into two kinds: moral virtues and intellectual virtues. (See Bk. I, Ch. 13, p. 348c-d.) Aristotle begins by considering moral virtue in general (Bk. II), and then goes on to consider the particular moral virtues, courage (Bk. III, Ch. 6ff.), temperance (Bk. III, Ch. 10ff.), and justice (Bk. V). In Book IV, he deals with such things as liberality, magnificence, pride, ambition. In Book VI he considers the intellectual virtues: art, prudence, science, understanding (sometimes called intuition), and wisdom.

It is interesting to note that Plato does not distinguish between the moral and the intellectual virtues. He enumerates four cardinal virtues: courage, temperance, justice, and wisdom. Of these Aristotle regards the first three as moral virtues, and the fourth as an intellectual virtue.

Justice and law are, of course, two different things, though it is clear that they are closely related. We shall first consider, in Section II, what Aristotle has to say about justice; and then, in Section III, we shall relate our findings to the subject of law. Section IV will be devoted to a number of questions.

II

As we might expect, Aristotle begins by trying to tell us in a very general way what justice is. He does not give us a philosophical or technical definition of justice. Rather he reports the general opinion of mankind concerning justice. It is characteristic of Aristotle's method to begin by reciting what others have said about the subject under discussion. Often those to whom Aristotle refers are earlier philosophers or scientists; but in this case he simply refers to "all men."

"All men," he writes, "mean by justice that kind of state of character which makes people disposed to do what is just and makes them act justly and wish for what is just" (p. 376b). This statement seems deceptively simple, or perhaps even simple-minded. There appears to be a circular definition here: justice is defined in terms of justice. But the definition does accomplish something. It tells us that justice is a state of character. The kind of actions men perform are determined by their character. Justice, then, is the state of character which disposes men to act justly. In brief, justice is the habit of acting justly.

All virtues are habits or dispositions, as Aristotle points out earlier in the *Ethics*. (See Bk. II, Ch. 5-6, pp. 351b-352d.) Some of the virtues are habits of the intellect or understanding; these are the intellectual virtues. And some of the virtues are habits of feeling or action; these are the moral virtues. Courage and temperance, for example, are habits that discipline the emotions or passions. Only justice is a habit of action.

Aristotle calls our attention to a significant difference between habits of knowledge and habits of passion or action. Habits of knowledge relate to opposites or contraries, but habits of passion or action do not. Thus, the man who has the habit of scientific mathematical knowledge knows about continuous quantities (like lines and areas) as well as about discrete quantities (like numbers). The man who has the habit of prudence knows which are the good means to a certain end, and also which are the bad means. But the man who has the habit of acting justly only acts justly. If for some reason or other he does not act justly, he is then not acting in accordance with his virtue. He is, as we say, acting "out of character."

After this very general statement about justice, which indicates that it is a moral virtue, Aristotle proceeds to a more detailed definition of it. He suggests that it is easier to begin with the meaning of "injustice" and derive the meaning of "justice" from it. Accordingly, he proceeds as follows:

> Let us take as a starting-point, then, the various meanings of 'an unjust man.' Both the lawless man and the grasping and unfair man are thought to be unjust, so that evidently both the law-abiding and the fair man will be just. The just, then, is the lawful and the fair, the unjust the unlawful and the unfair. (p. 376d)

It is important to understand that Aristotle is here giving us two meanings of justice. One meaning is that the just act is a *lawful* act. The other meaning is that the just act is a *fair* act. These two meanings of justice are related. The lawful is to the fair as justice in general is to a special form of justice. In a large or general sense, justice is to be found in all lawful acts. In a particular or special sense, to be just is to deal fairly with others. Aristotle again begins by explaining this matter in terms of injustice:

> . . . since the unfair and the unlawful are not the same, but are different as a part is from its whole (for all that is unfair is unlawful, but not all that is unlawful is unfair), the unjust and injustice in the sense of the unfair are not the same as but different from the former kind, as part from whole; for injustice in this sense is a part of injustice in the wide sense, and similarly justice in the one sense of justice in the other. (p. 378a)

Justice in the general sense, therefore, signifies that state of character which disposes a man to perform lawful acts habitually. Of lawful acts, some are also fair; the state of character which disposes a man to perform these fair acts is justice in the special sense. Similarly, the man who is unjust in the general sense performs unlawful acts; while the man who is unjust in the special sense performs unfair acts. And again we must observe that all unfair acts are unlawful, but not all unlawful acts are unfair.

One further thing must be noted about justice in general. Justice in this sense is almost exactly the same thing as complete virtue. But the virtues can be looked at in two ways: in relation to the individual's own perfection, and in relation to the good of others. General justice consists of all the moral virtues when they are exercised in relation to the good of others or the common good of society.

The fact that law aims at the common good explains the identity of general justice (which is the lawful) with virtue in its social bearings. The laws, Aristotle tells us, "in their enactments on all subjects aim at the common advantage either of all or of the best or of those who hold power" (p. 377a). Lawful or just acts, therefore, are those which tend to produce happiness in a political society. And since happiness, in Aristotle's view, depends on virtue, lawful acts must be those which are in accord with virtue. He points out that the laws command men to perform virtuous acts.

> . . . the law bids us do both the acts of a brave man . . . and those of a temperate man . . . and those of a good-tempered man . . . and similarly with regard to the other virtues and forms of wickedness, commanding some acts and forbidding others . . . (p. 377a)

Aristotle properly concludes that "This form of justice [*viz.*, general justice] . . . is complete virtue, but not absolutely, but in relation to our neighbour" (p. 377b). Furthermore, Aristotle thinks that general justice is virtue in the highest sense, precisely because it is exercised in a man's relation to other men.

Now let us turn to special justice, that state of character which disposes us to act fairly. This kind of justice is also divided into two kinds.

> . . . (A) one kind is that which is manifested in distributions of honour or money or the other things that fall to be divided among those who have a share in the constitution . . . and (B) one is that which plays a rectifying part in transactions between man and man. (p. 378b-c)

These two kinds of special justice are commonly referred to as (A) distributive justice, and (B) rectificatory or commutative justice.

In Book II of the *Ethics*, Aristotle points out that each moral virtue is a mean between two extremes. He gives a reason for saying this.

> . . . virtue is concerned with passions and actions, in which excess is a form of failure, and so is defect, while the intermediate is praised and is a form of success . . . Therefore virtue is a kind of mean . . . (p. 352b)

Since general justice is identical with all virtue (*i.e.*, disposes us to acts in accord with all the virtues), it does not consist in a mean that is distinct from the mean of each of the particular virtues. But special justice, being a particular virtue, is itself a mean between extremes. Indeed, distributive and commutative justice differ in that, though each is a mean, each is a mean of a different kind.

Distributive justice aims at a mean having to do with rewards and punishments. Each person should receive as much honor, money, or other reward as he deserves; punishments should similarly be meted out in accordance with the severity of the offense committed. Justice in this sense, therefore, demands a proportionality; two men are rewarded justly if their rewards are proportional to their merits. Let us suppose that the following proportion holds.

Reward given to A: Reward given to B:: Merit of A: Merit of B. Justice in the distributive sense has then been done. If, on the other hand, the reward given to A is out of proportion to his merit, then A and B are being treated unjustly; A because he receives too much, and B, too little.

The same kind of proportionality has to hold in the case of punishments, if justice is to be served. Criminal law takes cognizance of this and assigns more severe penalties to more serious crimes. The punishment for manslaughter is less than the punishment for murder, because manslaughter is a less serious crime than murder. And in a well-arranged criminal code, the punishment for manslaughter should be to the punishment for murder as the seriousness of manslaughter is to the seriousness of murder.

Commutative or rectificatory justice aims at a different sort of mean, namely, that of simply equality. Commutative justice rules transactions between men, especially commercial transactions.

. . . justice in transactions between man and man is a sort of equality indeed, and the injustice a sort of inequality . . . the law looks only to the distinctive character of the injury, and treats the parties as equal, if one is in the wrong and the other is being wronged, and if one inflicted injury and the other has received it. Therefore, this kind of injustice being an inequality, the judge tries to equalize it . . . (p. 379c)

When one person has injured another and redress is sought for the injury, commutative justice comes into play. The damage done must be rectified. Justice will be done when the inequality caused by the injury has been removed and equality is re-established.

Another and perhaps more important area in which commutative justice applies is buying and selling. Here there is no question of re-establishing equality; instead, as Aristotle points out, equality must be preserved. This occurs when each person involved in the sale gives as much as he receives. Justice in this sense, Aristotle says, "consists in having an equal amount before and after the transaction" (p. 380b).

Aristotle shows us an example of a commercial transaction.

> Let A be a house, B ten minae, C a bed. A is half of B, if the house is worth five minae or equal to them; the bed, C, is a tenth of B; it is plain, then, how many beds are equal to a house, viz. five. That exchange took place thus before there was money is plain; for it makes no difference whether it is five beds that exchange for a house, or the money value of five beds. (p. 381c)

The example also indicates how money facilitates exchange. ". . . all things that are exchanged," Aristotle writes, "must be somehow comparable. It is for this end that money has been introduced . . ." (p. 380d). Money is the common denominator, enabling us to express the value of a house and the value of a bed in such a way that a commutatively just exchange of a house for beds can take place.

Common linguistic usage supports Aristotle in saying that, in commercial transactions, the just is the fair. We are accustomed to speak of a fair price or of a fair wage (which is the price paid for someone's labor). In the United States we have laws prohibiting certain practices in selling and in advertising as unfair. In some cases there exist laws requiring all retailers to sell certain goods at the same price; these laws are called "fair trade laws."

Finally, we must note two peculiarities about the way in which justice is a mean. (1) Justice is a mean between two extremes that are called by the same name, injustice. This is true of both distributive and commutative justice. In the case of other virtues the two extremes are opposite vices; courage, for instance, is a mean between cowardice and rashness. (2) Justice is an absolute mean. What is just in a given case depends only on the circumstances. It does not depend on the person who is acting. Justice, therefore, is an objective, not a subjective, mean.

In the case of the other moral virtues, the mean that constitutes the virtue is subjective. What is courage for one man may not be courage for another; consequently, the mean between cowardice and rashness will be different for two men. Similarly, the mean which is temperance will vary from person to person. Let us take eating as an example. Consider two different men of quite different physical constitutions. Suppose that one of them is short, slight, and works at a sedentary occupation, while the other man is a tall, robust lumberjack. The amount of food which the first man needs in a day is obviously a great deal less than what the second man needs. Hence, what would be overindulgence and gluttony for the first man might very well be a moderate diet for the second man.

But the just course of action in given circumstances is the same for office-worker and lumberjack, for a tall man and a short man, and so on. No subjective considerations need to be taken into account; only the objective facts.

III

Aristotle relates justice to law in three ways. (1) He defines the just, in the general sense, as the lawful. (2) He makes a distinction between legal and natural justice. (3) He indicates how legal justice needs to be corrected by equity.

(1) We saw above (pp. 33-34) that Aristotle identifies the just (in its general sense) with the lawful. Justice in this sense is the same as complete virtue exercised with respect to other men and for the common good.

Men do in general identify the just with the lawful. If someone is suspected of having broken a law, a court determines his guilt or innocence. A court, it should be noted, is presided over by a person called a "justice." We feel that justice has been done when a man has been duly tried in a court of law and, if found guilty, is punished according to the law. A whole set of words employed in the language of law reminds us that the business of law has to do with justice: judge, jury, justice, adjudication, judgment, and so on.

(2) Aristotle distinguishes between natural and legal justice as follows:

> . . . natural [justice is] that which everywhere has the same force and does not exist by people's thinking this or that; legal, that which is originally indifferent, but when it has been laid down is not indifferent. . . (p. 382c)

Aristotle's distinction parallels that between *mala in se* and *mala prohibita* in the common law. *Mala in se* are those things which are bad in themselves; no law is needed to declare them evil. Obvious examples are murder or theft; these are actions that are bad in themselves, and are bad always and everywhere. In Aristotle's language, they offend against natural justice.

The phrase *mala prohibita,* on the other hand, designates acts that are bad only because they have been prohibited by law. If no law concerning them existed, these things would be perfectly all right. For instance, federal law in the United States imposes an excise tax on jewelry; we are thereby forbidden to purchase jewelry without paying this tax. There is no intrinsic reason for paying the tax. It is the law which makes it bad and unjust to avoid paying it. In Aristotle's terms, obedience to the law serves legal justice.

It is obvious that things which are *mala prohibita,* or legally unjust, may change from time to time, as the laws are changed, and that what is a *malum prohibitum* in one place need not be so in another. But the naturally just and unjust are unchangeable and are the same everywhere, in the same way, Aristotle says, "as fire burns both here and in Persia" (p. 382d).

(3) Now we come to the third way in which justice and law are related. This has to do with equity. "The equitable," Aristotle writes, "is just, but not the legally just but a correction of legal justice" (p. 385d). Legal justice is occasionally in need of correction.

> The reason is that all law is universal but about some things it is not possible to make a universal statement which shall be correct. (p. 385d)

But even though legislators may recognize the fact that it is not possible for a universal law to be correct in all cases, the laws must still be written universally. There is no other form in which they could possibly be cast.

> When the law speaks universally, then, and a case arises on it which is not covered by the universal statement, then it is right, where the legislator fails us and has erred by over-simplicity, to correct the omission—to say what the legislator himself would have said had he been present, and would have put into his law if he had known. (p. 386a)

Thus the equitable is superior to that which is legally just, for equity corrects the defects arising from the universality of law. However, the equitable is clearly not superior to that which is naturally just. Rather, the correction of what is legally just by equity is done in terms of what is naturally just. For instance, if a man shoots a bear out of season in order to save a child that is being attacked by the bear, he would, according to legal justice, be doing something unjust. Yet under the circumstances, not envisaged by the law, it would not be just to punish him for shooting the bear. Natural justice declares that it is right and just to save a child from harm by a wild animal. Equity corrects the precepts of legal justice accordingly.

Since the need for equity arises from the universality of law, it is clear that, in Aristotle's sense of equity, there can be no law of equity. Rules of equity would themselves have to be universal and would therefore be subject to correction. In modern legal usage, equity no longer means what it did for Aristotle. Although equity started out, in England, as a correction by the court of chancery of the justice dispensed by the courts of common law, equity itself became rigid and codified, until there were two concurrent bodies of law, and two kinds of courts: courts of common law and courts of equity.

IV

In addition to asking whether an action is lawful and therefore just, can we also ask whether a law itself is just?

When we ask whether a law is just, we have in mind, of course, the laws made by human legislators. If this is the only kind of law, then the question whether a law is just is not meaningful. For that which is just, we must remember, is the same as the lawful. If there is no law besides that which is made by men, the question "Is this law just?" can only mean "Is this law lawful; *i.e.,* in accordance with man-made law?" But obviously any man-made law is in accord with itself and so no distinction could be drawn between just and unjust laws.

This, as we have already pointed out in the guide to the First Reading, is the position of Hobbes. Justice, he says, depends on man-made law.

> . . . where there is no Commonwealth, there nothing is unjust. So that the nature of justice consisteth in keeping of valid covenants, but the validity of covenants begins not but with the constitution of a civil power sufficient to compel men to keep them. . . (*Leviathan,* Vol. 23, p. 91b)

Aristotle, however, has a different view. We recall that some things in Aristotle's opinion are naturally just, while others are legally just. A man-made law may, therefore, be called just; namely, when it proscribes something that is naturally unjust or is a *malum in se.*

In what way does it make sense to call a man-made law just or unjust, if the action which it forbids is a *malum prohibitum, i.e.,* something which, but for the law, would not be prohibited? Even though we cannot fall back on the standard of natural justice in this case, we are not left completely without criteria by which to judge such a law. There are at least two conditions which any such law must fulfill. In the first place, it must serve the common good. A law decreeing that the speed limit for cars in residential neighborhoods is 25 miles per hour serves the common good; on the other hand, a law that commands everyone to paint his house green does not. The latter law is, therefore, not just. In the second place, the law must be properly made. It must be made by the person or persons who have the duty of making laws, and it must be made in the right way. Federal laws must be made by the Congress of the United States; the President, for instance, cannot make laws. Furthermore, Congress must make laws in the proper way. Both the House of Representatives and the Senate must pass identical bills, and the President must sign the new law; if any of these steps are omitted, what results is an unjust law, or really no law at all.

Are there any other standards by which man-made laws can

be judged just or unjust? Is the condition that a law must be properly made an important one or is it trivial?

How does Aristotle classify transactions between men?

In the first place, Aristotle distinguishes between voluntary and involuntary transactions. Voluntary transactions are exemplified by ordinary, commercial dealings such as buying and selling. Involuntary transactions are those which one of the parties to the transaction does not wish to happen. Sometimes involuntary transactions occur clandestinely, as when a man becomes the victim of theft or adultery. Other things happen to a man against his will, as when he is assaulted, robbed, etc. (See p. 378c). We see that both parties act voluntarily in voluntary transactions; while in involuntary transactions, the patient (the man who is robbed or otherwise victimized) acts involuntarily, although the agent (the robber, etc.) acts voluntarily.

A little later Aristotle offers another scheme for classifying acts. He considers only the voluntariness or involuntariness of the agent in acts resulting in injury to the patient. Voluntary acts are those done by choice, after deliberation. Involuntary acts are done without choice or deliberation.

Involuntary injurious acts may be either (1) misadventures—when things happen contrary to reasonable expectation; or (2) mistakes—caused by a man because of some accident; or (3) acts of injustice—caused by a man, but not because of any habitual vice. Voluntary injurious acts, finally, are those in which a man acts from choice; in this case the agent "is an *unjust man* and a vicious man" (p. 383d).

Is this an adequate formulation of the different kinds of injurious action? Does the law take account of these kinds of involuntariness? Can there also be degrees of voluntariness?

How can we determine what is fair (and therefore just) in exchange?

This question deals with the particular form of justice that plays a role in exchange. We wish to inquire particularly about what constitutes fair commercial exchange. We want to determine what is commutatively just. What constitutes a fair or just price for a commodity? What constitutes a fair or just price for labor?

The just, in this sense, "consists in having an equal amount before and after the transaction" (p. 380b). If it is desired to exchange a house for a number of beds, and if five beds are equivalent in value to one house, then it is fair to exchange one house for five beds. But how do we determine whether a house is equivalent to four, or five, or ten beds? How can different things be made commensurable so that we can tell how many of one thing should be exchanged for how many of the other?

To introduce money does not solve the problem. Suppose we knew that the price of the house is $1,000 and that each bed costs $200; then of course it is clear that one house is equal in value to five beds. But we have really circumvented, not solved, the problem. For how did we know that the fair price for the house was $1,000, while the fair price for the beds was $200 each?

Aristotle solves the problem as follows.

> All goods must therefore be measured by some one thing, as we said before. Now this unit is in truth demand, which holds all things together (for if men did not need one another's goods at all, or did not need them equally, there would be either no exchange or not the same exchange); but money has become by convention a sort of representative of demand. . . (p. 381a)

Demand or, as we would say, "supply and demand" determines the fair value to be placed on different goods, in Aristotle's view. Marx asks the same question as Aristotle, but gives a different answer. "What is that equal something, that common substance, which admits of the value of the beds being expressed by a house?" Marx gives this answer.

> Compared with the beds, the house does represent something equal to them, in so far as it represents what is really equal, both in the beds and the house. And that is—human labour. (*Capital,* Vol. 50, p. 25c)

Here we have two radically opposed ways of determining the value of things to be exchanged. One theory bases value on supply and demand; the other, on labor. Both theories agree, however, that different goods must be capable of being valued in commensurable terms so that justice in exchange—having as much after the transaction as before—can be observed.

Which theory of value seems right to you? Does it make any difference from the point of view of justice which theory is followed?

SELF-TESTING QUESTIONS

The following questions are designed to help you test the thoroughness of your reading. Each question is to be answered by giving a page or pages of the reading assignment. Answers will be found on page 238 of this Reading Plan.

1 Are household justice and political justice the same thing?

2 Does Aristotle think that simple revenge–*i.e.*, the law of an eye for an eye and a tooth for a tooth–produces justice?

3 Are all involuntary acts excusable?

4 Can a man treat himself unjustly?

5 What is it that measures all things in commercial transactions?

6 What is a voluntary act?

7 How does Aristotle define political justice?

8 Is an action done from anger considered malicious by Aristotle?

Fourth Reading

OLD TESTAMENT

Exodus

19-20

Deuteronomy

5-6

NEW TESTAMENT

Matthew

15:1-20, 22:15-40

Romans

7-8

In the tradition of most peoples, the men who initially institute laws command high reverence. Solon, about whom we shall learn in the next reading, achieved his fame as the man who gave Athens laws that endured for many years. Most ancient of the lawgivers known to us is Hammurabi, a Babylonian king who reigned in the twenty-first century B.C. Hammurabi ranks as a rival in fame to Moses, probably the greatest lawgiver. Even today, millions of people still obey the Mosaic laws.

Moses himself did not make the laws for the children of Israel; he received them directly from God. A remarkable passage in the Old Testament bears witness to the special favor which Moses had received in the eyes of God. "The Lord spake unto Moses face to face, as a man speaketh unto his friend." We can hardly imagine a man more intimate with God than this.

God gave the law of the Old Testament to the Jewish people, though he spoke through Moses. Christ himself instituted the law of the New Testament, resulting in even more direct communication between God and men. In spite of the fact that the laws we read about in the Bible are divine laws, directly instituted by God, they are by no means punctiliously obeyed. On the contrary, both Old and New Testaments contain many instances of disobedience to God's law. Even the first injunction of the Decalogue, which forbids the Jews to worship any other gods, is broken time and again, and in the New Testament Christ is again and again disbelieved.

Punishment follows disobedience; forgiveness follows punishment. This cycle sums up man's relationship to God. No matter how explicitly Moses or Christ tells the people what to do, they fail to do it. But God gives men ways to redeem themselves. The law we read about here is both more stringent and more severe than human law; yet at the same time the divine lawgiver, unlike human legislators, applies it with infinite mercy and forgiveness.

GUIDE TO

Fourth Reading

I

This reading treats of the divine law or, as it should more properly be called, the divine positive law. It is positive law, because it is explicitly promulgated by God, just as the human positive law is the law that is explicitly made by human legislators. There may be another divine law—implicit in the workings of nature or the whole universe—but we are not concerned with it here.

The readings come from the Old Testament, from one of the four Gospels, and from one of the epistles written by St. Paul. Exodus and Deuteronomy tell how God gave his commandments to the Jews at Mount Sinai. In Matthew, we learn about the New Law which God promulgated through his son Jesus Christ. In Romans, St. Paul explains how the New Law supersedes the Old Law and how the New Law applies to all mankind, not just to the Jews. We will examine these three accounts in the order mentioned.

II

Let us note the historical point at which God reveals his law to the people of Israel. It occurs, according to Exodus, in the third month of their deliverance from Egypt. The Israelites have already crossed the Red Sea, and for many days God has fed them with quail and manna. Now they have reached the desert of Sinai. At this point God, through Moses, makes a proposal to the children of Israel.

> . . . if ye will obey my voice indeed, and keep my covenant, then ye shall be a peculiar treasure unto me above all people: for all the earth is mine: And ye shall be unto me a kingdom of priests, and an holy nation. (Exodus 19:5-6)[1]

---

[1] All direct quotations in this Guide are taken from the King James version of the Bible.

In return for obedience to the Law, God promises to make the children of Israel His "chosen people."

After this, God gives the Ten Commandments to the people. Deuteronomy 5 contains the same listing as Exodus 20, but in a slightly different form. The difference between these two versions of the Decalogue reflects the fundamental difference between the books of Exodus and Deuteronomy. Exodus, as the title indicates, primarily records the history of the Jews' flight from Egypt under the leadership of Moses. Deuteronomy, which means the Second Law, primarily sets forth the divine laws and ordinances. It places much more emphasis on obedience to the law and love of God than Exodus does. The themes of religious reform and of exaltation of God run through Deuteronomy. Thus Moses, who is the narrator in all of Deuteronomy, exhorts the people:

> Hear therefore, O Israel, and observe to do it; that it may be well with thee, and that ye may increase mightily, as the Lord God of thy fathers hath promised thee, in the land that floweth with milk and honey.
>
> Hear, O Israel: The Lord our God is one Lord:
>
> And thou shalt love the Lord thy God with all thine heart, and with all thy soul, and with all thy might. (Deuteronomy 6:3-5)

It is noteworthy that the divine law as laid down in Deuteronomy promises very explicit rewards for obedience to God. Furthermore, the exhortation to love God, in Verse 5, does not occur in Exodus. But this is the very verse which Christ picks out, in Matthew 22:37, as constituting the fundamental commandment of God. Between these two verses the writer of Deuteronomy placed Moses' acknowledgment of God's unity: "Hear, O Israel: The Lord our God is one Lord."

We find nothing like this verse in Exodus, or indeed elsewhere in the Bible. To be sure, the Decalogue in both versions contains God's admonition: "Thou shalt have no other gods before me" (Exodus 20:3, Deuteronomy 5:7). This, taken together with God's punishment of the people when they worship the golden calf (see Exodus 32), indicates that the Jewish religion was monotheistic. The verse in Deuteronomy, however, goes beyond this. Not only does it affirm the existence of only one

God, but it shows that this God is also essentially and wholly one. The conception of God here expressed is definitely unitarian.

Chapter 6 of Deuteronomy deserves special mention. In both Exodus and Deuteronomy, the Decalogue is followed by a multitude of other laws and ordinances, mostly of a ceremonial nature. But in Deuteronomy, Chapter 6 intervenes between the Decalogue and the other laws; it contains comment about the law and what it means to the children of Israel. Again and again this chapter reiterates that all will be well with Israel if the people obey the law of God; again and again it exhorts the people to fear and to love Him.

The past, the present, and the future of the people of Israel are related to the law which God has given them. Moses reminds the people that God promised to Abraham, Isaac, and Jacob that their children would inhabit a rich and fertile land. And now Moses adds that if the children of Israel will keep God's law, they will indeed inherit this land and God will be merciful to them. This one chapter, therefore, sums up the relationship of the people of Israel to the law. They must obey it, both to honor God for the good He has in the past bestowed on them (such as leading them out of Egypt) and to make themselves worthy of His gifts in the future.

III

The two passages from the Gospel according to St. Matthew deal with the problem of the meaning of the Old Law as interpreted by Jesus Christ. For hundreds of years prior to the appearance of Christ, the Jews had lived with the idea that God wished them to obey the law in the most minute and strict fashion. The last verse in Chapter 6 of Deuteronomy reads:

> And it shall be our righteousness, if we observe to do all these commandments before the Lord our God, as he hath commanded us. (Deuteronomy 6:25)

In Chapter 15 of the Gospel according to St. Matthew, Christ appears to contradict the words of Deuteronomy, and to tell the Jews that they need not observe God's law. The

Pharisees, at least, interpret Christ's words in this fashion. In order to understand what Christ means, we must investigate in some detail the rules and ordinances of the Old Law.

In the first place, the Old Law includes much more than the Ten Commandments. In both Exodus and Deuteronomy we find, following the Ten Commandments, enumerations of other laws and decrees that take up several chapters. In the second place, the commandments of the Old Law are of several kinds. Aquinas distinguishes between three classes of precepts.

We must therefore distinguish three kinds of precept in the Old Law; namely moral precepts, which are dictated by the natural law; ceremonial precepts, which are determinations of the Divine worship; and judicial precepts, which are determinations of the justice to be maintained among men. (*Summa Theologica,* Vol. 20, p. 248c)

Aquinas mentions "Thou shalt not kill" and "Thou shalt not steal" as examples of moral precepts of the Old Law. God intends to make men good by his law. "But," Aquinas writes,

the goodness of man is virtue which makes its possessor good. Therefore it was necessary for the Old Law to include precepts about acts of virtue, and these are the moral precepts of the Law. (*Ibid.,* p. 246d)

The moral precepts of the divine law command the same actions as the precepts of the natural law. The need for the moral precepts of the divine law arises from the defects of human reason. Men do not always or easily recognize what the natural law commands them to do; but the commandments of the divine law are explicit and clear.

. . . human reason could not go astray in the universal principle, that is, as to the most common principles of the natural law; but through being habituated to sin, it became obscured in the point of things to be done in detail. But with regard to the other moral precepts, which are like conclusions drawn from the common principles of the natural law, the reason of many men went astray, to the extent of judging to be lawful things that are evil in themselves. Hence there was need for the authority of the Divine law to rescue man from both these defects. (*Ibid.,* pp. 246d-247a)

The ceremonial precepts of the Old Law, Aquinas tells us, deal with "certain external works, whereby man makes profession of his subjection to God"; these works "are said to belong to the Divine worship." Aquinas concludes that "those precepts of the Law which refer to the Divine worship are specially called ceremonial" (*Ibid.*, p. 247c-d).

The judicial precepts regulate the conduct of men with respect to one another. The "determination of the general precepts of that justice which is to be observed among men is effected by the judicial precepts" (*Ibid.*, p. 248c).

In the light of these distinctions, let us now look at what Christ says about the Old Law and the New Law in Matthew 15. Certain Pharisees complained to Christ about infractions of the law by his followers.

> Why do thy disciples transgress the tradition of the elders? for they wash not their hands when they eat bread. (Matthew 15:2)

Christ condones the actions of his disciples and denies that they have sinned. He tells the Jews: ". . . to eat with unwashen hands, defileth not a man" (Matthew 15:20).

Yet this does not mean that Christ rejected the Old Law as a whole. The law concerning washing one's hands belongs to the ceremonial precepts. These precepts lost their validity with the coming of Christ. For the ceremonies of worship signified the faith of the Jews in God and in the future coming of the Messiah. But after Christ was born the need to indicate belief in His future coming disappeared. In fact, observance of the ceremonies would show a lack of faith in Christ as the true Messiah and son of God. Consequently, Aquinas argues that the ceremonial precepts not only need not, but must not, be obeyed any longer.

> . . . the ceremonies of the Old Law signified Christ as having yet to be born and to suffer, but our sacraments signify Him as already born and having suffered. Consequently, just as it would be a mortal sin now for anyone, in making a profession of faith, to say that Christ is yet to be born, which the fathers of old said devoutly and truthfully, so too it would be a mortal sin now to observe those ceremonies which the fathers of old fulfilled with devotion and fidelity. (*Summa Theologica,* Vol. 20, p. 302c-d)

The judicial precepts of the Old Law were also superseded by the coming of Christ and by the New Law. For these precepts were instituted "that they might shape the state of that people who were ordered to Christ" (*Ibid.*, p. 306b). With the coming of Christ, the state of that people (the Jews) changed and the need for these judicial precepts disappeared. Since, however, the judicial precepts regulated the relations of men from the point of view of justice, they may still be obeyed (unlike the ceremonial precepts), even though they have lost their utility in preparing the way for Christ.

The moral precepts of the Old Law, however, remain in full force even after Christ laid down the New Law. For, Aquinas writes, "the moral precepts, distinct from the ceremonial and judicial precepts, are about things pertaining of their very nature to good morals" (*Ibid.*, p. 251c-d). A little later he writes:

> . . . since good morals are those which are in accord with reason, and since also every judgment of human reason must be derived in some way from natural reason, it follows, of necessity, that all of the moral precepts belong to the law of nature. . . (*Ibid.*, pp. 251d-252a)

But the law of nature does not change "so that what previously was according to the natural law ceases to be so. In this sense," Aquinas writes in the question on natural law, "the natural law is altogether unchangeable in its first principles" (*Ibid.*, p. 225b). Consequently, if the natural law does not change, then the moral precepts of the Old Law also do not change.

Now, with the help of a great Christian theologian, we can understand how a Christian interprets the answer which Christ gave to the Pharisees. Christ not only condoned but encouraged His disciples to break the ceremonial precepts of the Old Law, such as the command to wash one's hands before breaking bread. But He upheld the precepts of the moral law.

> . . . out of the heart proceed evil thoughts, murders, adulteries, fornications, thefts, false witness, blasphemies:
> These are the things which defile a man. (Matthew 15:19-20)

Murder, adultery, theft, and so on are all prohibited by moral precepts of the Old Law; and Christ maintains that these acts remain sins and offenses against the New Law.

The passage from Chapter 22 contains two points that interest us here. In Verses 15-22, the Pharisees confront Christ with the problem of the relation betwen human law and divine law. Human law—in this case, the law of the Roman Empire to which Judea belonged as a province—decreed that tribute be paid to Rome. The problem is this: in paying tribute to Rome, do the Jews acknowledge Rome and Caesar as the highest authority in their lives? Are they substituting the temporal authority of Rome for God's authority? Does obeying the law of Rome imply disobedience to the law of God? This question was especially serious for the Jews, since the divine law as given to Moses directed their lives in the same detailed and intimate way in which human law regulated the conduct of Roman citizens. The ceremonial and judicial precepts of the Old Law included rules concerning food, clothing, marriage, inheritance, and similar matters.

The answer which Christ gives to the Pharisees is deceptively simple.

> . . . Render therefore unto Caesar the things which are Caesar's; and unto God the things that are God's. (Matthew 22:21)

This passage makes two related points. In the first place, Christ acknowledges that there are some things which are Caesar's. Secular authority has a definite place in human life. With the coming of the New Law, the divine law no longer extends to every aspect of human life, as the Old Law did which included ceremonial and judicial precepts as well as moral precepts.

But, in the second place, Christ also points out that there are some things which are not Caesar's but God's. This second point serves to balance the first one. Just as Christ disavows the monolithic theocratic state when He tells men to "render unto Caesar the things which are Caesar's," so He condemns the completely secular state when He reminds us that some things are God's. A totalitarian state that tries to rule all of a man's life and make the state the supreme authority in all matters offends against Christian teaching.

Both church and state have a function in man's life. Their authority extends to different kinds of human actions. Conflict occurs when divine law and human law each claims authority to regulate one and the same action, and when the precept of the divine law differs from the precept of the human law.

Then it becomes necessary to decide whether the action in question belongs properly to the realm of the state or of God.

In Verses 34-40 of Chapter 22, Christ takes up another question put to Him by the Pharisees. They want to know which is the greatest—that is, the most fundamental—precept of the law. Christ answers as follows.

> . . . Thou shalt love the Lord thy God with all thy heart, and with all thy soul, and with all thy mind.
> This is the first and great commandment.
> And the second is like unto it, Thou shalt love thy neighbour as thyself.
> On these two commandments hang all the law and the prophets. (Matthew 22:37-40)

This command to love God, we noted above, almost exactly repeats the words of Deuteronomy 6:5. Instead of pointing to one of the commandments of the Decalogue, which were written by God himself on the stone tablets given to Moses, Christ chooses the law of love as the basic commandment. Paul reflects this view in his first epistle to the Corinthians, when he calls charity—another word for love—the greatest of the theological virtues.

What does Christ mean by saying that the law bids us to love God? How can love be commanded? How do we recognize true love of God, and how do we distinguish it from hypocrisy? Christ offers no solution of these difficulties, and indeed shows no awareness of them. Nevertheless, this leaves unaltered the fact that "all the law and the prophets" hang on love toward God and neighbor. (See Matthew 22:40.)

IV

We now come to the last portion of our reading, two chapters from the Epistle to the Romans. Here Paul attempts to answer a question that must have bothered many early Christians, especially those who were converts from Judaism. As the other readings in this assignment show, the New Law as taught by Christ differs considerably from the Old Law. The latter contains moral, ceremonial, and judicial precepts. These precepts, especially the latter two kinds, contain highly detailed commands and injunctions concerning external actions. In the New Law, by contrast, much more emphasis is placed on the "law of love" in which the spirit counts for more than the letter of the law. We have already encountered Aquinas' view that the ceremonial and judicial precepts of the Old Law lost their validity with the coming of Christ. Thereafter, obedience to the judicial precepts lost its utility, while abidance by the ceremonial laws became positively sinful.

Quite naturally, then, the question arises: What is the relation between the Old and the New Law? Does the latter supersede the former? Do these laws supplement or oppose one another? Must the Old Law be despised now? How can it be despised, since it, too, comes from God?

Paul answers by citing the analogy of a married woman. As long as her husband lives, she is bound to him; but when he dies, she is free to marry someone else. Similar reasoning applies to those who were bound to the Old Law. The Old Law is now dead, and therefore men are now free from it and can adhere to the New Law.

Yet the Old Law and the New Law also have much in common. To understand this, let us examine Aquinas' analysis of the relation between two laws.

> . . . two laws may be distinguished from one another in two ways. First, through being altogether different, from the fact that they are ordered to different ends. . . Secondly, two laws may be distinguished from one another through one of them being more closely connected with the end and the other more remotely. . . (*Summa Theologica,* Vol. 20, p. 326b)

He then applies this distinction to the divine law in the following manner.

> . . . according to the first way the New Law is not distinct from the Old Law, because they both have the same end, namely, man's subjection to God. . . According to the second way, the New Law is distinct from the Old Law, because the Old Law is like a pedagogue of children. . . while the New Law is the law of perfection, since it is the law of charity. (*Ibid.,* p. 326c)

Thus, we must by no means think that the Old Law was bad, for it served the same end as the New Law does. "What shall we say then? Is the [Old] law sin? God forbid" (Romans 7:7).

On the contrary, Paul tells us a little later that "the law is holy, and the commandment holy, and just, and good" (Romans 7:12).

But the New Law takes better account of man's weaknesses. Man failed continually to obey the Old Law, because of his sinfulness. The punishment of sin being death, man was condemned to death as long as God judged him by the Old Law. With the coming of the New Law, man was freed from the Old Law and hence also from death. Man *can* obey the New Law; he need only love God. Paul explains the matter.

> For the law of the Spirit of life in Christ Jesus hath made me free from the law of sin and death.
>
> For what the law could not do, in that it was weak through the flesh, God sending his own Son in the likeness of sinful flesh, and for sin, condemned sin in the flesh:
>
> That the righteousness of the law might be fulfilled in us, who walk not after the flesh, but after the Spirit. (Romans 8:2-4)

The Old Law and the New Law are not antagonistic. On the contrary, "the New Law fulfils the Old" (*Summa Theologica*, Vol. 20, p. 327d). The Old Law indicated what men should do; but the New Law makes it possible for men actually to do it. God's love, which requires only man's love in return, saves men from sin and death. Paul sums up his certainty of salvation when he says, "If God be for us, who can be against us?" (Romans 8:31).

V

Are the commandments of God, as set forth in the Old Testament and in the New Testament, properly called laws?

In order to answer this question we must first state what a law is. Different definitions of law are, of course, possible. Let us take a definition which we shall encounter in the Sixth Reading—the *Treatise on Law* by Thomas Aquinas, which we have already consulted in this Guide. Leaving aside the problem whether this is the only definition, or the best definition, of law, let us merely see whether it fits the divine law, Old or New.

Aquinas writes:

> Thus . . . the definition of law may be gathered; and it is nothing other than an ordinance of reason for the common good, made by him who has care of the community, and promulgated. (*Summa Theologica*, Vol. 20, p. 208a)

Do the precepts of the Old Law fit this definition of law? Clearly they do. They are made for the good of mankind by God, Who has care of men. God knows what is good for men; He decrees accordingly. The precepts therefore stem from the divine reason. God promulgated the Old Law to the Jews by giving the law to Moses.

The same considerations apply to the New Law. We can see the reasonableness of the law in the very substitution of the New for the Old Law, since the latter no longer applied after Christ had come. The New Law is promulgated to all men since it applies to all men. That is why Christ sent His disciples to teach not just the Jews, but all mankind. (See Matthew 28:19-20.)

Both human and divine law conform to Aquinas' definition of law. How do these two kinds of law differ? Obviously, men make human law and God makes divine law. But do the two kinds of laws differ in any other way?

Which are the things that are Caesar's and which are the things that are God's?

It does not suffice to say that some things fall under human secular authority and law, and others directly under God's authority and law. We must be able to decide whether something is a proper subject for human legislation, or whether the state should leave it to God or His representatives on earth.

We begin with some easy cases. The manner of worshipping God should be decided by God and by the churches, not by the state. Similarly, the question of which side of the road cars ought to drive on should be decided by the state. But between the extremes that clearly belong to the one or the other sphere, there lies a vast middle area.

On what principle can we decide whether something belongs to the province of church or state? Everything which has to do with man's desire to be saved comes properly under the New Law. The problem of church and state does not arise under the Old Law. Through its ceremonial and judicial precepts, it regulated all of man's conduct in the Jewish theocracy. But in the Christian state this problem must be faced. If some human law interferes with man's preparation for salvation, such a law, in the Christian view, is invalid and without force.

This puts a great deal of human conduct under the rule of divine law. For the Christian religion regards all of man's life as a way toward God. Some actions must, of course, be regulated by human law, as long as such law is in accordance with the divine law and does not contravene it. Still, on this principle, every action that has consequences for man's moral perfection ultimately becomes a matter for the divine law. What is left for human law, except trivial matters? How does this condition differ from that in the Jewish state, where almost all of a man's actions were regulated by the Old Law?

Why is there any need for divine positive law?

We have already touched on this question earlier in the Guide. But it may be well to review this problem systematically. The question gains force if we ask it in this way: Why is there any need for divine positive law, over and above the natural law and the human positive law?

Before considering what function divine positive law performs, we must realize that there are a number of reasons why there seems to be no need for it. Aquinas, for instance, notes that in the first place, men live under the natural law. Through the natural law, men participate in the eternal law. The eternal law, however, is a divine law, consisting of the precepts of divine reason. This seems to obviate the need for divine positive law.

In the second place, man himself possesses the power of reason. Through this reason, he gives himself human positive law. This seems to leave no need for other positive law.

In the third place, the rest of nature needs no divine positive law, but depends simply on instinct and natural inclination. Why, then, should man need divine positive law, especially since he possesses the power of reason, an advantage denied to the lower parts of creation?

Aquinas considers the need for divine law in the *Summa Theologica,* Part I-II, Q. 91, A. 4. (See Vol. 20, pp. 210c-211c.) He begins by noting three reasons why the divine law seems not to be necessary. We have paraphrased these reasons above. You may be interested in trying to solve this problem yourself and comparing your solution with that of Aquinas. Here we will give only the following hint of how Aquinas solves the problem. The need for the divine positive law arises from (1) man's superior status in the hierarchy of creation, and (2) the fallibility and weakness of his rational powers.

SELF-TESTING QUESTIONS

The following questions are designed to help you test the thoroughness of your reading. Each question is to be answered by giving a page or pages of the reading assignment. Answers will be found on page 238 of this Reading Plan.

1 Through how many generations does God say He will punish the sins of men?

2 Do the people of Israel desire to speak to God directly?

3 What was the belief of the Sadducees with respect to resurrection?

4 Does man do those things which he wants to do?

5 What is the punishment for those who place the body above the spirit?

6 What kind of altar does God desire the people of Israel to build for Him?

7 How are the people of Israel to remember the words of God?

Fifth Reading

ARISTOTLE

The Athenian Constitution

Vol. 9, pp. 553-584

PLUTARCH

Lives of the Noble Grecians and Romans, "Solon"

Vol. 14, pp. 64-77

Laws and lawgivers, especially if they are ancient, customarily command esteem and respect. Socrates, when faced with the question whether he should flee from prison or remain and endure his unjust sentence, decided that he must stay out of reverence for the laws. He thought of the laws of Athens as persons, and found that he could not endure the prospect of facing them, if he should disobey them.

Not only ancient or primitive peoples feel this way about their lawgivers. The people of the United States hold the Constitution in awe and respect. The men who signed the Constitution are held in such honor that their biographers never fail to mention the fact that these men were among the signers.

The man whose life Plutarch writes and who is also

prominently mentioned by Aristotle in our present assignment belongs to the group of lawgiving heroes. Solon was famous even in antiquity for his wisdom and judgment. The most famous story concerning him —his encounter with King Croesus—is found not only in Plutarch but also in the history of Herodotus. Solon, in his travels, came to the court of Croesus, who asked him to name the happiest man in the world. Fully expecting to hear himself nominated, Croesus suffered disappointment when Solon explained that no living man could be called happy, because misfortune might still befall him. This answer, Plutarch says, gave "Croesus some pain, but not instruction."

Many years later Croesus' kingdom was overrun by the Persians under King Cyrus. Croesus was condemned to be burned publicly; thereupon he remembered Solon and loudly cried out three times "Solon!" Cyrus inquired why he invoked this name, and Croesus told how this present calamity had made him see the wisdom of Solon's earlier words. Plutarch finishes the tale as follows:

> When this was told Cyrus, who was a wiser man than Croesus, and saw in the present example Solon's Maxim confirmed, he not only freed Croesus from punishment, but honoured him as long as he lived; *and Solon had the glory, by the same saying, to save one king and instruct another.* (Vol. 14, p. 75c, italics added)

GUIDE TO

Fifth Reading

I

Newspaper stories about legislative bodies in the United States frequently refer to the legislators as "solons." It is not always clear whether the reporter is being sarcastic or whether he means the term to be as flattering as it should be. Along with such illustrious figures as Hammurabi and Moses, Solon is the prototype of the lawgiver. Almost without assistance he carried out a complete reform in the laws of Athens, the greatest and most enlightened city of classical Greece.

Flattering as the epithet "solon" is or should be, it really does not apply to legislators. For they make laws, while Solon made a constitution. Solon's achievement corresponds to that of the Constitutional Convention in Philadelphia in 1787. Some justification for Solon's fame can be seen in the fact that he accomplished alone a task equivalent to that performed by 55 delegates to the Constitutional Convention. In addition to framing a constitution for Athens, Solon also made a great many particular laws.

The reason why so much power and so much opportunity came to Solon lies in the political condition of Athens at the time. There existed a deep, almost irreconcilable, split between two parties in the city. Aligned against one another stood, on one side, the rich who favored an oligarchical form of government, and on the other side, the poor who wanted a democratic government. Plutarch describes the situation:

> Then the wisest of the Athenians, perceiving Solon was of all men the only one not implicated in the rtoubles, that he had not joined in the exactions of the rich, and was not involved in the necessities of the poor, pressed him to succour the commonwealth and compose the differences. (Vol. 14, p. 69a)

Solon was given complete powers. The Athenians

chose Solon to new-model and make laws for the commonwealth, giving him the entire power over everything, their magistracies, their assemblies, courts, and councils; that he should appoint the number, times of meeting, and what estate they must have that could be capable of these, and dissolve or continue any of the present constitutions, according to his pleasure. (*Ibid.*, p. 70c-d)

Solon, although endowed with such complete powers, chose not to become a despot, but to set up a constitutional government instead. Aristotle praises Solon for his restraint.

[He] was so moderate and public-spirited in all his . . . actions, that when it was within his power to put his fellow-citizens beneath his feet and establish himself as tyrant, he preferred instead to incur the hostility of both parties by placing his honour and the general welfare above his personal aggrandisement. . . (Vol. 9, p. 555b)

Plutarch tells us that Solon himself was aware that he could easily have become a tyrant. That he refrained, Solon wrote in a poem, "will be my chiefest fame" (Vol. 14, p. 69c).

Lawgivers such as Solon (*i.e.*, men who originate or completely change a constitution) played an important role in Greece and Rome. In Plutarch's *Lives,* there is not only a biography of Solon, but also one of Lycurgus, the lawgiver of Sparta, and one of Numa Pompilius, an early lawgiving king of the Romans. (See the Sixth Reading in *A General Introduction to the Great Books.*) Plato, in the *Republic* and the *Laws,* has Socrates and the "Athenian Stranger" act as lawgivers for ideal states. Aristotle, in Book II of the *Politics,* discusses not only the ideal states of Plato but also those of Phaleas and Hippodamus. In the *Athenian Constitution,* he remarks that there have been, up to his time, eleven significant changes in the constituion of Athens. All the early reforms were brought about by single men and are associated with their names. He cites Theseus, Draco, Solon, Pisistratus, and Cleisthenes as responsible for the first five changes. The last of these initiated constitutional reforms in the year 508 B.C.

Chief recognition as a legal figure during Roman times must be accorded to the Emperor Justinian I, who lived from 483 to 565 A.D. Justinian did not originate or even reform Roman law. He did, however, bring order out of the chaotic state in which he found the law. Justinian's achievement lay in consolidating a body of law that had grown up haphazardly out of many different sources. His laws are collected in the *Corpus juris civilis,* the chief part of which is the *Digest.*

In more modern times, the Code Napoleon bears the name of a single man. Napoleon did not, however, make the code himself. He had in fact only a little part in the task which was accomplished by a council. The code is now generally referred to simply as the Code Civil.

Great lawgivers—as distinguished from men who compile or consolidate bodies of law—require unusual gifts of mind and character. Rousseau discusses the qualities necessary for such a person (whom he calls a "legislator") in Book II of the *Social Contract.* (This work will be discussed in the Eleventh Reading.)

> . . . if great princes are rare, how much more so are great legislators? The former have only to follow the pattern which the latter have to lay down. The legislator is the engineer who invents the machine, the prince merely the mechanic who sets it up and makes it go. (*Social Contract,* Bk. II, Ch. 7, Vol. 38, p. 400c-d)

Rousseau emphasizes the difficulty of the legislator's task. He must almost change human nature so that man, accustomed to living in solitude and independence, can learn to live in society. The office of legislator, as Rousseau conceives it, precedes the state.

> This office, which sets up the Republic, nowhere enters into its constitution; it is an individual and superior function. . . (*Ibid.,* p. 401a)

Rousseau, we should remember, considers an imaginary situation, when a people, totally without government, makes the transition from a state of nature to civil society. The task which actual legislators, like Solon, perform is less dramatic, more moderate, and more possible.

II

We shall now examine some of the Athenian laws and legal institutions. Much of our most reliable information concerning them comes from Aristotle's *Athenian Constitution*. In his later years, Aristotle compiled a large collection of works describing the constitutions of Greek cities, but only the one dealing with Athens has survived. The book begins with a historical part (Chapters 1-41) in which Aristotle describes the work of Solon and other lawgivers; in the remaining chapters (42-69) Aristotle outlines the constitution of Athens as it functioned in his time, *i.e.*, during the fourth century B.C.

There are in general three functions that have to be performed with respect to laws: (1) the laws have to be made; (2) they have to be executed or enforced; (3) they have to be applied to particular cases. These three functions of government are usually distinguished as (1) legislative, (2) executive, and (3) judicial. The Constitution of the United States assigns these three functions to three separate branches of the government. The Congress, consisting of the House of Representatives and the Senate, makes the laws. The President, together with his cabinet and the administrative departments headed by the cabinet members, executes and enforces the laws. The Federal Courts, made up of District Courts, Courts of Appeal, and the Supreme Court, as well as some other specialized courts, handle the judicial application of the laws. At the same time the Constitution contains a careful system of checks and balances, so that no branch of government can seize control at the expense of the other two branches.

Who exercised the lawmaking functions under Solon's constitution? Neither Aristotle nor Plutarch is very clear about this. Both convey the impression that all the laws thought to be necessary were made by Solon and that thereafter the only problem was one of interpreting the laws. "All his laws," Plutarch writes, "he established for an hundred years. . . The council all jointly swore to confirm the laws" (Vol. 14, pp. 73d-74a). Evidently, Solon believed that his laws should remain in force without alteration for at least a century. To avoid the pressure of public opinion for changing them, he left the country.

When he had completed his organization of the constitution in the manner that has been described, he found himself beset by people coming to him and harassing him concerning his laws, criticizing here and questioning there, till, as he wished neither to alter what he had decided on nor yet to be an object of ill will to every one by remaining in Athens, he set off on a journey to Egypt . . . giving out that he should not return for ten years. (Vol. 9, p. 557a)

With the laws not susceptible to either alteration or addition, their interpretation and application became all the more important. These functions belong to the courts. Under Solon's constitution, all citizens had the privilege and the duty of serving in the courts. In this provision lies the democratic character of Solon's constitution; it gave great power to the people, poor as well as rich. Only citizens of substantial wealth could serve in the administrative positions, but the courts were open to all.

. . . since the laws were not drawn up in simple and explicit terms (but like the one concerning inheritances and wards of state), disputes inevitably occurred, and the courts had to decide in every matter, whether public or private. Some persons in fact believe that Solon deliberately made the laws indefinite, in order that the final decision might be in the hands of the people. (Vol. 9, p. 556d)

Two hundred years later, when Aristotle described the constitution then current in Athens, the power of the people had become even greater. The function and make-up of the courts had not appreciably changed, but apparently the lawmaking power had been given to the people; namely, to the Assembly which was composed of all the citizens, without regard to any requirements of wealth. Furthermore, all the administrative officers were selected from the citizenry by lot.

Thus we see that in Aristotle's time the legislative, executive, and judicial power were all in the hands of the people. "The franchise" [*i.e.*, membership in the Assembly], Aristotle writes, "is open to all who are of citizen birth by both parents" (Vol. 9, p. 572b). Legislative power, in other words, was given to all citizens. Aristotle, a little later, tells us that there are no special qualifications for executive positions: "All the magistrates that are concerned with the ordinary routine of administration are elected by lot . . ." (Vol. 9, p. 572d). Neither is there any requirement except citizenship for membership on a jury. "The juries for the law-courts are chosen by lot by the nine Archons . . ." (Vol. 9, p. 581d). These crucial passages reveal where the governmental power lay in Athens; the rest of the Athenian Constitution treats of the duties of particular offices.

III

What functions do the three powers of government have with respect to law?

The legislative power makes the laws; the executive power enforces them; the judicial power applies them. The Constitution of the United States, we have noted, provides a separate branch of government for each of the three powers. In only very limited ways can one branch of the government exert influence on another branch. Such overlapping of functions as the Constitution provides is for the sake of providing checks on the power which any one branch of the government may acquire. The President, for example, cannot make any laws; he can, however, veto a law passed by Congress, if it seems bad to him. This checks the power of Congress. On the other hand, the Congress can check the President's power somewhat. The President appoints his cabinet officers and other high government officials; but these appointments must be made with the "advice and consent" of the Senate.

In what fashion do the legislative and judicial powers exert influence and checks on one another? Although Congress makes all the laws, it operates under some restrictions concerning the matters about which it may legislate. The Bill of Rights provides that "Congress shall make no law respecting an establishment of religion . . ." (Vol. 43, p. 17a). In the main body of the Constitution itself, we read that "No bill of attainder or ex post facto law shall be passed" (Vol. 43, p. 13d). Who enforces these provisions of the Constitution? For the most part, of course, Congress simply abides by the language and intent of the Constitution.

Nevertheless, occasionally a question arises whether a law is in keeping with the Constitution. Such a question is settled by the courts. If a law is not in keeping with the Constitution, if it is "unconstitutional," then the law cannot be applied and no one can be convicted under it. In the American system, therefore, the courts serve as boards of review, passing on the constitutionality of laws made by Congress. The courts have this reviewing function in addition to their regular duties of hearing cases under the law. The Constitution acts as a standard against which human positive laws are measured by the courts.

The Athenian constitution seems to have functioned in a somewhat similar fashion. The ultimate power of interpreting the laws lay in the law courts. This, as both Plutarch and Aristotle mention, was particularly important because of the obscurity and vagueness of many laws. Furthermore, any person who made a motion in the Assembly (*i.e.*, any citizen who acted in his capacity as legislator) could be indicted for making an illegal proposal, if his motion was not brought up in the right fashion or if it seemed to be against the best interests of the state. (See Vol. 9, p. 580a-b.) The courts decided cases like these also.

In the Athenian constitution, then, the courts had great power, ruling on both the interpretation and on the constitutionality of laws. We must remember that the same persons served in the Assembly and in the courts. All of the citizens belonged to the Assembly, and the juries for the courts were selected from the citizens. The juries numbered 500, 1,000, or even 1,500 members. (See Vol. 9, p. 583b-c.) This number constituted a large percentage of the citizens of a small city like Athens. Hence the Athenian citizens must often have found themselves in the position of first making a law and then interpreting it or judging its constitutionality.

Do you think that this concentration of power in the hands of the citizens made for good government? Was anything lost by having the same institution, *i.e.*, the Assembly, act in both a legislative and a judicial capacity? Is it an essential part of democratic government to place the judiciary in the hands of *all* the people?

Is the cancellation of debts, as enacted by Solon, legally justifiable?

One of Solon's first acts as head of the government consisted in cancelling all debts that had been contracted. These debts had threatened to disrupt the state; the poor were being gradually enslaved by the rich, since the loans were made upon the security of the debtor's person. Plutarch describes the situation vividly:

> All the people were indebted to the rich; and either they tilled their land for their creditors, paying them a sixth part of the increase, and were, therefore, called Hectemorii and Thetes, or else they engaged their body for the debt, and might be seized, and either sent into slavery at home, or sold to strangers; some (for no law forbade it) were forced to sell their children, or fly their country to avoid the cruelty of their creditors... (Vol. 14, pp. 68d-69a)

This passage makes clear the need for credit reform. Obviously, Solon's action in cancelling the existing debts helped to preserve the Athenian state. However, we may still ask whether his action was legal, or just.

Since the debts in question were legally contracted, does Solon's action not amount to expropriation? Why could Solon not have settled on a compromise, making debts secured by the person of the debtor illegal in the future, but continuing to honor existing debts? Does not Solon's action set a precedent for future disavowal of past contracts?

The United States Constitution explicitly forbids ex post facto laws. Such laws are made after an event has happened, but are applicable nevertheless to the prior event. If such laws have legal force, no man is safe in performing any action. The fact that an action is not prohibited by law does not mean that a later law might not prohibit it and, after the fact, make the action illegal. Ex post facto laws obviously destroy any incentive to abide by the laws; for it makes impossible any certainty about what is and what is not legal.

Does Solon's cancellation of debts constitute an ex post facto law?

SELF-TESTING QUESTIONS

The following questions are designed to help you test the thoroughness of your reading. Each question is to be answered by giving a page or pages of the reading assignment. Answers will be found on page 238 of this Reading Plan.

1. Why did Solon repeal Draco's laws?
2. For how long did Solon intend his laws to last?
3. What was Solon's law with respect to those who remain neutral in a revolution?
4. What sort of person was the tyrant Pisistratus?
5. Who introduced the law that the jurors in Athens should be paid?
6. What kind of government was established when Athens lost the Peloponnesian War?
7. At what age did Athenians, in Aristotle's time, become full-fledged citizens?
8. What were the duties of the archons in Aristotle's time?
9. What was the procedure for choosing jurors?
10. What was the voting procedure of the jurors?

Sixth Reading

AQUINAS

Summa Theologica

Part I-II, QQ. 90, 94

Vol. 20, pp. 205-208, 220-226

"The laws of a nation form the most instructive portion of its history. . . ." These words are Gibbon's, taken from the beginning of the chapter in the *Decline and Fall of the Roman Empire* in which he discusses the achievement of Justinian, the emperor responsible for the collection and codification of Roman law. Justinian's *Digest* and *Institutes* were published A.D. 533. Such was the fame of Justinian that Aquinas in the *Summa Theologica,* written almost 750 years after the *Digest,* does not refer to him by name, but simply calls him "the Jurist." In the eyes of Aquinas, Justinian's fame rivals that of Aristotle, whom he called "the Philosopher," and that of Maimonides, whom he called "the Rabbi."

Justinian's great accomplishment lay in the collection and consolidation of thousands of laws and decrees issued over hundreds of years by various authorities. Aquinas does not deal with particular laws or edicts; he is concerned with the principles of law. Whereas Justinian is a jurist, Aquinas is a philosopher of law.

Aquinas' interest extends to all law, not just to Roman law or the law of any one country. He is not content to consider only human law; all kinds of law come under his purview—human, divine, eternal, and natural law.

In this assignment we read the question dealing with the "Essence of Law" (Q. 90) and the question treating "Of The Natural Law" (Q. 94). In the next assignment, we shall turn to Aquinas' consideration "Of Human Law" (QQ. 95-97).

The questions which Aquinas asks are typical philosophical questions. What is a law? Who makes it? What is its purpose? In *Great Books of the Western World,* Aquinas shares the title of "Philosopher of Law" with Immanuel Kant. Aquinas and Kant were not jurists in the narrow sense of the word; both of them were concerned with the underlying principles of law.

GUIDE TO

Sixth Reading

I

Question 90 of the *Treatise on Law*[1] deals with the essence of law, that is, with what law is. In the concluding article of the question, Aquinas arrives at a definition of law. Before turning to it, however, let us examine some definitions of law offered by predecessors of Aquinas. Plato, even in the long work called *Laws,* never arrives at a formal definition of law. He contents himself with figurative remarks, as, for instance, when he compares man to a puppet drawn by strings and cords. ". . . there is one among these cords," he says, "which every man ought to grasp and never let go, but to pull with it against all the rest; and this is the sacred and golden cord of reason, called by us the common law of the State . . ." (Vol. 7, p. 650a).

Aristotle, too, though generally more given to precise definitions than Plato, tells us what law is only in passing. In the last chapter of the *Nicomachean Ethics,* in the course of discussing how law and the state train the youth in virtue, he writes that "... law *has* compulsive power, while it is at the same time a rule proceeding from a sort of practical wisdom and reason" (Vol. 9, p. 435a).

Cicero, writing in the first century B.C. during the dying days of the Roman Republic, presents us with a conception of law that reflects his study of Plato and of the Stoic philosophers.

[1] Part of the *Treatise on Law* constitutes the sixth assignment of the Reading Plan entitled *Development of Political Theory and Government.* We refer the reader to that place for a discussion of the general plan and arrangement of the *Summa Theologica* and the place of the *Treatise on Law* in it, as well as for some explanatory remarks about the structure of each question and article.

. . . Law is the distinction between things just and unjust, made in agreement with that primal and most ancient of all things, Nature; and in conformity to Nature's standard are framed those human laws which inflict punishment upon the wicked but defend and protect the good. (*De Legibus*, Bk. II, Ch. 5, pp. 385-387)[2]

Near the beginning of Justinian's *Institutes*, the author enumerates all the different kinds of written human laws.

The written law consists of statutes, plebiscites, senatusconsults, enactments of the Emperors, edicts of the magistrates, and answers of those learned in the law. (*Institutes*, Bk. I, Title II, 3, p. 5)[3]

This, of course, is no definition of law but rather an enumeration of various things that are called by the name "law." The author goes on to explain what each of the terms enumerated means; for instance, "a senatusconsult is a command and ordinance of the senate." Most interesting is the fact that, according to the *Institutes*, the commands of an emperor have the status of law. "Whatsoever pleases the sovereign," we read, "has the force of law" (*Institutes*, Bk. I, Title II, 6). Aquinas quotes this definition in Q. 90, A. 1, Obj. 3. We shall consider this definition later on. (See p. 86.) Now let us turn to Aquinas' own definition.

. . . [Law] is nothing other than an ordinance of reason for the common good, made by him who has care of the community, and promulgated. (Q. 90, A. 4, Ans., p. 208a)

Compared with the other statements about law, Aquinas' definition is a model of precision and neatness. The four parts of the definition indicate four conditions that are essential to the nature of a rule of law. In the Aristotelian tradition which Aquinas here follows, the definition states the four *causes* of law.

Question 90 consists of four articles, one on each of the four parts in the definition of law. Article 1 states the *formal cause* of law: Law is an ordinance of reason. This is the unchanging

---

[2] Cicero, *De Re Publica, De Legibus,* trans. by C. W. Keyes. Cambridge, Mass., 1951: Harvard University Press (Loeb Classical Library).

[3] *Imperatoris Justiniani Institutionum Libri Quatuor,* ed. and trans. by J. D. Moyle. 2 vols. Oxford: At the Clarendon Press, 1883.

form which any law has, no matter what its content; law is something reasonable. Article 2 gives us the *final cause* of law, namely, that it is directed to the common good. This is the purpose of a law, the end (*finis*) which it serves. In Article 3, Aquinas tells us the *efficient cause* of law: It is made by him who has care of the community. The efficient cause is the thing or person who immediately initiates a given action or motion—in this case the action of lawmaking. Article 4 finally presents the *material cause* of law. The material cause is that with which or upon which the other causes operate. Here it is the written or spoken words which are a law, provided that what the words state is something reasonable, is directed to the common good, and is declared by him who has care of the community. Promulgation is thus, in a sense, the material cause of law.

Each of the four parts in Aquinas' definition of law needs to be examined a little further. First, consider that law is said to be a thing of reason. The purpose of law is to cause men to act properly or to prevent them from acting wrongly. But that whereby one man causes another man to act in a certain way is his will. The father imposes his will upon his children; the sovereign's will must be obeyed; the Lord's Prayer contains the line "Thy will be done." A law, it seems, ought to be called a "fiat of the will" rather than "an ordinance of reason."

This objection contains much truth. On the basis of Aquinas' own analysis of how the faculties and powers of the human person operate, the will is that which initiates movement. It causes all other powers to move, even the faculty of reason. Insofar as a law results in action, it expresses the sovereign's will, not his reason. Yet the sovereign's reason is also involved, for the resulting action is lawful action, not merely willful or arbitrary action. Vicious or unlawful actions may result from the operation of the will; but what characterizes lawful actions is that they are in accordance with reason. According to Aquinas, not everything which the sovereign wills is law; on this point he clearly differs from the Roman view set down in the *Institutes*.

Second, we can question the notion that law must necessarily be directed to the common good. We may grant that law being a thing of reason should be directed to something good. But why does it have to be the common good? Does not law serve the happiness of individuals as well as the welfare of the community?

Here again the answer concedes the truth contained in the objection. The end of the law is the happiness of men, but only insofar as happiness is a common human good, a good in which all men should share and not one that is possessed by certain men to the exclusion of others. The law also serves the good of the human community. It promotes and preserves the welfare of the state. But even in this way, the law contributes to the happiness of the men who are members of the community. Aquinas writes:

> Now the first principle in practical matters, which are the object of the practical reason, is the last end; and the last end of human life is happiness or beatitude . . . Consequently the law must regard principally the relationship to happiness. Moreover, since every part is ordered to the whole, as imperfect to perfect, and since one man is a part of the perfect community, the law must properly look to the relationship to universal happiness. (p. 206c)

Then Aquinas adds a little later:

> . . . since the law is chiefly ordered to the common good, any other precept in regard to some individual work, must be empty of the nature of a law, save in so far as it regards the common good. (p. 206d)

Third, we can ask why laws have to be made by some special person or persons. Would any person's pronouncement be a law if it is reasonable and aims at the common good? Aquinas answers in the negative. Common opinion seems to agree with this view.

A private person's opinion concerning what ought to be done does not have the force of law no matter how good it may be. Even if such an opinion were promulgated (as it might be through newspapers, television, or other media of mass communication), it does not have the sanctions of the state behind it. It thus remains on the level of counsel or advice. Individuals or pressure groups may try to promulgate their opinions and persuade others to act in accordance with them; but they cannot make laws. No punishment, for instance, is imposed on those who do not follow such advice.

Aquinas tells us the reason why not everyone is capable of making laws. Laws, he reminds us, look to the common good. But the common good is the good of the whole people. Hence it also belongs to the whole people to make laws.

> And therefore the making of a law belongs either to the whole people or to a public personage who has care of the whole people; for in all other fields the directing of anything to the end concerns him to whom the end belongs. (p. 207b)

According to this passage, the lawmaking power essentially belongs to the whole people. A single person can make laws only if he acts for the whole people; such a person is called a "vicegerent," *i.e.*, someone who acts in the behalf of others.

Fourth, we may raise a question as to the need for the promulgation of law. At first, it seems quite obvious that a law must be proclaimed; otherwise, how can people know about it and obey it? But, though this point seems obvious as long as we speak only of the human law, some doubt is introduced when we realize that Aquinas means his definition of law to apply to all kinds of law. Thus, for Aquinas, natural law definitely belongs to the category, "law." Here we do not seem to find any promulgation. Aquinas writes:

> For the natural law above all has the character of law. But the natural law needs no promulgation. Therefore it is not essential to a law that it be promulgated. (p. 207d)

Yet Aquinas answers this doubt which he himself has raised:

> The natural law is promulgated by the very fact that God instilled it into man's mind so as to be known by him naturally. (p. 208a)

Natural law, in other words, is promulgated. The manner of promulgation, however, is different from that employed for human laws. God Himself, according to Aquinas, promulgates the natural law. He does not use newspapers or town-criers to promulgate it. The fact that this law is implanted in the nature of each man, so that he can come to know it without the help of verbal promulgation, is what makes this law a *natural* law.

The objections that we have considered concerning Aquinas'

definition of law are taken from those which Aquinas himself raises in the four articles of Question 90. Each article in a question of the *Summa Theologica,* the reader will remember, contains several objections, *i.e.,* statements of opinion contrary to Aquinas' own views. Each objection is considered and answered by Aquinas. In the foregoing pages we have paraphrased the following objections and answers: In Article 1, Objection 3 and its Answer; in Article 2, Objection 3 with its Answer; in Article 3, the body of the article itself; in Article 4, Objection 1 and its Answer.

II

Now let us turn to Question 94, devoted to a detailed consideration of the natural law. This is the most sustained examination of natural law in *Great Books of the Western World,* and probably the first such treatment anywhere. Stoic philosophers refer in their writings to Law of Nature, but what they mean by "Nature" is quite different from what Aquinas means. Furthermore, we do not find in the writings of the Stoics an extended treatment of natural law.

The closest anticipation of Aquinas' conception of natural law occurs in Aristotle's *Nicomachean Ethics.* There we find a discussion not of natural law, but of natural justice. Indeed, the notion of "natural law" could hardly be expressed in the Greek language. "Nomos," the word for law, connotes that which is conventional and hence opposed to the natural. To speak of a natural law would, therefore, be as self-contradictory as to speak of a natural convention.

Aquinas begins his discussion of natural law by noting that it is *not* a habit (Q. 94, A. 1). Like any other law, ". . . the natural law is something appointed by reason, just as a proposition is a work of reason" (Q. 94, A. 1, Ans., p. 221b). Natural law consists of a number of precepts, *i.e.,* propositions cast in the imperative mood. Even though the natural law is not itself a habit, the precepts of which it consists may be habitually acknowledged. In the same way, we sometimes call the indemonstrable principles of the speculative reason "habits" because these principles are propositions which we habitually affirm.

Article 1 of Question 94 contains a peculiarity that is rarely found in the *Summa Theologica.* As in all articles of this work, the statement of objections is followed by an argument—"On the contrary"—which states the position that Aquinas ultimately is going to take. In this case, however, the argument—"On the contrary"—evidently proves too much, for Aquinas feels constrained to give an answer to it as well as to the regular objections. The argument in the contrary sense attempts to show that the natural law cannot be a habit because possession of a habit enables a man to act in accordance with it. But the natural law is possessed by all men, even by children and by those who are damned. Yet neither children nor the damned act in accordance with the natural law. And so, the argument in the contrary sense concludes, natural law cannot be a habit.

Although Aquinas agrees that it is not a habit, he denies the validity of this argument. It is possible, he maintains, to possess a habit and yet not be able to use it because of some impediment. Thus a sleeping man cannot use any of his habits because of the impediment of sleep, and a child cannot use some of his habits because of the impediment of his youth.

In the second article of Question 94, Aquinas considers whether the natural law consists of only one precept or of several. He answers that the natural law contains many precepts but that they all flow from one first precept. The precepts of the natural law are the first principles of the practical reason, *i.e.,* reason concerned with action. As such, they are self-evident and undemonstrable, just as the first principles of the speculative reason are self-evident. Aquinas tells us what the first principle in the realm of human action is.

> . . . good is the first thing that falls under the apprehension of the practical reason, which is directed to action; for every agent acts for an end, which has the aspect of good. (p. 222b)

The first principle in the practical order, therefore, concerns the good.

Hence this is the first precept of law, that good is to be pursued and done, and evil is to be avoided. All other precepts of the natural law are based upon this, so that whatever the practical reason naturally apprehends as man's good belongs to the precepts of the natural law as something to be done or avoided. (p. 222c)

Articles 1 and 2 cover the most important points concerning the natural law. The problems raised in the succeeding articles are solved in terms of what has been said so far. For instance, since the first precept of the natural law is to do good, we can immediately answer in the affirmative the question posed at the beginning of Article 3: "Whether All Acts of Virtue Are Prescribed by the Natural Law?" All virtuous acts aim at the good; and for that reason they are prescribed by the natural law. Article 4 raises the question "Whether the Natural Is the Same in all Men?" Here, too, the answer is affirmative. But Aquinas adds an important caution. The first principles of reason are the same for all men, in the sphere of both the speculative and the practical reason. In the case of the speculative reason, however, not only are the first principles the same for everyone, but so also are the conclusions. That the whole is greater than its parts holds for all men and all times; and from this, together with other principles and definitions, conclusions follow which similarly hold for all men. Such, for example, are the conclusions of geometry. In the case of the practical reason, the first principles are also the same for all men. But the conclusions drawn from them are not the same for all men because they involve contingent matters. Aquinas gives us an example of what he means:

. . . it is right and true for all to act according to reason. And from this principle it follows as a proper conclusion that goods entrusted to another should be restored to their owner. Now this is true for the majority of cases, but it may happen in a particular case that it would be injurious, and therefore unreasonable, to restore goods held in trust; for instance if they are claimed for the purpose of fighting against one's country. (p. 224b)

Hence we can say that what ought to be done is the same for all men only when we consider the most general principles of action. But when we consider the contingent details involved in particular actions, we find that what ought to be done may be the same for the majority of men, but not for all. And even when what ought to be done is the same for all men, it may not be known by all men. This, however, is a defect which the practical reason shares with the speculative reason. Even though it is true for all men that the three interior angles of a triangle in Euclidean space are equal to two right angles, this is not known to all men.

These same considerations also serve to outline the answer to the next problem (Article 5), "Whether the Natural Law Can be Changed?" Obviously, the first principles of the practical reason, which are and remain the same for all men, cannot be changed. But the secondary precepts of the natural law, which may differ from man to man according to the contingent circumstances of a particular time and place, are not unchangeable. Indeed, to say that these principles may differ is to say that they are alterable.

Finally, in Article 6, Aquinas asks "Whether the Law of Nature Can Be Abolished from the Heart of Man?" The previous article established that the first precepts of the natural law are unalterable; now in this article we read that these same first precepts can in no way be erased from the heart of man. This means that man always is aware of them; he knows that he should pursue the good. Sometimes, however, Aquinas adds, these first principles are blotted out as far as a particular action goes, because of the intrusion of a strong passion, such as concupiscence. Thus a man may, through passion, pursue evil even though he knows that he should pursue good.

The so-called secondary precepts of the natural law can actually be themselves erased from the human heart. Such a precept as "Thou shalt not steal" can be eradicated and forgotten if inveterate custom among a people has made stealing acceptable.

III

Is there a natural law for Man?

Although we have reviewed in some detail Aquinas' remarks about what natural law is, we have not yet discussed whether there actually is a natural law. Obviously, the author of the *Treatise on Law* thinks that there is. We find his defense of this point of view in Question 91, Article 2, entitled "Whether There Is in Us a Natural Law?" This article, in turn, depends on the previous one in which Aquinas undertakes to prove that there is an eternal law. We must, therefore, give a moment's consideration to the eternal law.

In the Christian view, the world is ruled by Divine Providence.

> Therefore the very Idea of the government of things in God, the Ruler of the universe, has the nature of a law. And since the Divine Reason's conception of things is not subject to time but is eternal . . . this kind of law must be called eternal. (p. 208c)

Aquinas makes an easy transition from the eternal to the natural law. ". . . since all things subject to Divine providence are ruled and measured by the eternal law . . . it is evident that all things partake somewhat of the eternal law . . ." (p. 209b). Things partake of the eternal law by the inclinations to their proper ends which are implanted in them. This is also true of man. But the way in which the eternal law is implanted in man is more excellent than the manner in which other things are guided by Divine Providence. Because man is a rational creature, his inclination to his proper end is instilled in him as a command which he himself can consciously formulate. Through his own reason, man comes to understand the law of his own nature. Unlike brute animals and lower beings, which are moved toward their ends instinctually and almost automatically, man is inclined toward his end by knowledge of it which he can attain through his own reason.

The natural law, Aquinas writes, "is nothing else than the rational creature's participation of the eternal law" (p. 209c). In the reply to an objection, Aquinas explains the difference between the way in which man participates in the eternal law and the way in which other creatures do:

> . . . because the rational creature partakes of it [the eternal law] in an intellectual and rational manner, therefore the participation of the eternal law in the rational creature is properly called a law, since a law is something pertaining to reason . . . Irrational creatures, however, do

not partake of it in a rational manner, and so there is no participation of the eternal law in them, except by way of likeness. (p. 209c-d)

Is the natural law really law?

Aquinas' definition of law as given in Question 90 applies very clearly to human positive law. Does it apply equally to natural law, or is it only a figure of speech to call the latter by the name of "law"?

(1) Natural law is an ordinance of reason. Positive law, in addition, is also something emanating from the will of the lawgiver. What the lawgiver wills has to be reasonable in order that his command be lawful rather than lawless, but there is an element of the willful in human positive law. In fact, this willful element occurs because the making of a positive law involves a voluntary choice among several alternatives, each of which constitutes a somewhat arbitrary determination of a principle of natural law. Rules of positive law cannot be simply deduced from the precepts of natural law. They are derived from the natural law, but the derivation is by determination (which involves the will as well as the reason), not by deduction (which involves the reason alone). If reason alone could deduce human laws from the natural law, there would be no need for a lawgiver; each person's reason would suffice to deduce the law for given circumstances.

What natural law lacks is exactly this element of arbitrariness or willfulness which is so important in human law. The natural law is a product of reason alone; it does not need the cooperation of the will.

(2) Natural law is directed toward the common good. Nevertheless, the goods toward which the human positive law and the natural law are directed are different. The positive law aims at the good of the community, at the political common good. The natural law aims at the good common to all human beings which is happiness or beatitude. These two goods are both common although not common in the same sense.

(3) Natural law is made by a lawgiver if we consider God as one. But God is a lawgiver in a different sense than that in which a whole people or its vicegerent is a lawgiver. Again we

note that human positive law depends in part on the will of the human lawgiver, and that it is directed toward the political common good. When we call God the lawgiver of natural law, we do not imply that there is anything arbitrary about the natural law, or that it aims at anything except the individual person's happiness.

(4) The natural law is promulgated, but the mode of promulgation is quite different from that of the positive law. Human positive law is promulgated verbally, and human beings remember it. Lest they forget the law or be tempted to disobey it, sanctions in the form of punishment are provided.

The natural law is promulgated through being inscribed in the hearts of men. It can be learned by any man who applies himself to the task. Man's own reason can discover the dictates of the natural law. This is surely quite different from positive law: Reason does not suffice to discover what the human law is, because, as we must recall once again, there is something arbitrary about the rules of law which men institute for the government of the political community.

In Justinian's Institutes *we read that law is "that which pleases the prince." Is this a good definition of law?*

We referred to this definition of law in Section I above. It has attained fame or perhaps infamy, because it so unequivocally dissociates law from any considerations of reason or justice and simply makes law equivalent to the pronouncement of the sovereign. Gibbon ascribes this definition to Ulpian, a Roman lawyer of the third century A.D., or to Tribonian, the jurist largely responsible for the codification of laws under Justinian. Gibbon criticizes this conception of law in scathing words:

> . . . it was not before the ideas and even the language of the Romans had been corrupted that a *royal* law, and an irrevocable gift of the people, were created by the fancy of Ulpian, or more probably of Tribonian himself; and the origin of Imperial power, though false in fact and slavish in its consequence, was supported on a principle of freedom and justice. "The pleasure of the emperor has the vigour and effect of law, since the

Roman people, by the royal law, have transferred to their prince the full extent of their own power and sovereignty." The will of a single man, of a child, perhaps, was allowed to prevail over the wisdom of ages and the inclinations of millions, and the degenerate Greeks were proud to declare that in his hands alone the arbitrary exercise of legislation could be safely deposited. (*Decline and Fall of the Roman Empire,* Vol. 41, p. 74d)

But if Gibbon implies that this definition of law reflects the degeneracy of the Roman empire, we must in fairness point out that a similar statement about law can be quoted from *The Leviathan,* written by the English philosopher Hobbes:

The law is made by the sovereign power, and all that is done by such power is warranted . . . (Vol. 23, p. 157b)

A few lines farther down, Hobbes tells us what a good law is:

A good law is that which is needful, for the good of the people, and withal perspicuous. (*Ibid.*)

Let us compare Ulpian's and Hobbe's definitions with Aquinas' definition of law. All three writers would probably agree that the proper person, namely, the people or its vicegerent, has to make the law and that the law has to be promulgated.

Aquinas differs from the other two writers in regard to the role of reason in law. Aquinas makes law a thing of *reason.* For Ulpian and Hobbes, law is something purely arbitrary; that is, something which merely depends on the *will* of the sovereign. But Aquinas maintains that what the sovereign wills must be something reasonable if it is to be law. Ulpian and Hobbes, on the other hand, believe that anything emanating from the sovereign will has the force of law.

A second and related difference between the two definitions of law consists in the way in which they view an unjust law. For Aquinas, a law must be something reasonable and must be directed to the common good. Consequently, an unjust law is no law at all, or a law in name only. Aquinas quotes a statement of Augustine's that ". . . that which is not just seems to be no law at all . . ." and then continues by adding that ". . . the force of a law depends on the extent of its justice" (p. 227d).

In Aquinas' scheme of things, the justice of a human law is measured by the standard of natural law. Ulpian's definition of law leaves no room for the consideration of justice; anything which the prince wills because it pleases him has the force of law. What would be an unjust law (and therefore really no law at all) according to Aquinas' standards would still be a law for Ulpian simply because the emperor willed it and enforced it. For Aquinas, therefore, the validity of a law depends on the justice of its commands; for Ulpian, it merely depends on the force of him who makes it.

Is a definition of law that ignores justice a good one? Does the justice or injustice of a command determine whether it has the force of law, or is it the other way around; *i.e.*, is some action just because it is lawful? Another way of asking this question is this: Does justice determine what is lawful, or does the law determine what is just?

SELF-TESTING QUESTIONS

The following questions are designed to help you test the thoroughness of your reading. Each question is to be answered by giving a page or pages of the reading assignment. Answers will be found on page 238 of this Reading Plan.

1 Can a law be made by a whole people?

2 How is the natural law promulgated?

3 What are the two ways in which something may be self-evident?

4 Can God order man to do things which are against the natural law, such as killing, theft, and adultery?

5 How does Aquinas explain that theft, which is expressly forbidden by the natural law, is nevertheless not considered wrong by certain peoples?

6 Why can a private person not lead another man to virtue, as the law can?

7 In Aquinas' theory of the faculties, does the reason move the will, or does the will move the reason ?

Seventh Reading

AQUINAS

Summa Theologica

Part I-II, QQ. 95-97

Vol. 20, pp. 226-239

Most of the time when we use the term "law" we refer to human law—the positive law made by human legislators. Law in this sense seems a more obvious thing than the other varieties of law which receive much of Aquinas' attention, such as the eternal law, the natural law, and the divine law.

The human law traditionally commands respect and even awe from those subject to it. The majesty of the law is emphasized by the honor paid to the great lawgivers of antiquity. Socrates' speeches and actions in the *Apology* and *Crito* bear witness to the importance which he and Plato attached to human law. In modern times we still indicate the special respect due the law and all those in its service by such ceremonial trappings as the gowns and wigs worn in British and some American courts.

But if the laws are held in high esteem, this does not prevent them from being subject to change. On the contrary, one of the most apparent facts about a body of law is that it never stays the same. Both statutory law and common law undergo changes all the time. The changing content of the positive law raises a number of problems, especially the problem of whether the law is always improved when it is altered.

A highly placed Russian official in Tolstoy's *War and Peace* exclaims in exasperation at a proposed reform of military laws:

"You are proposing new military laws? There are many laws but no one to carry out the old ones. Nowadays everybody designs laws, it is easier writing than doing." (Vol. 51, p. 239c-d)

In a similar vein, Montaigne in the essay entitled "Of Custom, and That We Should Not Easily Change a Law Received" describes the following custom:

The legislator of the Thurians ordained, that whosoever would go about either to abolish an old law, or to establish a new, should present himself with a halter about his neck to the people to the end, that if the innovation he would introduce should not be approved by every one, he might immediately be hanged . . . (Vol. 25, p. 48c)

Aquinas considers the change in human laws in Question 97. His treatment is less colorful than Tolstoy's or Montaigne's, but his conclusion is the same.

GUIDE TO

Seventh Reading

I

Aquinas begins his discussion of human law with a question that is somewhat startling in its directness. What is the point of having human laws? he asks; what is their utility? Of course, we already know from Question 90 and the definition of law that the purpose of law in general is to serve the common good. But here in Article 1 of Question 95 Aquinas asks a more specific question; namely, what is the purpose of having man-made laws? The divine law directs men to their eternal beatitude; the natural law directs them to their happiness on earth. What function, then, is left for the human law to perform?

The answer is that human laws are needed in order to lead men to virtue. There is in man a natural aptitude for virtue; but this does not mean that every man is necessarily virtuous in all or even most of his actions. In order to assure that men in fact make use of their natural aptitude and act virtuously, they must be trained. The special function of human laws consists in their pedagogical influence—their role in training men to become virtuous. Some few and fortunate men, to be sure, do not need this kind of training because they simply respond to paternal or divine admonition. But for most men this is not the case. Concerning these, Aquinas writes:

> . . . since . . . [they] are found to be depraved, and prone to vice, and not easily amenable to words, it was necessary for such to be restrained from evil by force and fear, in order that at least they might cease from evil-doing and leave others in peace, and that they themselves, by being accustomed in this way, might be brought to do willingly what hitherto they did from fear, and thus become virtuous. Now this kind of training, which compels through fear of punishment, is the discipline of laws. (p. 227a)

One of the most important aspects of human law, therefore, is the punishment to which a lawbreaker is subjected. Though transgressions of the divine and natural law are also punished, the penalties are not so immediate.

This seems to make a rather crude thing out of human law; it appears that its essential point is the fear which it inspires. But Aquinas immediately corrects this impression. Although from the point of view of those subject to the law, the punitive sanctions are primarily what gives it its power, the case is different when the human law is considered in itself. From this point of view, we must realize that in Aquinas' theory the power of human law derives from the fact that it is based on the natural law. Only a just law is truly a law; and the justice of a human law depends on whether or not it is in accord with the law of nature.

> Consequently every human law has just so much of the character of law as it is derived from the law of nature. But if in any point it differs from the law of nature, it is no longer a law but a corruption of law. (p. 228a)

Aquinas notes that human law may be derived from the natural law in one of two ways. (1) A human law may be derived from the natural law in the way in which a conclusion is derived from the premises of an argument. (2) A human law may be a particular determination of one of the general precepts of the natural law.

> Some things are therefore derived from the common principles of the natural law by way of conclusions; for instance, that one must not kill may be derived as a conclusion from the principle that one should do harm to no man. But some are derived from these principles by way of determination; for instance, the law of nature has it that the evil-doer should be punished, but that he be punished in this or that way is a determination of the law of nature. (*Ibid.*)

The second mode of derivation is by far the more common. Very few human laws are direct conclusions from the natural law. When a human law is a specific determination of the general natural law, the determination involves an element of arbitrariness; *i.e.*, the will of the lawgiver decides that this particular determination shall become law. Until the lawgiver has arbitrarily picked out one determination as the law, the point subject to determination is indifferent so far as justice is concerned. But once the determination has been made, what had been a matter of indifference no longer remains so. What the law requires has now become legally just.

Do human laws bind a man as strictly as the natural or the divine law? The latter two bind, in Aquinas' phrase, in "the court of conscience." They must be obeyed not merely because of the evil consequences, such as punishment, which ensue upon disobedience, but also because man's conscience, *i.e.*, his moral sense, indicates that he ought to obey them.

We have already noted how important punishment or the threat of punishment is to human law. If we now take into account that most human laws are not direct conclusions from the natural law, but are merely specifications of it, and that the actions which they command are merely legally just (*i.e.*, indifferent before the law was made), it might seem plausible to say that human law should bind men through fear alone and not in conscience.

Aquinas, however, disagrees. His reasoning is very simple. All laws are just. Unjust laws are not laws but mere counterfeits of law. But any command which requires man to act justly binds him in conscience. Only unjust laws, which are merely expressions of force, do not bind in conscience.

II

In this section we turn to Question 97, which deals with the change in human laws. The question consists of four articles. (1) Should human law be changed at all? (2) Should human law always be changed as soon as something better occurs? (3) Can custom acquire the force of law? (4) Can he who made the law also occasionally dispense some men from obeying the law?

Everyone knows, as a matter of fact, that human law does change. Every session of a legislative body gives evidence of laws being repealed, amended, or replaced by entirely new ones. However, let us remember that Solon considered any change in his laws to be such an evil that he decreed that they should continue unchanged for one hundred years. Solon even departed from Athens lest he himself be coerced into making changes. Evidently, then, there is some question about the wisdom of changing laws.

Aquinas presents several reasons why human law should not be changed. (Cf. the objections of Article 1.) Human law is derived from natural law and so, like natural law, should remain unchanged. Furthermore, since law measures the quality of human acts (*i.e.*, whether they are right or wrong), law must remain the same, for only something unchanging can properly measure something as changing and various as human acts. What is right once is always right.

In spite of these objections, Aquinas points out that law must sometimes be changed, for law is a thing of reason, and it exists for the good of man. On both counts, laws may need to be changed. Consider, first, that law must be something reasonable. Just as there is progress in sciences like physics and mathematics, where new discoveries are always being made, so there is progress in ethics.

> . . . those who first endeavoured to discover something useful for the human community, not being able by themselves to take everything into consideration, set up certain institutions which were deficient in many ways; and these were changed by subsequent lawgivers who made institutions that might prove less frequently deficient in respect of the common weal. (p. 236b)

As time goes by, men know better what is good or useful; consequently, they should change their laws in accordance with their improved knowledge.

In the second place, there is change not only in what is *known* to be good or useful for man, but also in what *is* good or useful. This change is due to the altered conditions under which men find themselves. What is reasonable for one group of men may not be so for another group, if the conditions under which the two groups live are quite different. The laws suitable for a primitive band of nomads—illiterate and barely at the subsistence level—are clearly not suitable for urban civilizations where men live in luxury and leisure. Thus Aquinas concludes that

> . . . the law can be rightly changed on account of the changed condition

of man, to whom different things are expedient according to the difference of his condition. (*Ibid.*)

However, in Article 2, Aquinas adds that laws should be changed with care and caution. Even when progress gives man new ideas of what is good or useful, and even when the men for whom the laws are intended have changed, the law must not be changed precipitately. For, Aquinas points out,

> . . . to a certain extent, the mere change of law is of itself prejudicial to the common good, because custom avails much for the observance of laws, seeing that what is done contrary to general custom, even in slight matters, is looked upon as grave. (p. 237a)

Any change in law, therefore, diminishes the general respect for laws and so also decreases the effectiveness of even those laws that have remained unchanged.

> Therefore human law should never be changed, unless, in some way or other, the common welfare be compensated according to the extent of the harm done in this respect. Such compensation may arise either from some very great and very evident benefit conferred by the new enactment, or from the extreme urgency of the case, due to the fact that either the existing law is clearly unjust, or its observance extremely harmful. (p. 237a-b)

This discussion indicates the importance which Aquinas attaches to custom. Hence when we read the question that constitutes the title of Article 3, "Whether Custom Can Obtain Force of Law?" we are prepared to learn that ". . . custom has the force of a law, abolishes law, and is the interpreter of law" (p. 237d).

Objection 3 in this article touches on an important point. The objector maintains that custom cannot possibly make laws since custom grows by the actions of private persons. But laws, according to the definition, are not made by private persons, but by ". . . him who has care of the community . . ." (p. 208a). In answering this objection, Aquinas notes that the people concerned may be "free and able to make their own laws." In this case, the people have care of the community and the right to make laws. Their consent, Aquinas says, ". . . counts far more in favour of a particular observance than does the authority of the sovereign, who has not the power to frame laws except as representing the people. Therefore although each individual cannot make laws, yet the whole people can" (p. 238b). Here, then, we see Aquinas envisaging and defending a republican form of government—a position not ordinarily associated with his name.

In the fourth article, we read that the lawgiver may occasionally exempt men from obeying the law, but only for good and sufficient reasons. ". . . when the law fails in its application to persons or circumstances, he may allow the precept of the law not to be observed" (p. 238d). The lawgiver's dispensation serves the same function as equity does in Aristotle's *Nicomachean Ethics.* (See *loc. cit.*, Bk. V, Ch. 10, Vol. 9, pp. 385c-386b, and the Guide to the Third Reading.)

III

Is everyone subject to the human law?

Aquinas answers this question in Article 5 of Question 96. The answer is twofold. The first part is rather straightforward. Men are not subject to human laws that do not apply to them; for instance, inhabitants of France are not subject to the laws of Great Britain. Furthermore, higher authority takes precedence over lower. Inhabitants of the state of California are not subject to the laws passed by the California legislature if those laws conflict with laws passed by the Congress of the United States.

The second part of Aquinas' answer is more interesting. Here he distinguishes between two ways of obeying a law. A just and virtuous person obeys a law because he realizes that the common good requires it. Such a person is not really coerced, for coercion implies that the person is compelled to act against his will. But the virtuous man, who obeys a law not from fear of punishment, but rather from respect for law, complies willingly.

A wicked person, on the other hand, obeys a law only because he is threatened. He fears the consequences of disobedience. Were it not for those consequences, he would act contrary to the law. Such a person is, therefore, subject to the law in the sense that he feels himself subject to the sanctions of the law. ". . . the will of the good is in harmony with the law, while the will of the wicked is discordant from it. Therefore in this sense the good are not subject to the law, but only the wicked" (p. 234c).

Do you agree with Aquinas' view here? Is it an infallible sign of virtue that a man obeys the law willingly and does not feel coerced by it? What would you say about a man who willingly obeys an unjust law? Can a man be just and yet find himself in conflict with just laws?

Would it be better to have living judges than inanimate laws?

Even when there are laws, it is necessary, of course, to have judges who preside over courts. The sense of this question, however, is that it might seem possible to dispense with laws altogether and instead let each individual case be decided by the wisdom of the judge. In support of this position, Aquinas notes that ". . . animate justice is better than inanimate justice, which is contained in laws" (p. 226c). Furthermore,

> . . . since human actions are about singulars, which are infinite in number, matters pertaining to the direction of human actions cannot be taken into sufficient consideration except by a wise man, who looks into each one of them. Therefore it would have been better for human acts to be directed by the judgment of wise men than by the framing of laws. (p. 226c-d)

Although there is some plausibility to these arguments, Aquinas maintains that written laws are superior to the decrees of judges. In the first place, to find men wise and impartial enough to serve as judges is difficult. If such men can be found, their wisdom can be most effectively used by letting them make laws. Thus their insight into what is just and unjust will be preserved. Furthermore, in the process of making laws, the lawmaker can take his time and act slowly and dispassionately. If, however, a particular case has to be decided quickly, the passions of those involved may pervert the judgment. And the judge does not have the benefit of being able to consider many similar cases, as the lawmaker can when he makes laws about a certain *kind* of case. The judge has to decide one case and it alone.

Nevertheless, it is correct to say that no lawgiver can possibly take into account the infinite details that may enter into a given case. Of necessity, the law has to be general. Hence, there is still a function for the wise judge who considers the particulars of a case with an eye toward doing justice.

Which kind of law is better: one which is very general and leaves all the details to be settled by a judge, or one which takes into account as many particular conditions as possible, leaving only the minimum latitude to the judge?

Is paternal justice in the family based on written law or on the wisdom of the father? Is the common law, unwritten but based on the precedents of previous decisions, built on the wisdom of judges or on the wisdom of lawgivers? Would Aquinas seem to favor a body of common law or of statutory laws?

Is it ever permissible to act contrary to the law?

Since everyone is subject to the law, it would seem that no one can be permitted to act contrary to it. But what if observance of the letter of the law would be a disservice to the common good? Are such cases possible?

What is the role of equity in Aristotle's *Nicomachean Ethics?* Does equity, in correcting the injustice which would follow from a strict application of the law, encourage breaches of the law?

Does the frequent application of equity, or the frequent breach of law for the sake of the common good, weaken the strength of law?

SELF-TESTING QUESTIONS

The following questions are designed to help you test the thoroughness of your reading. Each question is to be answered by giving a page or pages of the reading assignment. Answers will be found on page 238 of this Reading Plan.

1 What are the four principles according to which the human law may be divided?

2 Is there any virtue whose acts cannot be prescribed by law?

3 Can anyone dispense from the divine law?

4 What are the three purposes of law?

5 Is every vice forbidden by human law?

6 Is change of law harmful?

Eighth Reading

HOBBES

Leviathan

Ch. 14-15, 26-28

Vol. 23, pp. 86-96, 130-148

The Leviathan referred to in the title is, according to Hobbes, the "Commonwealth, or State." It is, he tells us, ". . . an artificial man, though of greater stature and strength than the natural . . ." (p. 47a).

Because the commonwealth or state ought to be so strong that no one can resist it, Hobbes picked the name "Leviathan" for it. The name is taken from the forty-first chapter of the Book of Job:

> . . . God, having set forth the great power of Leviathan, calleth him *king of the proud.* "There is nothing," saith he, "on earth to be compared with him. He is made so as not to be afraid. He seeth every high thing below him; and is king of all the children of pride." (p. 148b)

The first edition of the *Leviathan,* published in 1651, carries on its title page a picture of the "Leviathan." He is a man of vast stature, towering over a landscape of cities and farms. He is taller than the mountains in the background and has a martial mien. In his right hand he carries a sword and in his left, a bishop's crosier. These two implements symbolize, respectively, the power of the state and the church and illustrate the full title of the book: *Leviathan, Or Matter, Form, and Power of a Commonwealth Ecclesiastical and Civil.*

Close examination shows that the body of the Leviathan consists of hundreds of human persons. This bears out Hobbes's view that the commonwealth is nothing but the multitude of its subjects united in one person. (See p. 100d.)

In the Introduction, Hobbes comments on the analogy between the artificial person of the Leviathan and the natural person of a man. In the *Leviathan* he writes,

> . . . the sovereignty is an artificial soul, as giving life and motion to the whole body; the magistrates and other officers of judicature and execution, artificial joints; reward and punishment (by which fastened to the seat of the sovereignty, every joint and member is moved to perform his duty) are the nerves, that do the same in the body natural; the wealth and riches of all the particular members are the strength; *salus populi* (the people's safety) its business; counsellors, by whom all things needful for it to know are suggested unto it, are the memory; equity and laws, an artificial reason and will; concord, health; sedition, sickness; and civil war, death. (p. 47a-b)

To the consideration of the reason and will of Leviathan—of laws and equity—we now proceed.

GUIDE TO

Eighth Reading

I

Several chapters from the *Leviathan* constitute the eighth assignment in the Reading Plan on *The Development of Government and Political Theory*. Indeed, Hobbes is primarily a political philosopher rather than a philosopher of law. However, his thoughts concerning law, which we encounter in the present assignment, are intimately connected with his political theory. In Chapters 14 and 15 Hobbes develops a theory of natural law. His views of why the state is necessary, how it comes to be, and what its nature is are based directly on his theory of natural law. In turn, Chapters 26-28 (in which Hobbes discusses civil law, crimes, and punishment) are based on his theory of the state.

Hobbes is a great believer in the supremacy of the state over the individual. When we have investigated his view of the laws of nature, we shall understand why that is so. For the moment we merely wish to remind the reader of the way in which, according to Hobbes, the state comes into existence. It results from a mutual agreement or contract by which every man gives up his right to govern himself on the condition that other men do likewise. This right is surrendered to one man or to an assembly of men.

> This done, the multitude so united in one person is called a COMMONWEALTH; in Latin, CIVITAS. This is the generation of that great LEVIATHAN, or rather, to speak more reverently, of that mortal god to which we owe, under the immortal God, our peace and defence. (p. 100d)

This Leviathan is the essence of the commonwealth, which Hobbes defines as follows:

> . . . *one person, of whose acts a great multitude, by mutual covenants*

one with another, have made themselves every one the author, to the end he may use the strength and means of them all as he shall think expedient for their peace and common defence. (pp. 100d-101a)

The Leviathan, or commonwealth, is, therefore, a person, though an artificial one. Hobbes continues:

> And he that carryeth this person is called *sovereign,* and said to have *sovereign power;* and every one besides, his *subject.* (p. 101a)

Since for Hobbes the nature and necessity of the commonwealth derive from the natural law, we shall begin in Section II by considering what he has to say on the subject. In Section III we shall be concerned with the justice of laws. Then, in Section IV we shall consider positive law, which gets its character from the nature of the state. Section V will be concerned with a number of specific questions about laws.

II

Hobbes begins with a definition of natural law. It is much less exalted and more direct than Aquinas'.

> A *law of nature, lex naturalis,* is a precept, or general rule, found out by reason, by which a man is forbidden to do that which is destructive of his life, or taketh away the means of preserving the same, and to omit that by which he thinketh it may be best preserved. (p. 86c)

A law of nature, therefore, places a certain obligation on man. Hobbes points out that every law does this; herein lies the difference between right and law (*ius* and *lex*). ". . . *right* consisteth in liberty to do, or to forbear; whereas *law* determineth and bindeth to one of them . . ." (p. 86c-d). What is especially noteworthy, however, is that the obligation is so definite and limited in its scope: man must preserve his life. Nothing is said by Hobbes about the good, about man's end, about happiness, or about man's relation to God. However important these may be, the law of nature does not relate to them.

In order to arrive at particular precepts of the law of nature, it is necessary to put together *natural right* and *natural law.* Man's natural right, Hobbes says, consists in

> . . . the liberty each man hath to use his own power as he will himself for the preservation of his own nature; that is to say, of his own life;

and consequently, of doing anything which, in his own judgement and reason, he shall conceive to be the aptest means thereunto. (p. 86c)

Immediately we face a difficulty. By natural right, every man is entitled to do whatever he pleases if he thinks it contributes to the preservation of his life. Since *every* man has this right, the exercise of this right on the part of all men could result in mutual destruction. Every man is concerned only with his own needs and is, by natural right, entitled to anything he needs in order to satisfy those needs. Without doubt, therefore, conflicts will arise between one man's desire (and right) to satisfy his needs and another man's similar desire and right.

Such a conflict of desires would result in warfare between the men involved. This, however, is contrary to the *law* of nature. The law of nature commands men to preserve their lives and therefore to avoid warfare which endangers life. The unlimited and unchecked exercise of men's natural rights is, therefore, contrary to the natural law. By reasoning such as this, Hobbes arrives at ". . . the first and fundamental law of nature, which is: *to seek peace and follow it*" (p. 86d).

This is the basic law of nature and every man is obliged to follow it as long as there is any hope of actually attaining peace. If, however, peace cannot be obtained by any means, then men must revert to the exercise of their natural right which can be summed up, Hobbes says, in the phrase: ". . . *by all means we can to defend ourselves*" (pp. 86d-87a).

The fundamental law of nature (to seek peace) leads immediately to the second law of nature which commands us to do that which is necessary to achieve peace. In Hobbes's opinion this second law commands us to yield up our natural right. He states this law as follows:

. . . *that a man be willing, when others are so too, as far forth as for peace and defence of himself he shall think it necessary, to lay down this right to all things; and be contented with so much liberty against other men as he would allow other men against himself.* (p. 87a)

The only thing which can induce a man voluntarily to give up his natural right, or liberty, to anything he wants is the benefit he acquires by doing so. That benefit consists, of course, in other men's giving up their rights. The condition of war which naturally exists between men is thus supplanted by a state of peace. It would be absurd to give up a right when nothing is gained by such action. "And therefore," Hobbes writes, "there be some rights which no man can be understood by any words, or other signs, to have abandoned or transferred" (p. 87c). He gives us the following examples:

> As first a man cannot lay down the right of resisting them that assault him by force to take away his life, because he cannot be understood to aim thereby at any good to himself. The same may be said of wounds, and chains, and imprisonment, both because there is no benefit consequent to such patience . . . as also because a man cannot tell when he seeth men proceed against him by violence whether they intend his death or not. And lastly the motive and end for which this renouncing and transferring of right is introduced is nothing else but the security of a man's person, in his life, and in the means of so preserving life as not to be weary of it. (p. 87c-d)

The right to defend one's life and person against assault is, therefore, inalienable. If a man, by what he says or does, seems nevertheless to give up these rights, he is not to be believed. It must be assumed, Hobbes declares, that the man did not know what his words or actions signified. No man would knowingly give up the right to life.

It should be noted that in Hobbes's theory there is only one inalienable right. This contrasts with the catalogue of inalienable rights which Locke gives us, *viz.*, life, liberty, and estate (see *Concerning Civil Government*, Vol. 35, p. 44a), or with the list in the Declaration of Independence, "life, liberty, and the pursuit of happiness." It is worth noting, too, that in spite of the differences all the lists include the right to life.

The law of nature, as we have so far examined it, may therefore be summed up in the commands (1) to seek peace and, in order to accomplish this, (2) to give up all rights and liberties (on the condition that other men do likewise) except the inalienable right to life. But the command to give up one's rights makes sense only if one can be assured that other men will do likewise. Consequently, Hobbes states a third law of nature—". . . *that men perform their covenants made* . . ." (p. 91a). It will be remembered that for Hobbes a law of nature is a command to do those things which preserve life. Covenants must be honored if life is to be preserved, for unless they are, men would not give up their natural liberty and hence would remain in a state of war.

These are the three major commands of the natural law. Hobbes lists twelve more commands to make a total of fifteen, but we need not enumerate them here. He himself says that they can all be summarized in one easy sentence which any man can understand.

> . . . *Do not that to another which thou wouldest not have done to thyself* . . . (p. 95c)

For the sake of contrast, let us recall some of the descriptions of the natural law given by Aquinas in the *Treatise on Law*. It is ". . . nothing else than the rational creature's participation of the eternal law" (*Summa Theologica,* Vol. 20, p. 209c). Furthermore, the many secondary precepts of the natural law are, for Aquinas, based on one first precept: ". . . that good is to be pursued and done, and evil is to be avoided" (*Ibid.,* p. 222c). Again, ". . . all acts of virtue are prescribed by the natural law" (*Ibid.,* p. 223a).

Thus while the over-all purpose of the natural law is the pursuit of good in Aquinas' theory, the purpose of natural law in Hobbes's scheme is primarily to preserve life, and secondly—for the sake of life—to get men associated in a civil society or a commonwealth. (All the precepts about relinquishing one's rights and keeping covenants are merely preliminary steps in the establishment of the commonwealth by covenant.) In Hobbes's way of looking at things, there are no goods to be pursued, no acts of virtue to be prescribed until and unless the commonwealth is established. We shall return to this point in the next section.

III

According to Hobbes, there is no natural law that commands us to do justice. The concept of justice is, in fact, meaningless and empty until the state has defined which actions are just and which are unjust. Without a commonwealth there can be no unjust action. In a state of nature ". . . no right [has] been transferred, and every man has right to everything; and consequently, no action can be unjust" (p. 91a). Justice comes into being when there are covenants:

. . . the definition of *injustice* is no other than *the not performance of covenant*. And whatsoever is not unjust is just. (p. 91a)

Nothing whatever is said about the content of the covenant. Evidently, the non-performance of any covenant is unjust, no matter what it binds the partners to. Any covenant, however, that would pledge the partners to do something contrary to the law of nature (*i.e.,* to do something that would endanger the life of one or both of them) is on the face of it invalid.

The mere making of covenants does not suffice to bring justice and injustice into being. Suppose that A has made a covenant with B requiring A to do X while B is required to do Y. It is then unjust on the part of A not to do X, provided he is assured that B will do Y. But in a state of nature, A cannot be assured that B will do Y, even if A has done X. Such a covenant is therefore void, and non-performance does not result in injustice.

For he that performeth first has no assurance the other will perform after, because the bonds of words are too weak to bridle men's ambition, avarice, anger, and other passions, without the fear of some coercive power; which in the condition of mere nature, where all men are equal, and judges of the justness of their own fears, cannot possibly be supposed. And therefore he which performeth first does but betray himself to his enemy, contrary to the right he can never abandon of defending his life and means of living. (p. 89a-b)

Justice and injustice can exist only in a commonwealth, where the performance of covenants is enforced by the coercive power of the state. The punishment for non-performance being greater than the good a man can hope to achieve for himself by failing to perform, it can be safely assumed that covenants will be properly executed. Thus in a civil society non-performance of covenants cannot be excused on the ground that one of the parties to the contract was not sure that the other party would fulfill his obligations.

Therefore before the names of *just* and *unjust* can have place, there must be some coercive power to compel men equally to the performance of their covenants, by the terror of some punishment greater than the benefit they expect by the breach of their covenant, and to make good that propriety which by mutual contract men acquire in recompense of the universal right they abandon: and such power there is none before the erection of a Commonwealth. (p. 91b)

Hobbes sums up the argument briefly a few lines later:

So that the nature of justice consisteth in keeping of valid covenants, but the validity of covenants begins not but with the constitution of a civil power sufficient to compel men to keep them . . . (p. 91b)

It follows from this theory that every law in a commonwealth is a just law. Hobbes reminds us that ". . . every subject in a Commonwealth hath covenanted to obey the civil law . . . and therefore obedience to the civil law is part also of the law of nature" (p. 131b). Every law in a commonwealth must be obeyed; disobedience–being non-performance of a covenant–is an act of injustice. Indeed, it is not surprising that there can be no unjust law. By what standard would the justice or injustice of a law be measured? The situation is reversed; it is law–the law of the state–which is the standard of justice and injustice. Whatever violates a law is unjust; every other action is just. In a state of war (*i.e.*, before the commonwealth has come into being by covenant) nothing is just or unjust.

The notions of right and wrong, justice and injustice, have there no place. Where there is no common power, there is no law; where no law, no injustice. (p. 86b)

In such a condition there exists only the natural right of every man to take for himself anything that he wants and can obtain. Laws abridge natural right or liberty.

. . . nay, the end of making laws is no other but such restraint, without which there cannot possibly be any peace. And law was brought into the world for nothing else but to limit the natural liberty of particular men in such manner as they might not hurt, but assist one another . . . (p. 131b-c)

IV

In Chapter 26 Hobbes turns his attention to positive law. Although the title of the chapter is "Of Civil Law," Hobbes at once points out that he is not going to discuss merely the law of the Roman *civitas* but any man-made law as such. His subject matter therefore is what we call human positive law. He begins with a definition:

Civil law is to every subject those rules which the Commonwealth hath commanded him, by word, writing, or other sufficient sign of the will, to make use of for the distinction of right and wrong; that is to say, of what is contrary and what is not contrary to the rule. (p. 130c)

Let us compare this definition with Aquinas': Law is ". . . an ordinance of reason for the common good, made by him who has care of the community, and promulgated" (Vol. 20, p. 208a). There are some similarities. Where Aquinas says that a law is made ". . . by him who has care of the community . . . ," Hobbes says that it is made by the "Commonwealth." We can interpret the latter remark to mean the sovereign who, in Hobbes's phrase, "carries" the person of the commonwealth. Both Aquinas and Hobbes agree that the law must be promulgated, that is, made known.

But there are also important differences between the two definitions. Whereas Aquinas calls law an ordinance of reason, there is no mention of reason in what Hobbes says. According to him, all laws ". . . have their authority and force from the will of the Commonwealth; that is to say, from the will of the representative . . ." (p. 131d). And a little later he adds that ". . . the law is a command, and a command consisteth in declaration or manifestation of the will of him that commandeth . . ." (p. 132b). To be sure, Hobbes also says that law can never be against reason; by this he means that what the law commands is automatically in accord with the sovereign's reason. If the law does not seem to be reasonable to a subject, that is quite irrelevant. The subject must obey the law since he has covenanted to do so. And, of course, no law can be disobeyed on the pretext that it is an unjust law. There are no unjust laws; in fact, the justice or injustice of men is entirely determined by their obedience or disobedience to laws. The only kind of law that a man may—in fact, must—disobey is one that contradicts the law of nature. Otherwise, the laws exact total obedience.

From his definition of law Hobbes draws several conclusions. We have already anticipated the first one, which is that the lawmaking power belongs to the sovereign. It makes no difference whether the sovereign is one person, or a group of persons such as a legislative assembly. The sovereign makes the laws, and, conversely, whoever has the legislative power in a state is, by that fact, the sovereign. Since only the sovereign can make laws, it also follows that only the sovereign is exempt from the laws. Nothing binds the sovereign except his own will, for he can make and repeal laws as he wills.

In the next place, Hobbes acknowledges that custom can become law. But he immediately adds that ". . . it is not the length of time that maketh the authority, but the will of the sovereign signified by his silence . . ." (pp. 130d-131a). This is important to Hobbes, for it is by no means to be inferred that customary usage has any force if it is opposed to the sovereign's will. No matter how time-honored a custom may be, if the sovereign explicitly states that it is no longer lawful, the customary action loses any semblance of legality. What custom permits is law only as long as ". . . the sovereign shall be silent therein" (p. 131a).

Aquinas also maintains that custom can obtain the force of law. He tells us that ". . . by repeated external actions the inward movement of the will, and concepts of reason are most effectually declared" (Vol. 20, p. 237d). In Aquinas' theory, custom may well prevail if the law as expressed by custom conflicts with the will of the sovereign:

> . . . if they [the people] are free, and able to make their own laws, the consent of the whole people expressed by a custom counts far more in favour of a particular observance than does the authority of the sovereign, who has not the power to frame laws except as representing the people. (Vol. 20, p. 238b)

The paragraph just quoted would make no sense at all to Hobbes. If the people have the lawmaking power, they then are the sovereign, and so there cannot be a conflict between the will of the people and the will of the sovereign. If, on the other hand, there is a sovereign distinct from the people, this means that the lawmaking power resides not in the people but in the sovereign. In that case the will of the sovereign is necessarily supreme.

Hobbes rejects as utterly false the notion that the sovereign has lawmaking authority only as representing the people. For him, the sovereign does not represent the people; nor does he represent anyone. The sovereign *carries* the person of the commonwealth, he does not represent it. (See p. 101a.) Thus custom can lawfully oppose the will of the sovereign in Aquinas' theory but not in Hobbes's.

When Hobbes turns to the relation between natural law and human law, he reveals another significant difference between himself and Aquinas. In the Thomistic theory positive laws are derived from natural law. Any "law" that does not participate in the natural law is ". . . no longer a law but a corruption of law" (Vol. 20, p. 228a). In the Hobbesian theory, however, things are quite different. "The law of nature and the civil law contain each other and are of equal extent" (p. 131a). Further on Hobbes writes:

> The law of nature therefore is a part of the civil law in all Commonwealths of the world. Reciprocally also, the civil law is a part of the dictates of nature. (p. 131b)

What Hobbes means by this statement is that the natural law commands us to have certain qualities such as equity, justice, and gratitude; but this precept is not a law until the commonwealth makes it one. Hobbes tells us why.

> For in the differences of private men, to declare what is equity, what is justice, and what is moral virtue, and to make them binding, there is need of the ordinances of sovereign power, and punishments to be ordained for such as shall break them; which ordinances are therefore part of the civil law. (p. 131b)

This indicates the way in which the natural law is a part of the civil law; it is not effective as law until it has been incorporated into the civil law. On the other hand, all civil law is a part of the law of nature insofar as the law of nature commands us to fulfill all our covenants. Every subject in a commonwealth has made a covenant to obey the civil law; but this civil law would have no force if it were not for the natural law that commands us to keep our covenants and therefore to obey the civil law. And so Hobbes concludes:

Civil and natural law are not different kinds, but different parts of law; whereof one part, being written, is called *civil,* the other unwritten, *natural.* (p 131b)

Another significant observation which Hobbes makes is that "All laws, written and unwritten, have need of interpretation" (p. 134a). Since we have just seen that the distinction between written and unwritten laws corresponds to the distinction between civil and natural laws, this means that both civil and natural laws need interpretation. Man's natural reason, Hobbes says, easily comprehends the natural law, but man's understanding of it is obscured by his passions; consequently, it has ". . . the greatest need of able interpreters" (p. 134a).

The need of the civil law to be interpreted arises from the obscurity of words.

The written laws, if they be short, are easily misinterpreted, from the diverse significations of a word or two; if long, they be more obscure by the diverse significations of many words . . . (p. 134a)

Hobbes then elaborates on the difficulty about words.

. . . the significations of almost all words are either in themselves, or in the metaphorical use of them, ambiguous; and may be drawn in argument to make many senses; but there is only one sense of the law. (p. 135c)

Thus the task of interpretation is to find the one sense of the law within the many meanings of the words in which it is expressed.

Although Hobbes emphasizes the need for the interpretation, he also feels that a great deal of so-called interpretation has no relevance to the law. For instance, he stresses that the interpretation of the natural law does not in any way depend ". . . on the books of moral philosophy" (p. 134b). What the authors of these books have to say, though it may well be true, does not have the force of law. Only the commonwealth can make laws. It would be absurd to say that the opinions expressed in books are part of the natural law, for the natural law, we must remember, is unwritten.

Interpretation of law, as Hobbes understands it, does not consist in enlarging upon the meaning of the law or in writing commentaries about it. "For commentaries," Hobbes tells us, "are commonly more subject to cavil than the text, and therefore need other commentaries; and so there will be no end of such interpretation" (p. 135b). Interpretation of law, according to Hobbes,

> . . . is the sentence of the judge constituted by the sovereign authority to hear and determine such controversies as depend thereon, and consisteth in the application of the law to the present case. (p. 134b)

All writers on law agree that law, being universal, must be applied to particular cases and that this application must be done by human judges, for only a person can take account of the peculiarities of a given situation and see how a law is to be applied to it. This activity of the human judge is not usually called "interpretation of the law," however, but rather "application." The judge derives the authority for his interpretation or application from the authority of the sovereign.

Interestingly enough, Hobbes gives no authority to precedent. In every case it is the task of the judge to discover the purpose of the law (*i.e.*, the intent of the lawgiver). If an earlier judge has made an error in his interpretation of the law, this can in no way bind a later judge: ". . . all the sentences of precedent judges that have ever been cannot all together make a law contrary to natural equity" (p. 134c). In other words, precedent has force only insofar as it correctly interprets the law; incorrect interpretation has no force whatever. Hence, no reliance can be placed on precedents, for we do not know whether the preceding judges interpreted the law correctly or not. Thus every case that comes before a judge must be judged on its own terms.

V

What does Hobbes mean by "equity"?

Aristotle has a meaning for equity (see Vol. 9, pp. 385c-386b), and English legal theory also employs the term in a somewhat different sense. We are not concerned with either of these meanings, but only with the way in which Hobbes uses the term.

In anybody's use of the words, "equity" is closely related to "justice." Let us briefly recall what Hobbes has to say about justice: ". . . *injustice* is no other than *the not performance of covenant.* And whatsoever is not unjust is just" (p. 91a). Hobbes then goes on to point out an important condition that must be fulfilled before the term "justice" can be meaningfully used. ". . . before the names of *just* and *unjust* can have place, there must be some coercive power to compel men equally to the performance of their covenants . . ." From this he concludes: ". . . therefore where there is no Commonwealth, there nothing is unjust" (p. 91b).

A short while later Hobbes discusses the distinction between commutative and distributive justice. That distinction goes back to Aristotle's *Nicomachean Ethics,* Bk. V, Ch. 3-4. (Cf. the Third Reading, pp. 34-36.) Hobbes's comment on these two kinds of justice is as follows:

> To speak properly, commutative justice is the justice of a contractor; that is, a performance of covenant in buying and selling, hiring and letting to hire, lending and borrowing, exchanging, bartering, and other acts of contract. (p. 93b)

Then he goes on to distributive justice which consists in

> . . . the act of defining what is just. Wherein, being trusted by them that make him arbitrator, if he perform his trust, he is said to distribute to every man his own: and this is indeed just distribution, and may be called, though improperly, distributive justice, but more properly *equity,* which also is a law of nature, as shall be shown in due place. (p. 93b-c)

Here equity is mentioned by Hobbes, and is said to be a law of nature. How can equity or distributive justice be a law? Perhaps this is merely abbreviated language, as Hobbes seems to indicate a little later. The law of nature directs us to seek peace; consequently, it also directs us to embrace the means to peace. These means are justice, gratitude, modesty, equity, mercy. (See p. 96a-b.) Hence, it seems more accurate to say that it is a law of nature to be equitable, than to call equity itself such a law. Hobbes himself in a later place admits as much.

> . . . the laws of nature, which consist in equity, justice, gratitude, and other moral virtues on these depending, in the condition of mere nature

. . . are not properly laws, but qualities that dispose men to peace and to obedience. When a Commonwealth is once settled, then are they actually laws, and not before . . . (p. 131a)

If we try to put all these passages together, we find that the commands to be just, to be equitable, etc., come into being as civil laws only when there is a commonwealth. Here they bind men externally, and non-performance of the command is punished. But these same commands to be just, equitable, etc., exist as laws of nature even where there is no commonwealth. In this condition, however, they do not bind men externally; *ie.*, non-performance is not punishable. They bind men internally; that is, they require men to desire justice, equity, etc.

The same laws, because they oblige only to a desire and endeavour, I mean an unfeigned and constant endeavour, are easy to be observed. For in that they require nothing but endeavour, he that endeavoureth their performance fulfilleth them; and he that fulfilleth the law is just. (p. 96a)

Let us note just a few more places where Hobbes mentions equity. A judge who applies a law to a particular situation ". . . doth no more but consider whether the demand of the party be consonant to natural reason and equity . . ." (p. 134b). In applying the law, the judge must remember that ". . . the intention of the legislator is always supposed to be equity . . ." (p. 135c). Finally, let us take note of the importance of equity. Hobbes refers to it as ". . . that principal law of nature called *equity* . . ." (p. 136b).

Can all these remarks about equity be interpreted in a consistent fashion? It seems difficult. On the one hand, Hobbes insists that justice does not exist until there is a commonwealth. On the other hand, however, he speaks of equity, which is a kind of justice (*i.e.*, distributive justice), in the state of nature. Furthermore, when he says that the legislator should always look to equity and that a civil law must be applied so that equity is served, he seems to be saying that there is a standard, namely, equity, in terms of which laws can be judged. But this goes against his positivistic contention that every law is just and that books of morality have no relevance to natural law.

Can this apparent inconsistency be resolved? In using the notion of equity, does Hobbes fall back on more traditional concepts of natural law than he employs elsewhere?

What is Hobbes's theory of punishment?

It is probably fair to describe the *Leviathan* as a very unsentimental book. Hobbes does not hesitate to proclaim the supremacy of the state over the individual, no matter how unpleasant the consequences may be. For instance, Hobbes declares that promises made under duress must nevertheless be fulfilled. Again he tells us that the sovereign must be obeyed, no matter how he came to power—by legitimate succession or by usurpation. Thus we might expect that in his theory of punishment Hobbes would permit the commonwealth or the sovereign to inflict any kind of punishment. But this expectation is not fulfilled.

Hobbes severely circumscribes the manner of legal punishment. He recognizes, of course, that men inflict all sorts of injuries on one another, but injuries are not punishments. Punishment must be preceded by public condemnation, must be inflicted by proper authority, and must have as its end to dispose men to obey the law. A crime should not be punished by a penalty greater than that provided for at the time of its commission, nor should any penalty be inflicted for an act which was not illegal at the time of its performance.

In general, Hobbes's theory of punishment is utilitarian.

> . . . all evil which is inflicted without intention or possibility of disposing the delinquent or, by his example, other men to obey the laws is not punishment, but an act of hostility, because without such an end no hurt done is contained under that name. (p. 145c)

What is Hobbes's reason for subscribing to the utilitarian theory of punishment (*i.e.*, the theory that all punishment must be either for the improvement of the criminal or the deterrence of other possible offenders)? Does not the sovereign have the right to mete out any kind of punishment without being accountable to anyone?

Does punishment for the sake of mere revenge accord with the primary law of nature which commands us to seek peace?

Is the utilitarian theory of punishment prescribed by a law of nature?

Does Hobbes believe in natural slavery?

Even though Hobbes believes that might makes right, we cannot assume that he would agree that some men are slaves while others are masters. We must remember that the question has to do with *natural* slavery. It may well be, as some writers maintain, that the subjects of Hobbes's commonwealth are little better than slaves. They have no rights or freedoms except those the sovereign chooses to grant them. They must obey without question all the laws of the state. The only right left to them is the right to self-preservation; they need not meekly consent to have their lives taken from them. Even slaves retain this right of self-defense.

Although this describes the condition of men in a commonwealth, there are no slaves in a state of nature. Hobbes refers explicitly to Aristotle's doctrine of natural slavery. He rejects it and scornfully exclaims, ". . . as if master and servant were not introduced by consent of men . . ." (p. 94b). The ninth law of nature commands men to recognize their natural equality:

> . . . for the ninth law of nature, I put this: *that every man acknowledge another for his equal by nature.* (p. 94c)

When men leave the state of nature in order to enter the commonwealth, they still remain equal. All men must equally give up their rights, so that nobody retains any right which would make him superior to some or all of his fellow subjects. Those who break this law are called *arrogant.* (See p. 94c-d.)

An obvious question remains. If all men are equal in the state of nature and if none in that condition is a slave, why do men leave the state of nature and form a commonwealth in which all are slaves? To be sure, in the commonwealth all are still equal in condition, since all alike are subjects or slaves, but why is the condition of subjection or civil slavery preferable to the freedom of nature?

SELF-TESTING QUESTIONS

The following questions are designed to help you test the thoroughness of your reading. Each question can be answered by giving a page or pages from the reading assignment. Answers will be found on page 239 of this Reading Plan.

1 How does Hobbes summarize the law of nature?

2 What enforces a contract in the state of nature?

3 Can a covenant be made with God?

4 Does the law of nature command us to rebel against secular power for the sake of eternal happiness?

5 How can a man know that another man has had a revelation from God?

6 What is the relationship of law to sin?

7 What sort of persons are exempt from the law?

8 What are the signs which signify that an alleged law truly proceeds from the will of the sovereign?

9 Why does Hobbes call the commonwealth a Leviathan?

Ninth Reading

SHAKESPEARE

The Merchant of Venice

Vol. 26, pp. 406-433

This is a "controversial" play—so much so that some people contend it should never be read or presented on the stage, while others consider it perfectly harmless and ascribe the former view to the anxieties of our age. One side contends that the play is anti-Semitic and arouses the worst passions in men; the other side maintains that this is a comedy, a casual tale of happy and wealthy people in love.

The play has all the ingredients of a delightful comedy: it takes place in romantic settings, in the exotic port city of Venice and on the luxurious estate of the wealthy Lady Portia; its main characters are all rich gentlemen of leisure and education; a major part of the plot deals with a kind of lottery for the hand of the beautiful Portia. The fifth act is, indeed, a romance all by itself—in the moonlit garden of Portia's estate, the two fair ladies, Portia and Nerissa, engage in a gentle game of mistaken identities with their lover-husbands, Bassanio and Gratiano.

But we cannot overlook the discordant note in this harmonious picture—Shylock. Jew, moneylender, usurer—Shylock is all of these and more. He is also the man who mourns the loss of his money more than the loss of his daughter, and the man who prefers revenge on the body of his debtor to the restitution of his debt.

It is Shylock who makes the play controversial. He bursts upon the world of genteel wealth and romance with great spasms of hate, of violence, and of despair. Thus the play becomes ambiguous. Are we to take pleasure in the happiness of Bassanio and Portia? Or are we to take pity upon Shylock who is robbed of his money, of his daughter, and, finally, of his revenge? Is Shylock a consummate villain, or is he a miserable member of a downtrodden people?

The reader must make his own decision if he can. But there is no doubt which picture of Shylock has come down to us traditionally. The very word "shylock" has become synonymous with "usurer"; and to exact the last "pound of flesh" has become a phrase indicative of insatiable greed. Let the reader judge, remembering that Portia's exhortation to be merciful should apply not only to Shylock but also to those who judge him:

> The quality of mercy is not strain'd,
> It droppeth as the gentle rain from heaven
> Upon the place beneath: it is twice blest;
> It blesseth him that gives and him that takes:
> 'Tis mightiest in the mightiest: it becomes
> The throned monarch better than his crown;
> His sceptre shows the force of temporal power,
> The attribute to awe and majesty,
> Wherein doth sit the dread and fear of kings;

But mercy is above this sceptred sway;
It is enthroned in the hearts of kings,
It is an attribute to God himself;
And earthly power doth then show likest God's
When mercy seasons justice. (Act IV, Sc. 1, p. 427c)

GUIDE TO

Ninth Reading

I

The Merchant of Venice is, of course, a play and not a treatise on law. Nevertheless, it has something to say to us about legal matters. Let us first briefly summarize the plot of the play insofar as it bears on the subject of law.

Bassanio, a gentleman of Venice, desires to court the beautiful and rich Lady Portia. However, he is in straitened financial circumstances and therefore turns to his friend Antonio, a merchant of Venice, for help. Antonio himself does not have any ready cash, since all of his fortune is tied up in various ships that are now at sea, but as soon as the ships return safely from their voyages, he will again be wealthy. Antonio's credit is quite good, and so he decides to borrow three thousand ducats for his friend Bassanio. To arrange the loan, Antonio and Bassanio go to Shylock, a Jew and professional moneylender. Apparently, there has been bad blood between Antonio and Shylock for some time. Antonio despises Shylock for lending money at interest, which is against Christian doctrine. Shylock in turn hates Antonio because the latter often has lent money without interest, thus driving down the rate of interest. Nevertheless, Shylock and Antonio finally agree on the terms of the loan: if it is not paid back within three months, Shylock shall have a pound of Antonio's flesh. Though Bassanio does not like the terms, Antonio readily agrees to them, since he expects to have several times the amount of the loan within two months.

The second and third acts of the play are taken up with Bassanio's courtship of Portia—he succeeds in winning her hand—and with the elopement of Shylock's daughter, Jessica, with a young Christian gentleman named Lorenzo. Interspersed with this action are various hints that things are not going well with Antonio's commercial ventures.

In Act IV things come to a head. The loan falls due, and Antonio cannot pay; Shylock demands his bond, and a court is convened a few days later to determine what should be done. Though Bassanio now appears with several times the borrowed three thousand ducats (given to him by his wife, Portia, whom he has left behind), Shylock insists that Antonio failed to repay the loan when it was due and that the bond be forfeited. Portia disguises herself as a male lawyer and appears in court. She carries with her a letter from a famous attorney praising her skill and recommending that she be permitted to settle this case. The Duke of Venice, presiding over the court, agrees. Portia begins by acknowledging that Shylock is entitled to demand his bond. She asks him to be merciful, but he refuses and prepares to cut his pound of flesh from near Antonio's heart.

Now the tables are turned on Shylock by Portia. She urges him to take his bond, but to be sure not to spill one drop of Antonio's blood. To spill a Christian's blood is a crime in Venice, punishable by confiscation of all worldly goods. Shylock thereupon decides to accept Bassanio's offer to pay three times the amount of the loan. But Portia will not let him accept this offer. She tells him to cut his pound of flesh, but if he cuts too much or too little, he will then forfeit all his goods. Shylock now offers to settle the debt by merely taking the principal sum from Bassanio who, again, is ready. But Portia refuses to permit this; Shylock must take his bond instead. Shylock now realizes he is trapped and prepares to take his loss and leave the court.

Shylock's troubles still keep mounting. Portia tells him that by insisting on his bond he has made an attempt on the life of a Venetian citizen, and this crime is punishable by death at the discretion of the Duke, and by forfeiture of all the criminal's goods. Half of his estate is to go to the person whose life he threatened; the other half, to the state.

Finally, some mercy is shown Shylock. The Duke spares his life, and upon Antonio's urging the terms of the fine are changed. Shylock keeps half of his goods, though he must promise to will his possessions to his daughter and son-in-law. The other half of his goods he must give to Antonio, who will also use them for the benefit of Jessica and Lorenzo. Furthermore, Shylock must consent to become a Christian. His exchange with Portia ends as follows:

Portia. Art thou contented, Jew? What dost thou say?
Shylock. I am content.
Portia. Clerk, draw a deed of gift.
Shylock. I pray you, give me leave to go from hence;
I am not well: send the deed after me,
And I will sign it.

(p. 429c)

Those are the last words which Shylock speaks in the play; he leaves us on the note of "I am not well."

The rest of the play is romantic and happy. Act V, containing only one scene, takes place during a moonlit night on Portia's estate. There is music and gaiety, as three couples are happily reunited—Lorenzo and Jessica, Gratiano and Nerissa, Bassanio and Portia.

II

In order to understand Shylock and what happens to him, we must examine the problem of usury. In contemporary speech "usury" refers to the practice of lending money at an excessive rate of interest. Many countries have laws forbidding usury; these same laws also define what is the highest rate of interest that may be charged.

In earlier times, however, "usury" simply referred to the practice of charging interest for money lent. The very word indicates that usury is payment for the "use" of money. Christian ethics in medieval Europe forbade usury as a sin. Aquinas, in that part of the *Summa Theologica* which treats of justice, devotes a whole question to "the sin of usury." (See Part II-II, Q. 78.)

The first article in this question asks "Whether It Is a Sin to Take Usury for Money Lent?" Aquinas begins his answer as follows:

I answer that, To take usury for money lent is unjust in itself, because this is to sell what does not exist, and this evidently leads to inequality which is contrary to justice. (*Summa Theologica,* Pt. II-II, Q. 73, A. 1, Ans.)

This brief paragraph does not give the reasons for Aquinas' position, but it indicates some of the passion that has always been felt against the moneylender: he sells and charges for something that is not there, something unreal. The borrower does not feel that he is buying something which commands a legitimate price; he feels that he is buying nothing and yet must, because of the circumstances in which he finds himself, pay for the purchase of "nothing."

Aquinas' full explanation is less emotional and more reasoned. He points out that there is nothing unjust in paying for the use of certain things. For instance, when a man rents a house from another person, the rent constitutes payment for the use of the house. Why, then, is there anything unjust or sinful when the moneylender demands payment for the use of money?

The explanation lies in the fact that things are used in different ways. Some sorts of things—such as houses—can be used without being destroyed by the use. There may be wear and tear on a house when it is being used, but the house subsists. Other things, however, must be destroyed when use is made of them, as, for example, when food is consumed. For this reason, Aquinas says such things and their use cannot be considered separately. It makes no sense, for instance, to sell separately the food and its use. In fact, it cannot be done, for there is no food to sell separately from its use.

But in the case of a house, the thing and its use can be considered and sold separately; I can sell the use of a house for a certain length of time to Person A, and then I can, if I wish, sell the house itself to Person B. (I must, of course, acquaint B with the fact that A has purchased the right to use the house for a certain period of time.)

To which class of things does money belong? Aquinas says that it is one of those things which is consumed in its use.

Now money, according to the Philosopher (*Ethic,* v. 5; *Polit.* i. 3) was invented chiefly for the purpose of exchange: and consequently the proper and principal use of money is its consumption or alienation whereby it is sunk in exchange. (*Ibid.*)

If I have a hundred dollars and want to use this sum of money in order to buy a suit, I can only do this by consuming or destroying the money. In other words, when I have used the money and bought the suit, I then no longer have the money.

Consequently, just as it would be immoral to sell the use of food apart from the food itself, so it is immoral to sell the use of money apart from the money itself. It is perfectly all right to sell money as such; *i.e.*, to sell $50 for $50 (provided anyone wants to make such a purchase), or to sell $50 for its equivalent in British pounds. But it is immoral to sell $50 for, say, $60 with the excuse that the purchaser gets not only $50 but also the right to use it.

Hence it is by its very nature unlawful to take payment for the use of money lent, which payment is known as usury: and just as a man is bound to restore other ill-gotten goods, so is he bound to restore the money which he has taken in usury. (*Ibid.*)

Question 78 contains another article that is relevant to *The Merchant of Venice.* In Article 4 Aquinas asks "Whether It Is Lawful to Borrow Money under a Condition of Usury?" We have already seen that it is sinful to *lend* money under conditions of usury. Now the question arises whether he who *borrows* from a usurer also commits a sin. Does not the borrower encourage the lender to commit a sin and therefore himself become guilty of sin? Aquinas answers that it would be a sin to induce someone to lend money at interest, but it is not a sin to borrow from him under those conditions, if he stands ready to do it.

Accordingly we must also answer to the question in point that it is by no means lawful to induce a man to lend under a condition of usury: yet it is lawful to borrow for usury from a man who is ready to do so and is a usurer by profession; provided the borrower have a good end in view, such as the relief of his own or another's need. (*Summa Theologica,* Pt. II-II, Q. 78, A. 4, Ans.)

This absolves Antonio from sin in borrowing from Shylock; and in general it absolves Christians from sin in borrowing at interest from Jews. Indeed, one of the reasons why the business of moneylending was largely in the hands of Jews during the Middle Ages was that Christians were forbidden to engage in it; but Christians were not forbidden to borrow from Jews, and so the Jewish moneylender filled a need in the community.

III

We turn from these more general considerations to the particular situation in the play. Does Shylock deserve his fate? Is he treated justly? Or is he ensnared and trapped so that he cannot extricate himself?

Let us begin by examining the characters of Shylock and of Antonio. We recognize immediately that Shylock is not an attractive person, whereas Antonio is. Suspiciousness and meanness characterize the lender, while the borrower shines with generosity toward his friend Bassanio. Although he knows that Antonio's fortunes depend on the successful return of his various ships, Shylock is willing to make the loan. "The man is, notwithstanding, sufficient," Shylock says to Bassanio, ". . . I think I may take his bond" (p. 409d).

But from here on things do not go smoothly. Quite reasonably Shylock asks to see Antonio before making the loan. Bassanio, in what appears to be a cordial manner, invites Shylock to dine with him and Antonio. But Shylock refuses the invitation. "I will buy with you, sell with you, talk with you, walk with you, and so following, but I will not eat with you, drink with you, nor pray with you" (*Ibid.*). The need to arrange a meeting disappears, however, since at that moment Antonio enters.

Shylock immediately tells us that he hates Antonio. The hatred is due in part to the fact that Antonio is a Christian, but the major reason for it lies in Antonio's habit of lending money without interest.

> He lends out money gratis and brings down
> The rate of usance here with us in Venice.
> If I can catch him once upon the hip,
> I will feed fat the ancient grudge I bear him.
> He hates our sacred nation, and he rails,

Even there where merchants most do congregate,
On me, my bargains, and my well-won thrift,
Which he calls interest. Cursed be my tribe,
If I forgive him! (p. 410a)

Shylock and Antonio quickly start an argument; first they dispute about the propriety of charging interest in general, but soon they discuss their personal relationship. Shylock recalls that Antonio has often berated him publicly, spat on him, called him a dog. How then does Antonio expect Shylock to do him a favor now and lend him three thousand ducats? Antonio has his answer ready:

I am as like to call thee so again,
To spit on thee again, to spurn thee too.
If thou wilt lend this money, lend it not
As to thy friends; for when did friendship take
A breed for barren metal of his friend?
But lend it rather to thine enemy,
Who, if he break, thou mayst with better face
Exact the penalty. (pp. 410d-411a)

These are strong words and Antonio openly invites Shylock to do his worst. Shylock does not fail to do so. He offers to charge no monetary interest for the loan, but demands the right to one pound of Antonio's flesh if the latter should fail to repay the loan in three months' time. Antonio unhesitatingly agrees:

Content, i' faith: I'll seal such a bond
And say there is much kindness in the Jew.
(p. 411a)

He has no fears about the bond and quiets Bassanio's apprehensions by pointing to the expected return of his ships. Shylock makes fun of Bassanio's fears and claims that only persons as ungenerous as Christians would take this agreement seriously and worry about it; in truth, Shylock says, he is making the loan out of friendship.

Pray you, tell me this;
If he should break his day, what should I gain
By the exaction of the forfeiture?
A pound of man's flesh taken from a man
Is not so estimable, profitable neither,

As flesh of muttons, beefs, or goats. I say,
To buy his favour, I extend this friendship . . .
(p. 411b)

Who is more to blame in this initial exchange? Certainly Shylock admits that he hates Antonio before the negotiations have even started, yet Antonio also admits that he has scorned and spurned Shylock in the past and will do so again. Neither side seems willing to make a concession to the other. Antonio's invitation to lend the money to him as an enemy is a pretty bald challenge. A better man than Shylock might have yielded to the temptation to take Antonio at his word. Yet it cannot be gainsaid that the terms which Shylock proposes are monstrous.

Most interesting is the speech in which Shylock points out how unprofitable the terms of the loan are to him. He will receive no interest whatever; and what, after all, is the utility of a pound of flesh? Who would even seriously imagine that he would insist on his bond? Is Shylock speaking the truth, when he claims he has no intention of collecting the bond in case Antonio misses the repayment date? It is hard to know; but if he does not mean to insist on his due here in Act I, something happens to him by the time we reach Act IV which causes him to be serious.

The elopement of Shylock's daughter, Jessica, with Lorenzo takes place between the time the loan is made and the time it falls due. Jessica becomes a Christian, and she absconds with gold and jewelry taken from her father. It is not hard to believe that his daughter's treachery hardens Shylock's heart and makes him hate Christians even more intensely than before. Apparently, no Christian sympathizes with him; instead he is mocked in the streets. Now when it is pointed out to him how useless and unprofitable it will be for him to insist on his bond, Shylock no longer thinks so. Salarino asks:

Why, I am sure, if he forfeit, thou wilt not take his flesh: what's that good for? (p. 419b)

And Shylock answers:

To bait fish withal: if it will feed nothing else, it will feed my revenge. (*Ibid.*)

He wants to be revenged on Antonio because he believes that Antonio hates him and hates him only because he is a Jew.

> I am a Jew. Hath not a Jew eyes? hath not a Jew hands, organs, dimensions, senses, affections, passions? fed with the same food, hurt with the same weapons, subjected to the same diseases, healed by the same means, warmed and cooled by the same winter and summer, as a Christian is? If you prick us, do we not bleed? if you tickle us, do we not laugh? if you poison us, do we not die? and if you wrong us, shall we not revenge? If we are like you in the rest, we will resemble you in that. If a Jew wrong a Christian, what is his humility? Revenge. If a Christian wrong a Jew, what should his sufferance be by Christian example? Why, revenge. (*Ibid.*)

Yet, can Shylock properly complain that Antonio hates him simply because he is a Jew? Earlier we saw that Shylock's first words about Antonio were "I hate him for he is a Christian."

No doubt, then, there exists deep personal hatred between Antonio and Shylock. It finds its climactic expression in the court scene in Act IV. But justice is supposed to be dispensed dispassionately. Does hatred interfere with the legal process, or is justice done?

The question is, does Shylock have the right to Antonio's pound of flesh? Apparently, it was established by law in Venice that the Duke must determine in open court that a loan had not been paid and that the bond should be forfeited. Must the Duke consent to this bond being collected? "I am sure the Duke/Will never grant this forfeiture to hold," says Salarino, but Antonio contradicts him:

> The Duke cannot deny the course of law:
> For the commodity that strangers have
> With us in Venice, if it be denied,
> Will much impeach the justice of his state;
> Since that the trade and profit of the city
> Consisteth of all nations. (p. 423c)

The facts are that the agreement was voluntarily entered into and that Antonio has failed to pay the debt. No one disputes these facts. The Duke does not deny Shylock's right to the bond, but asks him to be merciful. But Shylock insists on his right; he claims his demand is no more outrageous than the common assumption that slaves, although human beings, are the property of their masters.

> The pound of flesh, which I demand of him,
> Is dearly bought; 'tis mine and I will have it.
> If you deny me, fie upon your law!
> There is no force in the decrees of Venice.
> I stand for judgement: answer; shall I have it?
> (p. 426c)

Like Antonio, Shylock realizes that more is at stake here than the life of Antonio or his own cruel whim. The question is whether the state will enforce contracts made between merchants. The entire reputation and wealth of Venice was built on its trade. Even today no country will prosper commercially if the merchants of the world do not feel protected by its laws. No capital will be invested in a country which does not respect private property but seizes it willfully and without adequate compensation.

Portia—speaking in her disguise as a lawyer—joins Antonio and Shylock in emphasizing the importance of enforcing established law. Bassanio, less concerned with niceties of law and more with the realities of life and death, addresses her thus:

> And I beseech you,
> Wrest once the law to your authority:
> To do a great right, do a little wrong,
> And curb this cruel devil of his will. (p. 427d)

But Portia does not subscribe to this doctrine that the end justifies the means.

> It must not be; there is no power in Venice
> Can alter a decree established:
> 'Twill be recorded for a precedent,
> And many an error by the same example
> Will rush into the state: it cannot be. (*Ibid.*)

The law must reign supreme, she tells Bassanio; it cannot be bent or twisted even in a good cause because of the dangerous effects such a precedent would set.

The remainder of the court scene is taken up with Portia's insistence that Shylock take what is his due, but no more, and that he also be responsible for the consequences of his action. Just as Portia insisted earlier that she could not change the law for the benefit of Antonio, so now she insists on the letter of the law and refuses to show consideration or mercy for Shylock.

Is Portia being just in her treatment of Shylock? Why will she not allow him to change his mind, for instance, and receive the payment of his loan when he realizes what the consequences of his action will be? Is she being just or merely being vengeful? If the contract between Antonio and Shylock was lawful, how can Shylock be subject to punishment for making an attempt against the life of a Venetian citizen? We may also wonder about the mercy shown to Shylock by Antonio. It is made conditional on Shylock's embracing the Christian faith. Is this a legitimate demand, from the point of view of law and from the point of view of Christianity?

IV

Is Aquinas' theory of usury applicable under modern conditions?

Money must not be lent at interest; that is the sum and substance of Aquinas' theory. In the modern economy, however, money is constantly being lent and borrowed at interest, and it is fair to say that no modern industrial state could exist if the charging of interest were forbidden. It is also worth noting that Christian churches no longer condemn this practice. We are speaking here of the practice of charging reasonable rates of interest, not of usury in the sense of charging excessive rates of interest. No one—either now or in earlier times—condones the latter. Is Aquinas wrong, or can his theory be made to fit modern conditions? The theory applies perfectly as long as the only use of money consists in spending. If I can use money only to spend it in order to acquire goods, I must always consume money in its use. Under these conditions, it makes no difference who has my money (as long as I do not wish to spend it immediately); if I lend it to someone who returns it, I have lost nothing I would have had if I had not lent the money. For if I had not lent the money I would simply have had to safely keep it under my pillow or in a strongbox.

In modern society money has a second (and very important) use. Money may also be invested. This function of money is essential to the modern economy. The money invested becomes the capital for a business enterprise, and unless there were investments, there would be no capital formation and, consequently, no economic growth.

It follows that he who lends money to someone is, by that very fact, losing something even if the money is properly paid back. What the lender deprives himself of is the opportunity to invest his money. Since in the case of investment time is of the essence—that is, the value of the investment depends on when and for how long the money is invested—it cannot be maintained that the lender can just as well invest his own money when he gets it back from the borrower. This may be true when the use of money is to buy a refrigerator; it can as well be bought six months from now as at the present moment. But it is not true of investment; I may have no opportunity to invest in a business if I do not do it now. Even if the opportunity to invest should still exist six months from now, I may need more money in order to purchase an equal share in the business.

Under these conditions, therefore, he who charges for the use of money is charging for something. For now money and its use (in investment) can be separated; and in this use, money is not destroyed.

Is this reasoning convincing? Does Aquinas' theory mean that he would be opposed to the capitalist economy; *i.e.*, to a state which depends on capital formation for its growth? Could communist economy permit the practice of lending money at interest?

Was Antonio committing a sin by consenting to the bond proposed by Shylock?

We have already seen that Aquinas is ready to excuse him who borrows at interest from a professional moneylender. Thus Antonio committed no sin in going to Shylock for a loan.

But by agreeing to the particular bond proposed by Shylock, Antonio put his life in jeopardy. Was this not a sin? Knowing that Shylock had no love for him—indeed urging Shylock to lend the money as though to an enemy—was not Antonio inducing Shylock to commit the sin of killing? Or, since it was not known whether Antonio would be able to pay back the loan, was he not at least inducing Shylock to consider deliberate killing in return for money lent? Thus there seem to be two different sins which Antonio may have committed. First, he jeopardized his own life; and second, he induced Shylock to contemplate murder.

Is it a sin in Christian doctrine to risk one's own life? Clearly there are degrees of risk; some risks may be legitimately taken. For instance, it is not a sin to fly in airplanes or to ride in automobiles, even though both modes of transportation carry an inherent risk. It is permitted to do things which normal and reasonable expectation regards safe, even though occasional accidents happen. The question therefore arises, whether the risk Antonio was taking was a legitimate one or whether he was presuming on God's charity in order to remain alive.

Taking into account the uncertainties connected with sailing ships at the time of the play's setting, was the risk Antonio took great or small? Should a human life ever be risked for the sake of obtaining material goods? Antonio's purpose was to help out a friend; does that legitimatize his action? Bassanio was not in such need that *his* life depended on obtaining the three thousand ducats; he needed the loan in order to court Portia. Did Bassanio offend against justice by consenting to risk Antonio's life for this purpose?

SELF-TESTING QUESTIONS

The following questions are designed to help you test the thoroughness of your reading. Each question is to be answered by giving a page or pages of the reading assignment. Answers will be found on page 239 of this Reading Plan.

1 Which Biblical story does Shylock tell in support of his endeavor to prosper financially?

2 Which casket does the Prince of Morocco choose in his courtship of Portia?

3 What is written in the silver casket?

4 Why does Bassanio want to borrow money from Antonio?

5 What is the content of the letter in which Antonio informs Bassanio of his misfortune?

6 Who recommends that Portia be permitted to settle the legal dispute between Shylock and Antonio?

7 What reward does Portia demand from Bassanio for her legal services?

Tenth Reading

MONTESQUIEU

The Spirit of Laws

Books I, XIV-XVII, XXIX

Vol. 38, pp. 1-3, 102-125, 262-269

Referring to Montesquieu, Voltaire writes in the *Philosophical Dictionary,* "Europe owes him eternal gratitude" because ". . . he was always right against the fanatics and promoters of slavery." Yet Voltaire was no unqualified admirer of Montesquieu's. On the contrary, he was extremely hostile toward him and spoke ill of him in private. However, the fame of *The Spirit of Laws* had become so great by the time that the *Philosophical Dictionary* was published that even Voltaire felt obliged to praise it in public.

Yet it is worth noting that the words of approval we have quoted come at the very end of the article "Laws (Spirit of)." Everything that precedes the praise is designed to run down the author. "Montesquieu was almost always in error with the learned, because he was not learned . . .," Voltaire writes. He devotes nearly the entire article to listing errors in Montesquieu's books. Much of Voltaire's unfavorable appraisal is no doubt based on personal feelings. In general, however, it is true that *The Spirit of Laws* was not well received by the rationalists dominating the eighteenth-century French intellectual scene. Many of them, indeed, advised Montesquieu against publishing the work—advice which he fortunately ignored.

The Spirit of Laws was more congenial to British and American thought. Montesquieu was a great admirer of the British constitution; Chapter 6 of Book XI, the longest chapter in the work, is a separate little treatise on the constitution of England. The founders of the American republic deeply respected Montesquieu. In the forty-seventh paper of *The Federalist*, Madison, writing of the separation of the powers of government, tells us that "The oracle who is always consulted and cited on this subject is the celebrated Montesquieu." The remark is as applicable today as it was in 1788.

GUIDE TO

Tenth Reading

I

The Spirit of Laws was published in 1748. It thus belongs to the period of time called the "Enlightenment" and is one of the influential political treatises of that age. In general, the thinkers of the Enlightenment were interested in reforming and liberalizing government, in religious toleration, and in free expression. Montesquieu is one of the first writers in this tradition. Others are Voltaire, Rousseau, and the French Encyclopaedists such as Diderot, D'Alembert, Helvetius, and Holbach. The *Declaration of the Rights of Man* and the *Declaration of Independence,* the great documents of the French and American Revolutions, also belong to this tradition.

Montesquieu exemplifies the period of enlightenment. In *The Spirit of Laws,* he endeavors to bring the light of reason to the subject of law and to base its study on knowledge rather than on guesswork, hypotheses, or preconceived notions. The need for a reasonable approach to the subject can be seen from his definition of law:

> Law in general is human reason, inasmuch as it governs all the inhabitants of the earth: the political and civil laws of each nation ought to be only the particular cases in which human reason is applied. (p. 3c)

Since countries differ, however, the way in which reason is applied in different systems of law varies.

> [Laws] should be adapted in such a manner to the people for whom they are framed that it should be a great chance if those of one nation suit another. (p. 3c)

This last remark indicates the general task that Montesquieu sets for himself: What is the manner in which law ought to be applied to particular nations in particular circumstances? The laws, Montesquieu writes, ". . . should be in relation to the nature and principle of each government . . ." (p. 3c). He then continues:

> They should be in relation to the climate of each country, to the quality of its soil, to its situation and extent, to the principal occupation of the natives, whether husbandmen, huntsmen, or shepherds: they should have relation to the degree of liberty which the constitution will bear; to the religion of the inhabitants, to their inclinations, riches, numbers, commerce, manners, and customs. In fine, they have relations to each other, as also to their origin, to the intent of the legislator, and to the order of things on which they are established; in all of which different lights they ought to be considered . . . These relations I shall examine, since all these together constitute what I call the *Spirit of Laws.* (p. 3c-d)

Let us also note the utility which Montesquieu sees in his enterprise. It will show to every nation ". . . the reasons on which its maxims are founded . . ."; thus it will contribute to the instruction of mankind. (See Preface, p. xxic.) And, he remarks, "It is not a matter of indifference that the minds of the people be enlightened" (*Ibid.*).

> Could I but succeed so as to afford new reasons to every man to love his prince, his country, his laws; new reasons to render him more sensible in every nation and government of the blessings he enjoys, I should think myself the most happy of mortals.
>
> Could I but succeed so as to persuade those who command, to increase their knowledge in what they ought to prescribe; and those who obey, to find a new pleasure resulting from obedience—I should think myself the most happy of mortals. (p. xxid)

In the Reading Plan on *Development of Political Theory and Government,* where part of *The Spirit of Laws* constitutes the Tenth Reading, we concentrate mainly on Montesquieu's concern with liberty and with the arrangement of the constitution (for instance, the need for the separation of the powers of government). In this assignment we shall emphasize the spirit of laws; *i.e.,* the ways in which laws are applied to particular conditions.

II

As an example of Montesquieu's characteristic method, we have chosen Books XIV-XVII. These books deal with the role that climate plays in the laws of countries. Montesquieu discusses "Of Laws in Relation to the Nature of the Climate" (Book XIV); "In What Manner the Laws of Civil Slavery Relate to the Nature of the Climate" (Book XV); "How the Laws of Domestic Slavery Bear a Relation to the Nature of the Climate" (Book XVI); and "How the Laws of Political Servitude Bear a Relation to the Nature of the Climate" (Book XVII).

In Montesquieu's view, laws are by their very nature relative. They are not absolute, not unchanging, not eternal; they can only be studied in terms of the things to which they relate. That is why a subject like climate is so important to Montesquieu: climate is one of those things which affect the character of law. Hence we must study climate if we wish to understand law.

It follows from the relativity of law that the method by which we understand it cannot be pure exposition or simple rational deduction. The method must be empirical, or at least quasi-empirical. Montesquieu employs a device that bridges both time and space: His method is "historical" in that he illustrates the effect of such factors as climate on law by examples drawn from the entire range of history as well as from peoples in different parts of the earth. In evidence for some point, he is as likely to cite the laws of ancient Rome or of China, as those of eighteenth-century France.

Although Montesquieu firmly believes in the relativity of laws, he is not a relativist in the matter of basic moral values. The actual positive laws are of men's own making and these vary from place to place, and from time to time, according to factors such as climate and soil. Behind these actual laws, however, there exist certain relations which are fixed and unchanging. Such an unchanging relation is justice.

> Before laws were made, there were relations of possible justice. To say that there is nothing just or unjust but what is commanded or forbidden by positive laws, is the same as saying that before the describing of a circle all the radii were not equal. (p. 1c)

Montesquieu concludes:

> We must therefore acknowledge relations of justice antecedent to the positive law by which they are established . . . (*Ibid.*)

The "historical method," then, consists in showing how the possible relations of justice should be actualized in particular historical conditions.

At the beginning of Book XIV, Montesquieu indicates why he is concerned with climate:

> If it be true that the temper of the mind and the passions of the heart are extremely different in different climates, the laws ought to be in relation both to the variety of those passions and to the variety of those tempers. (p. 102b)

Montesquieu's main point concerning climate is that "People are . . . more vigorous in cold climates" (*Ibid.*). Hence, he concludes,

> The inhabitants of warm countries are, like old men, timorous; the people in cold countries are, like young men, brave. (p. 102d)

There follow some physiological arguments in support of this thesis. Then Montesquieu adduces historical evidence for his point. He begins with India and then turns to other parts of Asia, especially China. Montesquieu's habit of using laws passed hundreds of years ago on an equal footing with laws in force at the time of his writing is illustrated by his reference to the laws of Mahomet, the Carthaginians, the ancient Egyptians, Greeks, Romans, and Jews. Examples from ancient Rome are quite frequent in *The Spirit of Laws*. Here in the fourteenth book Montesquieu jumps in quick succession from the laws of Rome to those of England, and from the latter to those of ancient Germany.

From all these instances, Montesquieu concludes that the laws of a country ought to oppose the direction in which climate tends to influence people: That is, in northern (cold) countries, the laws ought to encourage repose and inaction; on the other hand, the laws of southern (warm) countries ought to try to encourage the people to action and vigor. (See Chapter 5, pp. 104c-105a.)

In the three remaining books having to do with climate, Montesquieu discusses its effects on civil (that is, legal) slavery, on domestic slavery (that is, the slavery in which women are held in some countries), and on political slavery (that is, the slavery of a people as a result of war or conquest).

We cannot leave this subject without pointing out that Montesquieu need not be right in his views that climate crucially influences laws. He may have overstated his case. His reasoning can be summarized as follows: Climate and similar physical causes influence the passions of men. Hence, most men living under similar physical circumstances will have the same general character. The laws for such a group of men must take into account their national character.

Voltaire claims that Montesquieu is simply mistaken in the view that cold climates promote courage and that warm climates tend to make men timid.

> We should take great care how general propositions escape us. No one has ever been able to make a Laplander or an Esquimaux warlike, while the Arabs in fourscore years conquered a territory which exceeded that of the whole Roman Empire. This maxim of M. Montesquieu is equally erroneous with all the rest on the subject of climate.[1]

David Hume's denial of Montesquieu's position is as sweeping as Voltaire's although somewhat more reasoned and calm. First of all, Hume indicates that the notion of a "national character" must be used with caution.

> The vulgar are apt to carry all *national characters* to extremes; and, having once established it as a principle that any people are knavish, or cowardly, or ignorant, they will admit of no exception, but comprehend every individual under the same censure.[2]

Hume is opposed to these judgments although he admits that the notion of national character is not totally without value.

> Men of sense condemn these undistinguishing judgments; though, at the same time, they allow that each nation has a peculiar set of manners, and that some particular qualities are more frequently to be met with among one people than among their neighbours.[3]

However, Hume sharply disagrees with Montesquieu on the causes that shape national character. He denies that physical

---

[1] *Philosophical Dictionary*, Article "Laws (Spirit of)." In *The Works of Voltaire*, Paris, 1901: E. R. DuMont. Vol. XI, pp. 104-105.

[2] "Of National Characters" in *Essays, Moral, Political and Literary*, London, 1904; Henry Frowde (The World's Classics), p. 202.

[3] *Ibid.*

causes such as climate have any appreciable effect on character. Instead, he ascribes such effects to moral causes. By these he means causes which work on man indirectly because they become motives for action. (Physical causes work on man directly, by bringing about physiological changes.) As examples of moral causes, Hume lists

> . . . the nature of the government, the revolutions of public affairs, the plenty or penury in which the people live, the situation of the nation with regard to its neighbours, and such like circumstances.[4]

There can be no doubt, Hume continues, that moral causes affect the character of men. As examples he mentions soldiers and priests. The different circumstances in which members of these professions find themselves produce different motives in them; consequently, their characters are also different. In Hume's view, soldiers are courageous, boisterous, and honest; priests are quiet, timid, and hypocritical.

But physical causes are unimportant to the formation of men's characters.

> As to *physical causes,* I am inclined to doubt altogether of their operation in this particular; nor do I think that men owe any thing of their temper or genius to the air, food, or climate.[5]

He sets forth a considerable array of arguments in support of his position. For instance, he notes that in a large country such as China where there are great climatic differences, the national character nevertheless seems to be the same. This is due to the fact that the Chinese character is formed by a moral cause which is the same throughout China, namely, the nature of their government. On the other hand, the populations of two neighboring cities, Athens and Thebes, which shared the same climate, displayed distinctly different national characters. Hume describes the Athenians as ingenuous, polite, and gay, while he calls the Thebans dull, rustic, and phlegmatic.

Hume derives another argument against Montesquieu from the example of the Jews. Because Jews keep close to one an-

---

[4] *Ibid.,* pp. 202-203

[5] *Ibid.,* pp. 205-206

other and do not freely mingle with other persons, Hume says that they have a distinctive character of their own and do not acquire the character of their host nation even though they obviously share the same climate. In a similar vein, Hume points out that Spanish, English, and Dutch colonists maintain the character of their native country and do not acquire the traits of the tropical people among whom they live.

Hume's arguments seem rather telling. We may wonder if Montesquieu could rebut them. Apparently, Montesquieu's reply would consist in a denial of Hume's facts. Whereas Hume cites China as an example of a country with one national character but several different climates, Montesquieu cites it in just the opposite way:

> In the north of China people are more courageous than those in the south; and those in the south of Korea have less bravery than those in the north. (p. 122a)

Whereas Hume refers to the Jewish people as one that has not been affected by the character of its hosts, Montesquieu tells us that ". . . the Jewish laws concerning the leprosy were borrowed from the practice of the Egyptians" (p. 106b). Again, Montesquieu appears to deny Hume's assertion that colonists keep their native temper and character; on the contrary, Montesquieu claims that ". . . even the children of Europeans born in India lose the courage peculiar to their own climate" (p. 104a).

Hume's remarks hardly constitute a refutation of Montesquieu's view that climate influences national character and therefore should be taken into account when laws are made. All we can conclude, after comparing what Montesquieu says with what Hume says, is that the influence of climate on national character is not as simple as Montesquieu appears to believe. If the facts are as Hume presents them, Montesquieu is wrong in thinking that all peoples in cold climates are vigorous.

However, it is still entirely possible that climate influences national character, although in much more subtle ways than Montesquieu imagines. Consequently, climate may indeed have to be considered when laws are made. In other words, Montesquieu's general proposition—that climate influences national character—cannot be refuted by mere examples. Neither, of course, can it be established in that way.

III

What are Montesquieu's views on slavery?

Books XV, XVI, and XVII treat the subject of slavery. Book XV deals with "civil slavery"; this is the kind of slavery we ordinarily have in mind when we use the term. It involves a master and a slave who is the former's property and performs services for him. In Book XVI Montesquieu speaks of "domestic slavery"; this refers to the slavish condition in which women are kept in some countries. In Book XVII, the topic is "political slavery"; this arises when one people conquers another and forces it into servitude.

The fact that Montesquieu discusses slavery in such detail does not mean, however, that he approves of the institution. Here as elsewhere in *The Spirit of Laws,* Montesquieu's historical method leads him to relate the facts—or what he believes to be the facts—that influence the customs and laws of countries. Since many countries have or have had the institution of slavery, Montesquieu is duty-bound to discuss it and to indicate how such a factor as climate affects it and the laws relating to it.

Montesquieu unequivocally denounces civil slavery as bad.

> Slavery, properly so called, is the establishment of a right which gives to one man such a power over another as renders him absolute master of his life and fortune. The state of slavery is in its own nature bad. It is neither useful to the master nor to the slave; not to the slave, because he can do nothing through a motive of virtue; nor to the master, because by having an unlimited authority over his slaves he insensibly accustoms himself to the want of all moral virtues, and thence becomes fierce, hasty, severe, choleric, voluptuous, and cruel. (p. 109a)

This argument of Montesquieu's deserves special attention because he insists that slavery is bad for the master. Few slaves would disagree that slavery is bad for the slave, but masters tend to think that slavery is good not only for themselves but also for their slaves. Montesquieu's reasoning is undoubtedly correct and can still be used against those who wish to perpetuate any kind of superiority for themselves. The master-slave relationship morally degrades the master.

Opposed to this entire view of slavery is, of course, Aristotle's theory that some men are natural slaves. According to Aristotle natural slavery is good for both the master and the slave. Natural slaves are in the same relation to their masters as animals are to men, or as the body is to the soul. Aristotle adds that

> . . . it is better for them as for all inferiors that they should be under the rule of a master. (*Politics,* Vol. 9, p. 448b)

He later reiterates that slavery is to the mutual advantage of master and slave when he says:

> . . . where the relation of master and slave between them is natural they are friends and have a common interest, but where it rests merely on law and force the reverse is true. (*Ibid.*, p. 449b)

Montesquieu is not impressed by Aristotle's argument:

> Aristotle endeavours to prove that there are natural slaves; but what he says is far from proving it. (p. 111b)

Although Montesquieu denies the existence of natural slavery, he then qualifies his denial. Apparently, he believes that in a few savage countries there may really be natural slaves. He is certain, however, that in civilized countries no one can or should be a natural slave.

> . . . as all men are born equal, slavery must be accounted unnatural, though in some countries it be founded on natural reason . . . (*Ibid.*)

He continues:

> . . . a wide difference ought to be made between such countries [where slavery is natural], and those in which even natural reason rejects it, as in Europe, where it has been so happily abolished. (*Ibid.*)

With the exception of a few countries, then, slavery is never natural, nor is slavery in any sense needed. All tasks that at one time were performed by slaves are much better performed by freemen.

If Montesquieu's position on natural slavery seems a little confusing, the author himself gives us a clue as to why this is so. He obviously would like to say that slavery is never natural but does not feel quite able to defend this position. "I know not," he writes, "whether this article be dictated by my understanding or by my heart" (p. 111c).

However, since civil slavery exists, Montesquieu turns to the laws having to do with it. Chapters 10-18 discuss the regulations concerning slavery. What is the purpose of these regulations? Does the slave retain any rights in Montesquieu's opinion? Does he think that slaves should be freed as much and as rapidly as possible?

What general purpose should lawmakers keep in mind?

This question may be rephrased as follows: What is the spirit of the legislator? Montesquieu raises this question in the first chapter of Book XXIX and answers as follows:

> I say it, and methinks I have undertaken this work with no other view than to prove it, the spirit of a legislator ought to be that of moderation; political, like moral good, lying always between two extremes. (p. 262a)

Any law that is well made, therefore, ought to bring about the effect of moderation. Montesquieu investigates historical examples of laws to find if they meet this criterion. He arrives at a number of surprising results. For instance, laws that appear to aim at extremes sometimes do nevertheless result in moderation. An example of this is Solon's famous law that in a civil strife no one ought to remain neutral, but everyone should take one or the other side. This law forced the more thoughtful and virtuous citizens to take part in rebellions. Without this law the mob who usually start rebellions might have succeeded simply because the responsible part of the citizenry would not bother to concern itself with the rebellion. This law, therefore, contributed to moderation, though at first it seemed to aim at the opposite.

Another important observation of Montesquieu's is that laws which seem to be the same do not always have the same effect. The circumstances of the people for which they are designed may cause the effects to be quite different. As an example,

Montesquieu cites a law of the Romans that no man could have more than a small amount of money in his house, and an almost identical law of France. The former law encouraged the economy and helped the poor; the latter law, however, simply confiscated people's property. Montesquieu's explanation of why these different effects resulted constitutes an illustration of his general thesis that laws must take into account the particular circumstances of time and place and the physical conditions of the country to which they apply.

Is Montesquieu correct in saying that moderation is the end of law? Are there any other ends which a law should serve? Are these always compatible with moderation? Should they be short or lengthy, simple or ornate in length? What are the external requirements that should be followed in making law?

What does Montesquieu think of the subjection of women?

Montesquieu seldom expresses his own opinions on a subject at great length; instead he reports the facts as he finds them. This is what he does with respect to the slavery of women. He devotes Book XVI to the topic, reporting on the laws of marriage, divorce, and government in the family. For the most part, Montesquieu finds that domestic government tends to imitate political government.

> . . . the slavery of women is perfectly conformable to the genius of a despotic government, which delights in treating all with severity. Thus at all times have we seen in Asia domestic slavery and despotic government walk hand in hand with an equal pace. (p. 118b-c)

Since the kind of government suitable to a people is influenced by the climate (hot climates, for instance, favoring despotic governments), we see that climate also exerts an influence on the relation between men and women. The warm weather of the East, for example, requires that women there be kept in separate parts of the houses from the men.

> These are things which ought to be decided by the climate. What purpose would it answer to shut up women in our northern countries, where their manners are naturally good; where all their passions are calm; and where love rules over the heart with so regular and gentle an

empire that the least degree of prudence is sufficient to conduct it? (p. 119c)

Immediately after this passage, Montesquieu permits himself one of the few value judgments to be found in this work; he congratulates himself and his reader on living in a moderate climate:

> It is a happiness to live in those climates which permit such freedom of converse, where that sex which has most charms seems to embellish society, and where wives, reserving themselves for the pleasures of one, contribute to the amusement of all. (*Ibid.*)

Do you think that Montesquieu is correct in saying that climate is at least partially responsible for such customs as polygamy and the confinement of wives? Could climate also influence the laws of divorce and repudiation? Does Montesquieu think that wives and husbands should have equal rights in the matter of divorce and repudiation?

SELF-TESTING QUESTIONS

The following questions are designed to help you test the thoroughness of your reading. Each question is to be answered by giving a page or pages of the reading assignment. Answers will be found on page 239 of this Reading Plan.

1 What are the kinds of civil slavery?

2 Does Montesquieu approve of polygamy?

3 Do men follow the natural law as well as inanimate beings do?

4 What are the physiological effects of cold on man, according to Montesquieu?

5 What regulations does Montesquieu favor in the freeing of slaves?

6 Does Montesquieu believe that women should be able to repudiate their husbands if husbands can repudiate their wives?

7 What physical causes favor liberty in Europe and despotism in Asia?

Eleventh Reading

ROUSSEAU

A Discourse On Political Economy

The Social Contract

Book II

Vol. 38, pp. 367-385, 395-406

Every revolution has its own thinkers and writers. John Locke was the philosopher of the English Revolution of 1688; Locke and Montesquieu were the foremost intellectual moving forces behind the American Revolution and the Constitution; Karl Marx and Friedrich Engels wrote the basic document for the European revolutions of 1848, the *Communist Manifesto*.

The name of Jean Jacques Rousseau is closely connected with the French Revolution. Although there have been many revolutions in France, when we speak of "the" French Revolution, we always mean the great upheaval that began on July 14, 1789, when the populace of Paris captured the Bastille. The French Revolution set in motion tremendous political and economic forces. Empires and kingdoms fell; the social structure of Europe was permanently changed. Perhaps the end of the changes initiated in 1789 has not yet been reached.

Such a cataclysm could not be caused by a single man. It would be foolish to pretend that Rousseau through his writings single-handedly brought about the French Revolution. Many forces and accidents combined to produce that result. But Rousseau's work does reflect the thinking about government, law, sovereignty, and similar topics current in the period immediately preceding the outbreak of the Revolution.

The French Revolution was a revolution of the middle class or *bourgeoisie*. The revolution was directed against the absolute rule of the French kings and against the privileges of the nobility. Before very long, the *bourgeoisie* itself became the object of revolutionary attack. In 1848 the *Communist Manifesto* called on the laboring classes to rebel against the exploitation by the *bourgeoisie.*

Compared with a revolutionary program like the *Communist Manifesto,* Rousseau's opinions are mild. Indeed, much of his political and economic thought would be termed conservative by the standards of the nineteenth and twentieth centuries. For instance, Rousseau places a very high value on obedience to law and on the rights of property. Both points are exemplified in our reading assignment.

GUIDE TO

Eleventh Reading

I

Few men could be more different than Montesquieu and Rousseau. At first glance there seem to be a few superficial similarities. Both writers were Frenchmen (although Rousseau was born in Geneva). They were nearly contemporaries; Montesquieu lived from 1689 to 1755; Rousseau, from 1712 to 1778. Both men were political philosophers, and both advocated republican government.

Their differences, however, were more striking. Montesquieu was a man of substance and reputation. He was a baron, a landowner, and an important figure in and around La Brède, his birthplace and estate. He studied law, became a counsellor to the parliament at Bordeaux, and, on the death of his uncle, inherited the office of President of the Bordeaux Parliament. Montesquieu was well-to-do financially, and his reputation as a writer and political thinker rose steadily throughout his lifetime. He was made a member of the French Academy, and was acquainted with many famous people in both France and England.

In contrast to Montesquieu's fairly placid and conventional life, Rousseau's life was turbulent and unconventional. He had very little formal education. For his livelihood he depended largely on his wit and his considerable attractiveness to women. He had several mistresses and sired a number of illegitimate children. Rousseau never had any difficulty in finding patrons, although he constantly quarreled with all of them. In France, he incurred the enmity of D'Alembert, Diderot, Voltaire, and the other Encyclopaedists. In England, Rousseau quarreled with David Hume who had invited him there when he was exiled from France as a result of the publication of *Émile*. In the last years of his life, he occupied himself with writing the *Confessions* and other autobiographical works (such as *Rousseau Juge de Jean-Jacques*), which are the main sources for the scandalous details of his life.

Rousseau's major writings, in addition to *The Social Contract*, the *Discourse on Political Economy*, *Émile*, and the *Confessions*, are the *Discourse on the Origin of Inequality* and a novel, *La Nouvelle Héloïse*.

II

The Social Contract is not a well organized book, nor can it escape the suspicion of inconsistency. Rousseau himself was well aware of this. When he begins to discuss sovereignty, he writes:

> Attentive readers, do not, I pray, be in a hurry to charge me with contradicting myself. The terminology made it unavoidable, considering the poverty of the language; but wait and see. (p. 397b, fn. 1)

Let us take Rousseau's advice and investigate his theory of sovereignty in some detail. By the social compact, Rousseau tells us in Book I of *The Social Contract*, a public person is formed.

> . . . it is called by its members *State* when passive, *Sovereign* when active, and *Power* when compared with others like itself. (p. 392a)

The sovereign being the state insofar as it is active, sovereignty is the activity of the state. This activity is ". . . nothing less than the exercise of the general will . . ." (p. 395a). The exercise of the general will results in *law*. (See also Book II, Chapter 6.)

Rousseau gives definitions (or perhaps they had better be called mere descriptions) of law in two places. In the first passage, he tells us what an act of sovereignty is; in the second, he actually uses the word "law."

> . . . every act of Sovereignty, i.e., every authentic act of the general will, binds or favours all the citizens equally . . . What, then, strictly speaking, is an act of Sovereignty? It is not a convention between a superior and an inferior, but a convention between the body and each of its members. It is legitimate, because based on the social contract, and equitable, because common to all; useful, because it can have no other object than the general good, and stable, because guaranteed by

the public force and the supreme power. So long as the subjects have to submit only to conventions of this sort, they obey no-one but their own will . . . (pp. 397d-398a)

So much for the first definition. Now let us look at the second one:

. . . when the whole people decrees for the whole people, it is considering only itself; and if a relation is then formed, it is between two aspects of the entire object, without there being any division of the whole. In that case the matter about which the decree is made is, like the decreeing will, general. This act is what I call a law. (p. 399d)

Rousseau draws several conclusions from this definition of law:

On this view, we at once see that it can no longer be asked whose business it is to make laws, since they are acts of the general will; nor whether the prince is above the law, since he is a member of the State; nor whether the law can be unjust, since no one is unjust to himself; nor how we can be both free and subject to the laws, since they are but registers of our wills. (pp. 399d-400a)

Let us examine the properties of law and of the lawmaking power. The latter (*i.e.*, the general will) is inalienable and indivisible. This means that only the general will can make laws; this power cannot be delegated to anyone else, nor can it be repudiated, nor can it be divided. The general will can never be exercised by a part of the people but only by the people as a whole.

The general will is general in two ways. In the first place, it must be directed to general aims; and in the second place, it must be the will of the whole people.

. . . the general will, to be really such, must be general in its object as well as its essence . . . it must both come from all and apply to all . . . it loses its natural rectitude when it is directed to some particular and determinate object, because in such a case we are judging of something foreign to us, and have no true principle of equity to guide us. (p. 397b)

This passage emphasizes the generality of the general will in the first way; the following words emphasize the generality of the will in the second way:

. . . the general will is always right and tends to the public advantage; but it does not follow that the deliberations of the people are always equally correct. Our will is always for our own good, but we do not always see what that is; the people is never corrupted, but it is often de-

> ceived, and on such occasions only does it seem to will what is bad.
>
> There is often a great deal of difference between the will of all and the general will; the latter considers only the common interest, while the former takes private interest into account, and is no more than a sum of particular wills . . . (p. 396b)

The first way is the more important of the two:

> It should be seen from the foregoing that what makes the will general is less the number of voters than the common interest uniting them . . . (p. 397c)

It is important to realize that the general will is infallible. By definition, the general will is that will which tends to the public good; ". . . it can have no other object than the general good . . ." (p. 397d), Rousseau writes, because any will that has as its object some particular good is by that very fact not the general will.

Since the general will is infallible, it can, of course, never be unjust. This explains how men are free, even though they are subject to the laws. The laws "are but registers of our wills" and so in obeying them we obey ourselves. For the laws being infallibly directed to the public good, they merely direct us to do that which we would want to do anyhow. But he who does what he wants, Rousseau implies, is free. Therefore the citizens of a republic which is governed by duly made laws are free.

The problem of the freedom of citizens concerns Rousseau deeply. He wants to find assurance that men may remain free, even though they are the subjects of a state. In his *Political Economy* he asks:

> By what inconceivable art has a means been found of making men free by making them subject; of using in the service of the State the properties, the persons and even the lives of all its members, without constraining and without consulting them; of confining their will by their own admission; of overcoming their refusal by that consent, and forcing them to punish themselves, when they act against their own will? How can it be that all should obey, yet nobody take upon him to command, and that all should serve, and yet have no masters, but be the more free, as, in apparent subjection, each loses no part of his liberty but what might be hurtful to that of another? (p. 370c)

Rousseau immediately answers his own questions:

> These wonders are the work of law. It is to law alone that men owe justice and liberty. (p. 370d)

Law is not antithetical to freedom; on the contrary, it constitutes the guarantee of freedom. Law is the work of the general will, and no individual person's will can be truly opposed to the general will. If a particular will *is* opposed to the general will, this arises from a particular person's misunderstanding of what the public good is. "When . . . [an] opinion that is contrary to my own prevails, this proves neither more nor less than that I was mistaken, and that what I thought to be the general will was not so" (p. 426d). Rousseau concludes that he is free only if his own will does not win out.

> If my particular opinion had carried the day I should have achieved the opposite of what was my will; and it is in that case that I should not have been free. (*Ibid.*)

This agrees with what Rousseau says in the first book: There he notes that if a person's particular will disagrees with the general will, he should be forced to obey the general will. "This means nothing less," he writes, "than that he will be forced to be free . . . " (p. 393b).

III

Rousseau discusses the aims of legitimate government in the *Discourse on Political Economy.* He begins by noting that the word "economy" originally referred to the government of the household, and was later extended to ". . . the government of that great family, the State" (p. 367a). In the latter sense, the word "economy" is usually accompanied by the adjective "political." The *Discourse on Political Economy* is a work dealing with political government and not primarily with what we usually think of as "economic" matters such as property, capital, wages, the production and distribution of goods, although some of these things are discussed briefly.

Rousseau makes an interesting distinction between the government and the sovereign.

> I must here ask my readers to distinguish also between *public economy,* which is my subject and which I call *government,* and the supreme authority, which I call *Sovereignty;* a distinction which consists in the fact that the latter has the right of legislation, and in certain cases binds the body of the nation itself, while the former has only the right of execution, and is binding only on individuals. (p. 368c-d)

Government is a much less exalted thing than Sovereignty. The government is simply charged with administering what the sovereign power commands. It is, Rousseau notes elsewhere, in an intermediate position between the subjects and the sovereign. (See p. 407a.)

The question concerning the aims of government must be understood in the light of Rousseau's conception of government. "What are the aims of government?" means "What must the administration do in order to execute the laws made by the sovereignty in the best and most efficient manner?" The answer consists in three rules which a good government ought to follow.

The *first* rule is ". . . to follow in everything the general will" (p. 370b). The *second* rule is to ". . . bring all the particular wills into conformity with it [the general will]; in other words, as virtue is nothing more than this conformity of the particular wills with the general will, establish the reign of virtue" (p. 372b-c). The *third* rule is to make "Provision for the public wants . . ." (p. 377b). Each of these rules requires some elucidation.

The first rule is the easiest to understand. In fact, it merely restates the duty of the government. To follow the general will means to obey the laws. "The most pressing interest of the ruler, and even his most indispensable duty . . . is to watch over the observation of the laws of which he is the minister, and on which his whole authority is founded" (p. 370d). In a well-governed state, the laws will be obeyed because of their wisdom, and not merely because of the threat of punishment: ". . . the first of all laws is to respect the laws . . ." (p. 371a). Rousseau expresses the same thought when he remarks that the most certain way of assuring obedience to the laws is to make men love the laws. (See p. 372a-b.)

In the course of urging obedience to the laws, Rousseau makes the remark, referred to earlier, that law promotes liberty. This correlation between law and liberty, which is also made in *The Social Contract,* ranks high in importance because liberty is one of the purposes for which men form a government.

> Look into the motives which have induced men, once united by their common needs in a general society, to unite themselves still more intimately by means of civil societies: you will find no other motive than that of assuring the property, life and liberty of each member by the protection of all. (p. 370b)

This view of the ends of government agrees well with Locke's opinion. He declares in the *Second Essay Concerning Civil Government* that

> The great and chief end, therefore, of men uniting into commonwealths, and putting themselves under government, is the preservation of their property . . . (Vol. 35, p. 53d)

Locke notes that "property" is his "general name" for the "lives, liberties and estates" of men (*Ibid.*). The Declaration of Independence also maintains that ". . . governments are instituted among men . . ." in order to ". . .secure these rights . . . ," among them being those to ". . . life, liberty, and the pursuit of happiness" (Vol. 43, p. 1a).

Rousseau's second rule was "to establish the reign of virtue." The reason for this consists in the fact that ". . . at bottom only good men know how to obey [the laws]" (p. 372c). Men who do not obey the laws out of a sense of duty and respect will not obey them from fear of punishment. To try to enforce the laws on such men by threats and penalties is useless.

> In such a situation, it is vain to add edicts to edicts and regulations to regulations. Everything serves only to introduce new abuses, without correcting the old. The more laws are multiplied, the more they are despised . . . (p. 372d)

Since the laws must be obeyed for the sake of justice and liberty, it is necessary that the citizens be virtuous. But, Rousseau adds,

> It is not enough to say to the citizens, *be good;* they must be taught to be so . . . (p. 373c)

As a result moral education becomes one of the most important tasks of government. The most efficacious way of making men virtuous is to instill patriotism in them. Because of his patriotism, Cato benefited Rome more than Socrates benefited Athens. Rousseau compares the two men as follows:

> A worthy pupil of Socrates would be the most virtuous of his contemporaries; but a worthy follower of Cato would be one of the greatest. The virtue of the former would be his happiness; the latter would seek his happiness in that of all. We should be taught by the one, and led by the other; and this alone is enough to determine which to prefer: for no people has ever been made into a nation of philosophers, but it is not impossible to make a people happy. (p. 374a)

This is probably one of the few recorded places in which Socrates is compared with another man and found second best.

Patriotism, or love of country, will spring up in the citizens if they find their country truly lovable. If their country gives and guarantees them their rights and liberties and if it treats them justly, men will become patriots. The virtue he is looking for, Rousseau tells us, is that of citizenship; if every inhabitant of a country feels and knows himself to be a citizen, he will love his country. To make citizens out of inhabitants, the state must control education.

> Public education, therefore, under regulations prescribed by the government, and under magistrates established by the Sovereign, is one of the fundamental rules of popular or legitimate government. (p. 376c)

The third rule was to make "provision for the public wants" (p. 377b). Rousseau explains that he does not mean that the state should simply supply the needs of its citizens without any effort on their part. He means that the government should so regulate the economy that every citizen can satisfy his needs, provided he is willing to expend the necessary effort and labor. The duty of the state is not

> . . . to fill the granaries of individuals and thereby to grant them a dispensation from labour, but to keep plenty so within their reach that labour is always necessary and never useless for its acquisition. (p. 377b-c)

In addition, the government must of course concern itself with ". . . the management of the exchequer, and the expenses of public administration" (p. 377c). Although Rousseau does not advocate a "welfare state," he recognizes that the government has a responsibility for the economic well-being of the citizens. Every step that is taken toward this end must, however, take into account that

> . . . the right of property is the most sacred of all the rights of citizenship, and even more important in some respects than liberty itself . . . (p. 377c)

Why is property so important in Rousseau's eyes?

> . . . because it more nearly affects the preservation of life, or because, property being more easily usurped and more difficult to defend than life, the law ought to pay a greater attention to what is most easily taken away; or finally, because property is the true foundation of civil society, and the real guarantee of the undertakings of citizens . . . (*Ibid.*)

In other words, because property is ". . . answerable for personal actions . . . ," men do not ". . . evade duties and laugh at the laws" (*Ibid.*). If they did, they would be faced with the threat of fines by the government or civil suits by injured persons. These remarks seem to contradict what Rousseau says in connection with the second rule. On page 164 above, we quoted his view that the threat of punishment does not induce men to obey the laws. (See p. 372.) Perhaps Rousseau considers the threat of physical pain ineffective but believes that the threatened loss of property may help bring about obedience to the laws.

Government must necessarily demand contributions from the citizens' property in order to run the state. Thus an unavoidable conflict arises between the sacred right of property and the government's need. In general, however, the government ought to leave property alone as much as possible and permit it to stay in the same family. Rousseau believes that this way of dealing with property will help preserve the state.

> . . . nothing is more fatal to morality and to the Republic than the continual shifting of rank and fortune among the citizens: such changes are both the proof and the source of a thousand disorders, and overturn and

confound everything; for those who were brought up to one thing find themselves destined for another; and neither those who rise nor those who fall are able to assume the rules of conduct, or to possess themselves of the qualifications requisite for their new condition, still less to discharge the duties it entails. (p. 378a)

IV

Is Rousseau's theory of law and liberty totalitarian in character?

In general, a totalitarian theory of the state proclaims the superiority of the state over the individual. In such a state, the individual serves the state rather than the state the individual. Liberty is not an important value in a totalitarian state.

The last point seems to imply that Rousseau cannot be a totalitarian. Liberty is certainly of great importance to him; again and again he returns to the subject. The end of government is "property, life and liberty." (See p. 370b.) Similarly, ". . . the end of every system of legislation . . . [reduces] itself to two main objects, liberty and equality . . ." (p. 405a). These are by no means the only places where the importance of liberty is emphasized.

Nevertheless, we must proceed with caution before proclaiming Rousseau as a champion of liberty. The major context in which Rousseau discusses liberty is that of law. "It is to law alone," he says, "that men owe justice and liberty" (p. 370d). This statement, if we take it seriously, would seem to mean that the more we are subject to law, the freer we are. Again, the problem which Rousseau sets himself in *The Social Contract* is that of reconciling man's natural freedom with the fact that in societies man is not free because he is subject to laws. The reconciliation is brought about very simply. Rousseau claims that being free and being subject to law are one and the same thing.

In Chapter 8 of Book I of *The Social Contract,* Rousseau indicates in a straightforward way what liberties a man has and does not have under law, and what liberty is desirable.

What man loses by the social contract is his natural liberty and an unlimited right to everything he tries to get and succeeds in getting; what

he gains is civil liberty and the proprietorship of all he possesses . . .
We might, over and above all this, add, to what man acquires in the civil state, moral liberty, which alone makes him truly master of himself; for the mere impulse of appetite is slavery, while obedience to a law which we prescribe to ourselves is liberty. (p. 393c)

Let us recall another remark of Rousseau's:

On this view, we at once see that it can no longer be asked . . . how we can be both free and subject to the laws, since they are but registers of our wills. (pp. 399d-400a)

What is the upshot of all this? Is Rousseau a liberal or a totalitarian? In a liberal theory of man and the state, must freedom and law be necessarily opposed? And conversely, is the identification of liberty and law an indication that "real" liberty is being denied?

In order to be free, must men be able to do what they want? Rousseau wants men to obey the laws and thinks that this requires virtue. Does Rousseau place a higher value on liberty or on law? Toward the end of Section III we quoted a remark by Rousseau that property is, perhaps, more important than liberty. Is this an illiberal point of view?

What is the office of the legislator?

Chapter 7 of Book II is devoted to this topic. The legislator must be sharply distinguished from the sovereign who has the legislative power. Every act of sovereignty or act of the general will is a legislative act; this says no more than that what the general will does is to make laws.

What then is the function of the legislator? He establishes the state; his office precedes the constitution because it makes the constitution. The legislator sets up the civil state and endows it with its constitution or fundamental law.

This office, which sets up the Republic, nowhere enters into its constitution; it is an individual and superior function . . . (p. 401a)

Obviously, it takes great skill to formulate the constitution for a people. Those legislators who have succeeded in framing successful constitutions are therefore rightly famous. They are such men as Solon and Lycurgus; Rousseau also names Calvin as one of them for his achievement as legislator for Geneva.

Because the legislator works prior to the existence of a constitution, he cannot rely on the constitution to authenticate his acts. There are as yet no laws that require the people to obey him; indeed there are no laws at all.

> Thus in the task of legislation we find together two things which appear to be incompatible: an enterprise too difficult for human powers, and, for its execution, an authority that is no authority. (p. 401c)

How then does the legislator go about getting his fundamental law or constitution accepted? Rousseau raises the question with respect to a time prior to any government or constitution; that is what makes the problem difficult. How is a constitution adopted, when there already is some kind of government? How, for instance, was the Constitution of the United States adopted by the people of the United States? Was the problem the same as Rousseau's?

To what purpose should the laws be directed?

The two main purposes, Rousseau says, are liberty and equality.

> . . . liberty, because all particular dependence means so much force taken from the body of the State and equality, because liberty cannot exist without it. (p. 405a)

Which liberty of the three kinds he mentions in Book I, Chapter 8 of *The Social Contract* does Rousseau have in mind here? We have already pointed out that for Rousseau we are free when we are subject to laws; does this mean that liberty is necessarily promoted by any law?

What does Rousseau mean by "equality"? Does he refer to political or to economic equality? Does he mean that all men should be absolutely equal in political or economic power?

Is the battlecry of the French Revolution—"Liberty, Equality, Fraternity"—one that Rousseau could have adopted?

SELF-TESTING QUESTIONS

The following questions are designed to help you test the thoroughness of your reading. Each question is to be answered by giving a page or pages of the reading assignment. Answers will be found on page 239 of this Reading Plan.

1 What is a Republic?

2 What are the three kinds of law?

3 Does Rousseau think that the death penalty is justified?

4 Is a declaration of war an act of sovereignty?

5 Are extremes of wealth and poverty good for the state?

6 Do the rich or the poor derive more advantage from living in Society?

7 Does the right to property extend beyond the life of the owner?

8 Must tax assessment be voluntary?

Twelfth Reading

KANT

The Science of Right

Part I

Vol. 42, pp. 403-434

In the popular view of the German national character, some of its outstanding traits are orderliness, adherence to routine, and perseverance. These Germanic characteristics are often thought to be best exemplified by the inhabitants of Prussia. Immanuel Kant was a German and a Prussian; he resided in Königsberg, the capital city of East Prussia.

Both in his personal life and in his writings, Kant displayed the characteristics mentioned above. His life proceeded in an orderly and routine fashion; so much so, in fact, that he never left his native city of Königsberg. The story is told that his neighbors set their watches by his daily walk; he missed making his regular appearance only on the occasion when he became engrossed in Rousseau's *Émile.*

Kant's writings display the same traits of precision and orderliness. Each of his works approaches its subject in a systematic manner; each book is carefully divided into parts, chapters, sections, subsections, paragraphs, and so forth. *The Science of Right* presents a good example of the structuring of a Kantian treatise. Unfortunately, we must add that occasionally Kant's devices seem to get the better of him; in *The Science of Right* the reader sometimes finds himself bewildered by the multiplicity of divisions that Kant uses.

In the language of certain authors, the meanings of "right" and "law" differ considerably. Hobbes, for example, sets law and right in opposition as being equivalent to freedom and obligation. In Kant's usage, however, the terms seem closely related. An alternate title for *The Science of Right* might be *Philosophy of Law*. Kant is interested in rights insofar as they give rise to laws.

The subtitles of the two major parts into which the work is divided indicate that each deals with a system of laws. The word "system" is important and again indicates Kant's approach to the subject: everything here is systematized, ordered, derived from *a priori* principles. The reader will find to his pleasure and to his despair that the Kantian system is based on reason alone; it has no room for the charming confusion of detail that Montesquieu presents nor for a candid admission, such as Rousseau's, that the author is caught in an apparent contradiction. Kant will never admit to a flaw in his systematic, philosophical writings.

GUIDE TO

Twelfth Reading

I

It is instructive to compare Kant's work on law with Montesquieu's. Even the titles indicate the contrast between them. Montesquieu's work is entitled *The Spirit of Laws;* Kant's is *The Science of Right.* Each author tells us what we are to understand by the title. Montesquieu writes:

> . . . [Laws] have relations to each other, as also to their origin, to the intent of the legislator, and to the order of things on which they are established; in all of which different lights they ought to be considered.
>
> This is what I have undertaken to perform in the following work. These relations I shall examine, since all these together constitute what I call the *Spirit of Laws.* (Vol. 38, p. 3d)

Contrast this with Kant's words:

> The Science of Right has for its object the principles of all the laws which it is possible to promulgate by external legislation . . . the theoretical knowledge of right and law in principle, as distinguished from positive laws and empirical cases, belongs to the pure science of right. . . . The science of right thus designates the philosophical and systematic knowledge of the principles of natural right. And it is from this science that the immutable principles of all positive legislation must be derived by practical jurists and lawgivers. (Vol. 42, p. 397a-b)

Montesquieu is concerned with whatever affects laws and tends to make them different from place to place and from time to time. His method is empirical or historical; it consists in assembling examples of laws from different countries throughout history.

Kant's interests aim in the diametrically opposed direction. Kant wants to discover the underlying principles of law and to grasp what is common to all laws. His method is non-empirical; instead of examining the vast diversity among laws, Kant seeks the principles which can systematize legal knowledge.

Kant divides *The Science of Right* into two parts. The first part is entitled "Private Right." Its subtitle indicates its subject matter: "The System of Those Laws which Require no External Promulgation. The Principles of the External Mine and Thine Generally." The second part is called "Public Right." Its subtitle reads as follows: "The System of Those Laws which Require Public Promulgation. The Principles of Right in Civil Society."

In the first part Kant discusses those rights and laws which are valid even in the state of nature. Of course, these rights and laws retain their validity in the civil state. The second part concerns itself with those laws which are valid only in the civil state. Much of the second part relates to the powers of government, to the constitution, to the various forms of government, and to the relations between governments. The second part constitutes the Twelfth Reading in *The Development of Political Theory and Government* and therefore is not included in the reading assignment here.

II

Kant's method, style, and terminology are quite different from anything else we have so far encountered in this Reading Plan. Because of this and the fact that *The Science of Right* is a very compact book, we shall summarize the text in simple outline. It will become apparent that the work is not nearly as formidable as it appears at first glance.

The portion of *The Science of Right* that we read contains just three chapters. Chapter I is entitled "Of the Mode of Having Anything External as One's Own." This complicated title could be replaced by the following question: "How can a man own something?" The chapter has nine numbered paragraphs dealing with various aspects of ownership.

The first paragraph discusses the meaning of ownership. What does it mean to own something rightfully?

> Anything is *"mine" by right*, or is rightfully mine, when I am so connected with it, that if any other person should make use of it without my consent, he would do me a lesion or injury. (p. 403a)

It is easy to see how this definition applies when I physically possess a thing. If someone uses the shirt I am wearing to clean a paint brush, I am injured by his use of it. But suppose that I own an automobile which is parked around the corner from where I live and that someone comes along and uses this automobile without my consent. How am I injured by this use since I am not in physical possession of the automobile at the moment in question? According to Kant the concept of ownership must be extended to include ". . . *rational* possession that is perceivable only by the intellect" (p. 403b). If possession need not be physical, then he who interferes with my rational possession of a thing injures me, and so the definition of ownership is applicable again.

Paragraph 2 states the "Juridical Postulate of the Practical Reason." This postulate maintains that any external thing may become mine. There is nothing in the world which cannot be owned. Everything may become an object of my free will.

Someone who owns a thing must be in possession of it; otherwise, use of the thing by someone else could not possibly injure him. But possession, as we have already seen, may be either physical or rational. Hence someone who owns a thing must be either in physical or in rational possession of it. (See paragraph 3.)

Kant next raises the question: Into what types can all external objects, capable of being owned, be divided? (See paragraph 4.) There are three sorts, Kant answers. The first of these is obvious; it is "A corporeal *thing* external to me . . ." (p. 404b). This category includes houses, cars, books, and so forth.

The other two categories are less obvious. The second is "The *free-will* of another in the performance of a particular act . . ." *(Ibid.)*; the third, "The *state* of another in relation to myself" *(Ibid.)*. Again, Kant's expressions are more obscure than they need be. The second category indicates that I may *own* the right to have another person perform certain acts for me. In some fashion or other—usually by paying money—I cause another person to do something, and, having paid money, I then own the performance even though it has not yet taken place.

For instance, I may pay somebody a sum of money to run an errand for me; I have then acquired and own the right to the performance of that errand. What I own and what the other person receives in return is settled by contract.

The third category is similar to the second but more inclusive. I may own not only a single act of free will (as in the second category) but the whole condition of a person as well. There are various ways of acquiring ownership of a condition of a person. Through marriage husband and wife acquire a right in each other's state of being so that they can speak, respectively, of "my wife" and "my husband." Through the act of procreation parents acquire children and, temporarily, ownership of their condition. Thus the parent speaks of "my child" and the child of "my parents." Finally, through a contract the master acquires a right in the condition of another person who agrees to act in a certain way, namely, for the benefit of the master, in return for monetary or other considerations. Again, it follows that the master can speak of "my servant" and the servant of "my master."

The husband possesses his wife's uxorial condition just as she possesses the husband's condition; the father possesses the offspring's condition of childhood; the master possesses the servant's condition of servitude. Kant, who likes to relate his various treatises to one another, points out that the three kinds of objects which may be owned (things, acts, and conditions) correspond to the three categories of relation that are discussed in *The Critique of Pure Reason.* Those three categories are substance, causality, and reciprocity. (See p. 42c.)

Paragraph 5 repeats the definition of "mine" or "ownership" and points out again that the possibility of "rational ownership" must be assumed. Kant then asks a question typical of his entire way of thinking (paragraph 6): "How is a *merely juridical* or *rational* possession possible?" (See p. 405b.) Kant answers this by reference to the juridical postulate of the practical reason. (Cf. paragraph 2.)

The possibility of such a possession, with consequent deduction of the conception of a non-empirical possession, is founded upon the juridical postulate of the practical reason, that "It is a juridical duty so to act towards others that what is external and useable may come into the possession or become the property of some one." (p. 406d)

In other words, if everything is capable of belonging to someone, then rational possession must be possible, for not every material thing can actually be in the physical possession of someone.

This discussion continues in paragraph 7 and arrives at an antinomy of possession—another concept that is typically Kantian. In an antinomy, reason affirms two contradictory propositions with equal force. In this case they are the following two:

Thesis . . . "*It is possible* to have something external as mine, although I am not in possession of it."

Antithesis . . . "*It is not possible* to have anything external as mine, if I am not in possession of it." (p. 408b)

Kant resolves this antinomy by pointing out that the thesis holds true if by possession we mean merely physical possession. It is possible to have something external as mine although I am not in physical possession of it, if I am in rational possession of it.

Similarly, the antithesis holds true if by possession we understand merely rational possession. If I am not in rational possession of a thing external to me, I cannot have it as mine, since, being external, it is not in my physical possession either.

The two preceding paragraphs discussed the assumptions that must be made if the notion of ownership of something external to the person is to be meaningful. Paragraph 8 goes further and discusses what must be the case if external ownership is to be actualized. Such ownership requires that I abstain from interfering with what belongs to other persons while they reciprocally abstain from what is mine.

. . . it is only a will that binds every one, and as such a common, collective, and authoritative will, that can furnish a guarantee of security to all. But the state of men under a universal, external, and public legislation, conjoined with authority and power, is called the civil state. There can therefore be an external mine and thine only in the civil state of society. (p. 408d)

The civil state guarantees ownership of something external

to the persons composing it. (See paragraph 9.) But if it guarantees ownership (*i.e.*, makes it secure), then ownership must already exist, though insecurely, prior to the civil state.

There may thus be a possession in expectation or in preparation for such a state of security, as can only be established on the law of the common will; and as it is therefore in accordance with the *possibility* of such a state, it constitutes a *provisory* or temporary juridical possession; whereas that possession which is found in reality in the civil state of society will be a *peremptory* or guaranteed possession. (p. 409a-b)

III

Now we turn to Chapter II. It is called "The Mode of Acquiring Anything External." This title, though complicated, simply raises the question: "How is anything acquired?"

Paragraph 10, the first one of the chapter, discusses acquisition in general. "I acquire a thing when I act so that it becomes *mine*" (p. 409d). This definition is unexceptionable if perhaps not very enlightening. Suppose that there is an object which as yet belongs to no person. There are then three steps which together constitute the process of original acquisition. First, there must be physical possession of the thing. Secondly, there must be a declaration of the possession of this object; in this fashion the will of the person taking possession interdicts other persons from using this thing as theirs. Thirdly, there has to be appropriation. This is ". . . the act . . . of an externally legislative common will, by which all and each are obliged to respect and act in conformity with [the owner's] act of will" (p. 410b). Through this last act the possession becomes valid as a purely rational and juridical possession.

After these preliminary remarks, Kant turns to acquisition that is not original. Here he proposes a division of the subject according to three different principles. We shall not be concerned with the third division. The first division is made according to the matter of the object of acquisition. This is the division that was used in Chapter I, where we saw that three kinds of objects can be acquired: a thing, the performance of an act, and the condition of a person.

The second division is made according to the form of the

acquisition. What is acquired is, in form, either a real right, a personal right, or a real-personal right. The first and second divisions can be put into one-to-one correspondence. In acquiring a thing, I acquire a real right; in acquiring the performance of an act, I acquire a personal right; in acquiring the condition of a person, I acquire a real-personal right.

In paragraph 11, Kant discusses the nature of real right, or right in a thing. He concludes that it is ". . . a right to the private use of a thing, of which I am in possession . . . in common with all others" (p. 411b). Right, even when it is right in a thing, requires more than one person; between a person and things no relationship of obligation exists, and therefore no rights can exist.

Before anything else can be acquired, land must be acquired. Every part of the land (just like any other thing) may be acquired and possessed (paragraph 13); and every part of the land is initially acquired by physical possession. (See paragraph 14.) Physical possession produces an empirical title of acquisition. The rational title of acquisition cannot be produced except in the civil state of society. Only in such a state can an obligation be conferred upon all to respect the acquisition of a particular thing. (See paragraph 15.)

Paragraphs 16 and 17 continue this line of thought. We read again that in the state of nature acquisition of the soil is only provisory and that rational possession requires ". . . the *axiom* of freedom, the *postulate* of right, and the universal *legislation* of the common will, conceived as united *a priori*" (p. 414d). Kant also points out that a person cannot acquire right to a piece of land by cultivating it or otherwise improving it if that land belongs to another person and adds several other corollaries following from the notion of real right. He ends paragraph 17 with a brief appendix entitled "Property," which contains the following definition:

> An external object, which, in respect of its substance can be claimed by some one as his own, is called the *property* of that person to whom all the rights in it as a thing belong—like the accidents inhering in a substance—and which, therefore, he as the proprietor can dispose of at *will* . . . (p. 415c)

This definition adds one new note to the concept of ownership: Property always refers to a thing, something corporeal. Whereas possession can be of persons (for one person can acquire a personal or real-personal right in another), one person can never be the property of another. A man cannot acquire a real right in another man.

Paragraph 18 begins the second section of the chapter which deals with the principles of personal right. I acquire a personal right when I acquire possession of the free will of another person. Such acquisition always must be the result of an exchange whereby he who gives up his personal right acquires something else in return. Consequently, the acquisition of personal right never can be primary; that is, it must be preceded by the acquisition of things so that these may be exchanged for personal rights. "Such transference of the *property* of one to another is termed its *alienation*. The act of the united wills of two persons, by which what belonged to one passes to the other, constitutes *contract*" (p. 416b).

Kant next turns to a discussion of contract. There are two acts which together constitute a contract: promise and acceptance. One of the two persons involved promises to perform something, and the other party to the contract accepts this promise. These two acts of promise and acceptance must be simultaneous; otherwise, all sorts of embarrassing possibilities can be envisaged that might invalidate the contract in the time between the promise and the acceptance. The simultaneity of the two constitutive acts of a contract is possible only if we consider the acts as purely juridical and rational. Such acts proceed from a common will; namely, the common will of the two parties to the contract united in a common purpose. (See paragraph 19.)

What is acquired directly in a contract is not a real right in a thing but rather a personal right; namely, the right to have another person perform a certain act. Of course, this act may itself be the transference of a thing. (See paragraph 20.) The contract is not fulfilled merely by the acceptance of the promise; there must also be delivery of the object promised; that is, the performance promised must actually be performed. Kant acknowledges that there may be a lapse of time between the contract (promise and acceptance) and delivery. (See paragraph 21.)

We now come to Section III, "Principles of Personal Right that is Real in Kind." This is defined in paragraph 22 as follows:

> Personal right of a real kind is the right to the *possession* of an external object as a thing, and to the *use* of it as a person. (p. 418c)

The "object" mentioned in the definition is a person. What makes this kind of right special is that in this relationship a person is possessed as though he or she were a thing but used as a person. (To use a person as though he or she were a thing would of course be contrary to all principles of right.)

The three kinds of persons that can be possessed as things and used as persons are a wife, children, and domestic servants. (See paragraph 23 and also paragraph 4.) Kant proceeds to discuss in detail the rights involved in each of the three relationships.

Marriage, according to Kant,

> . . . is the union of two persons of different sex for life-long reciprocal possession of their sexual faculties. (p. 419a)

Though the producing and education of children is a natural end of marriage for the partners, this need not be the purpose of marriage for the partners. (See paragraph 24.) As each person gives himself or herself up to be enjoyed by the other person, he or she has the right to enjoy the other person. (See paragraph 25.) Thus the two marriage partners are in a state of equality, and, consequently, only monogamy truly realizes marriage. (See paragraph 26.) Marriage is a relation that arises not merely from the fact of cohabitation, nor merely by the marriage contract; it is a relation of right that exists only when there has been a marriage contract followed by mutual sexual enjoyment. (See paragraph 27.)

The second kind of real-personal right is parental. Parents have certain duties toward their offspring such as that of preserving and rearing them. Conversely, the children have the right to be preserved and reared by their parents until they are capable of maintaining themselves. (See paragraph 28.) The parents also have rights corresponding to their duties: to manage, train, and command the child until he reaches the age of emancipation. At that time all parental rights and duties cease. (See paragraph 29.)

The third real-personal right is household right which Kant discusses in paragraph 30. This is similar to parental right except that it involves the father as the head of the household and other free persons who are of age. The relationship is established by contract, and this contract is subject to certain definite limitations. The servant never becomes the property of the master, for this would make the servant into a thing; he must always be used as a person.

> This contract, then, of the master of a household with his domestics, cannot be of such a nature that the *use* of them could ever rightly become an *abuse* of them . . . the servants . . . ought never to be held in bondage or bodily servitude as slaves or serfs. Such a contract cannot, therefore, be concluded for life, but in all cases only for a definite period, within which one party may intimate to the other a termination of their connection. (p. 422a-c)

IV

Kant follows the discussion of real-personal right with another discussion of contract. He indicates how many different kinds of contracts there are and then illustrates the validity of his division by two examples; namely, the kind of contract involved when we make use of money, and the kind of contracts relating to the making and publishing of books.

At the end of Chapter II there is an "episodical section" dealing with ideal acquisition which Kant defines as acquisition ". . . which involves no causality in time, and which is founded upon a mere idea of pure reason" (p. 426b). There are three kinds of such ideal acquisition. There is acquisition by usucapion, which occurs when

> I . . . acquire the property of another merely by *long possession* and use of it. (p. 426c)

Then there is acquisition by inheritance; and, thirdly, there is the right to a continuing good name after death.

Chapter III is called "Acquisition Conditioned by the Sentence of a Public Judicatory." We must remember that in this entire first part Kant is discussing natural right; *i.e.*, that right which exists prior to and without the civil state. But there are certain juridical acts established by natural right which nevertheless require the sanction of the public judicatory; *i.e.*, of the courts. They are the contract of donation, the contract of loan, the action of revindication of what has been lost, and the acquisition of security by the taking of an oath.

After this, Kant begins the transition to the Second Part, namely, from ". . . the Mine and Thine in the State of Nature to the Mine and Thine in the Juridical State Generally" (p. 433c). He ends the First Part with "The Postulate of Public Right" which he expresses as follows:

"In the relation of unavoidable coexistence with others, thou shalt pass from the state of nature into a juridical union constituted under the condition of a distributive justice." (p. 434b)

V

Is there such a thing as purely rational or noumenal possession?

In the Kantian doctrine, as stated in *The Critique of Pure Reason,* a distinction is made between phenomena and noumena. The former are things as they appear to us through the senses under conditions of space and time. To say, therefore, that I empirically or phenomenally possess a thing is to say that I have or hold it in a physical way that can be perceived by the senses. Thus, when I say that my wallet is in my possession, I mean that it is in my pocket and therefore in my physical or phenomenal possession.

Why is there any need to go beyond empirical possession and say that there must also be purely rational or juridical possession? And what is meant by rational possession? Kant develops this doctrine in response to an obvious fact: we do seem to speak of possessing things which we are not actually holding in a physical way. Thus I may speak of a house I own even though I am a hundred miles away from it. In what sense can I be said to possess that house since I do not have physical control of it?

Such ownership or possession can be understood only through a discussion of right and wrong. When I am said to possess something over which I have no physical control because it is removed from me in time or space, what is meant is that I would be *wronged* if someone else did with the thing as he pleased. In other words, it is *right* that I and I alone should control what is mine even if I am remote from it.

Rational or noumenal ownership means ownership by right. Physical or empirical ownership is ownership in fact. Kant simply points out that a man who owns something is entitled to control it or do with it as he pleases no matter what his physical relation to the thing. Kant sometimes calls such ownership by right "juridical possession." This name is preferable to "rational" or "noumenal" possession since it sounds less mystifying.

In accordance with his method in *The Critique of Pure Reason* and other works, Kant investigates how juridical possession is possible. There is no need, however, for us to pursue his investigation in great detail. His solution, which mirrors his findings in earlier books, consists in asserting that the possibility of rational or juridical possession cannot be proved on theoretical grounds but must be postulated on practical grounds. What this means in plainer language is that the reality of juridical possession cannot be proved but must be assumed lest the system of morality be incomplete.

Granted that I may possess some object which I do not now physically have in my power, how can I be secure in this possession? What gives me a guarantee that my right to own this object and do with it as I please will be respected? Without such a guarantee my right to the possession of this object seems to be empty and meaningless. Kant recognizes this and concludes that such possession requires a civil society. Here each person guarantees to every other person that he will respect what is his.

> This guarantee of reciprocal and mutual abstention from what belongs to others does not require a special juridical act for its establishment, but is

already involved in the conception of an external obligation of right, on account of the universality and consequently the reciprocity of the obligatoriness arising from a universal Rule. (p. 408c-d)

"Rational" or "noumenal" possession may therefore be summed up as the recognition that possession means more than the physical holding of an object. It means the ability, guaranteed by the state, to dispose of something that is mine according to my will, whether or not I am physically able to do so.

Is there anything unusual in Kant's conception of possession? Does his insistence on the need for the civil state mean that without a state there is no possession by right?

Does Kant have a theory of natural law?

To answer this question, we must look at the Introduction to *The Science of Right*. "The Science of Right," the book begins, "has for its object the principles of all the laws which it is possible to promulgate by external legislation" (p. 397a). The important word here is "principles." The science of right does not deal with all laws in their complexity, but only with their principles. Kant continues as follows:

. . . the theoretical knowledge of right and law in principle, as distinguished from positive laws and empirical cases, belongs to the pure science of right. The science of right thus designates the philosophical and systematic knowledge of the principles of natural right. And it is from this science that the immutable principles of all positive legislation must be derived by practical jurists and lawgivers. (p. 397a-b)

It appears that Kant has a theory of natural right, not a theory of natural law. Natural rights are the principles of good positive laws. Bad laws, of course, are not based on natural right.

When Kant speaks of natural right he means right that is based ". . . upon pure rational principles *a priori* . . ." (p. 401b). Natural right is far more extensive than innate right which is ". . . that right which belongs to every one by nature, independent of all juridical acts of experience" (p. 401b); in fact, Kant points out there is only one innate right, the birthright of freedom. This is the right of every human person to be independent of the compulsory will of another.

It is important to note that what Kant discusses in the remainder of *The Science of Right* is not innate right but acquired right. All acquired rights are external rights; innate right, by contrast, is an internal right, and not, of course, acquired. Rights, in other words, are divided as follows. On one side are external, acquired rights; on the other side, internal, innate rights. External, acquired rights are again divided into private and public rights. The former of these are those rights and laws which require no external promulgation; they exist in the state of nature. The latter are those rights which require external promulgation and exist only in the civil state.

In a sense, therefore, Kant has a theory of natural law or natural right. The entire *Science of Right* deals with natural right, namely, the rational principles of acquired, external right. This is a science, because it defines rights simply in terms of the nature of the things involved without regard to any empirical circumstances. Thus Kant's *The Science of Right* is directly opposed to Montesquieu's *The Spirit of Laws*, which is a catalogue of the circumstances that affect laws.

Kant's theory of natural law is quite different from more traditional theories. Kant gives us no precepts of the natural law as Aquinas does, for instance. Commands, such as "Do good," do not belong to the natural law in Kant's view. The system of natural law consists of those *a priori* principles which are discoverable by reason. "Do good" does not belong to that system, for the discovery of what is good requires more than the employment of pure reason.

In the preceding discussion we have spoken of both natural right and natural law. Does Kant use these two terms interchangeably? If he does not, how are they related? Is the one and only innate right which Kant acknowledges a natural right in other theories with which you have become acquainted? In Kant's theory, if natural law rests on and proceeds from pure principles of reason, what is the basis of positive law?

How can a person be possessed by another person?

There seems to be little difficulty in understanding that a person can possess a thing. Things exist, in fact, to be owned and used by persons. They exist as means and not for their own sake.

Kant envisages the possibility of one person possessing "... the active free-will of another person ..." (p. 416a); this is what we acquire when we acquire a personal right. Furthermore, he speaks of a personal right of a real kind. This is "... the right to the *possession* of an external object as a thing, and to the *use* of it as a person" (p. 418c). When I acquire a personal right, I acquire the right to have another person perform some action; when I acquire a personal right that is real in kind, I acquire a whole person in a condition such that I may use him in a certain way, as my spouse, my child, or my servant.

Are personal rights in accordance with the dignity of the human person? Kant is a great believer in the proposition that no man should ever be used as a mere means. Every person is an end in himself. When I acquire a personal right, do I use the person as a means or as an end? In speaking of personal right that is real in kind, Kant makes a distinction between possession and use. What is the distinction?

SELF-TESTING QUESTIONS

The following questions are designed to help you test the thoroughness of your reading. Each question is to be answered by giving a page or pages of the reading assignment. Answers will be found on page 239 of this Reading Plan.

1 What is the juridical postulate of Practical Reason?

2 What are the four juridical acts involved in a contract?

3 Does cultivation of land give the worker a right to the land?

4 Is the wife the equal of the husband in marriage?

5 How does Kant define money?

6 How many kinds of contract does Kant enumerate?

7 Can a court enforce a gratuitous promise?

8 Can a court demand that a person swear that he believes something?

9 What is the postulate of public right?

10 Is a borrower responsible for damage to the thing he has borrowed?

Thirteenth Reading

Articles of Confederation

Vol. 43, pp. 5-9

The Constitution of the United States of America

Vol. 43, pp. 11-20

The Constitution of the United States is the supreme law of the land. Yet how many of us actually know in detail what the Constitution says? High school students, while taking a course in civics, are probably well acquainted with its major provisions, but few other persons can make the same claim. Even smaller is the number of people who have read the Articles of Confederation, the basic law of the United States of America prior to the Constitution. Knowledge of the Articles of Confederation is of more than antiquarian interest; many provisions in the present Constitution remedy defects in the Articles of Confederation, which made the latter unworkable.

The Articles of Confederation came into effect in 1781 when the Revolutionary War was still in progress. According to Article Three, the thirteen states ". . . hereby severally enter into a firm league of friendship with each other . . . ." Just six years later (in 1787) the Constitutional Convention met in Philadelphia and adopted the Constitution. The preamble to the Constitution states its purpose:

> We, the People of the United States, in order to form a more perfect union, establish justice, insure domestic tranquillity, provide for the common defense, promote the general welfare, and secure the blessings of liberty to ourselves and our posterity, do ordain and establish this Constitution for the United States of America. (p. 11a, c)

The Constitution became effective in 1789 and, with remarkably few changes and additions, continues in effect today. Aside from the first ten amendments (the so-called Bill of Rights which became effective in 1791 and which is almost part of the original Constitution) only thirteen amendments have been added in more than 170 years. We must admire the wisdom of the Founding Fathers; the Constitution which they devised in 1787 for an agricultural country of less than 4,000,000 inhabitants still serves an industrial nation of 180,000,000 people.

GUIDE TO

Thirteenth Reading

I

What is omitted from the Articles of Confederation deserves as much attention as what is included in them. The men who fought the Revolutionary War and who wrote the state and federal constitutions were obviously jealous of government and its powers. The American colonists had complained that British rule was not representative and that it encroached on areas which did not properly concern government. When the thirteen colonies achieved independence, the people did not intend to saddle themselves with a similar kind of government. Consequently, the Articles of Confederation begin by noting the name of the Confederacy in Article One and then immediately go on to state the powers, rights, and privileges which do *not* belong to the United States:

Article Two

EACH State retains its sovereignty, freedom, and independence, and every power, jurisdiction, and right, which is not by this Confederation expressly delegated to the United States in Congress assembled. (p. 5a-b)

The powers not expressly granted to the United States remain with the individual states. The body of the Constitution does not contain a similar provision "protecting" the states against the federal government. However, the Tenth Amendment does:

THE powers not delegated to the United States by the Constitution, nor prohibited by it to the States, are reserved to the States respectively or to the people. (p. 18a)

We should note that while the Articles of Confederation reserve powers only to the states, the Constitution reserves them to either the states or the people. This points to an important difference between the Articles of Confederation and the Constitution. The Articles of Confederation established a league of thirteen sovereign states, deriving its power from the states. The Constitution, however, established a new sovereign government, deriving its power directly from the people. The preamble to the Articles speaks of a ". . . confederation and perpetual union between the states of . . ." (p. 5a); the preamble to the Constitution notes that "We, the people of the United States . . . do ordain and establish this Constitution . . ." (p. 11a).

We find evidences of this difference in many other places in the two documents. For example, Article Five of the Articles of Confederation describes the Congress of the United States and its members. The delegates to the Congress are to be appointed annually by the legislatures of the several states and may at any time be recalled by the states and replaced. In contrast, the Constitution provides that "The House of Representatives shall be composed of members chosen every second year by the people of the several States. . ." (p. 11b). Senators originally were chosen by the legislatures of the several states; but the Seventeenth Amendment places the election of senators in the hands of the people also.

In Article Eight of the Articles of Confederation, we read about the method for raising taxes to defray the expenses of the United States. Each state will pay a share of the expenses proportional to the value of land and improvements found in the state. The revenue for paying this share shall be raised by taxation in each state. Thus, under the Articles of Confederation, the United States itself did not have the power of raising taxes. Contrast this with Section 8 of Article One of the Constitution:

> The Congress shall have power to lay and collect taxes, duties, imposts, and excises, to pay the debts and provide for the common defense and general welfare of the United States . . . (p. 13a)

According to the Constitution, the United States deals directly with the people in the matter of taxation.

In the Congress as set up by the Articles of Confederation,

each state has one vote. The Constitution changed this arrangement in the following manner: each state has two votes in the Senate; in the House of Representatives, the number of votes a state has is proportional to its population. Again we see that the Constitution attaches greater importance to the people than to the states.

The president, according to Article Nine of the Articles of Confederation, merely presides over a "Committee of the States" (p. 8b). Article Two of the Constitution, on the contrary, declares that "The executive power shall be vested in a President of the United States of America" (p. 14b) and that he shall be elected by the people, although indirectly.

All of these examples indicate that, according to the Articles of Confederation, each of the states remains fully sovereign and grants to the United States only certain rights which it may withdraw. In this earlier setup, the United States was a creature of the states. By contrast, the Constitution creates a government which derives its sovereignty directly from the people. The rights which the people have given the United States cannot be taken back by the individual states since they are not the donors of these rights. The source of sovereignty and authority is firmly placed in the people.

II

In previous readings we have learned much about natural law, natural rights, and the justice of laws. Is the Constitution of the United States concerned with these topics? Among the purposes to be achieved, the preamble to the Constitution lists the establishment of justice. (See p. 11a, c.) Although natural law and natural rights are not mentioned in the Constitution, we do find them referred to in the Declaration of Independence: ". . . the laws of nature and of nature's God . . ." entitle a people to a separate and equal station in the world, Jefferson writes. A few lines later he speaks of certain unalienable, *i.e.*, natural, rights such as ". . . life, liberty, and the pursuit of happiness." Furthermore, justice is mentioned, too, since governments whose aim is ". . . to secure these rights . . ." derive

". . . their just powers from the consent of the governed . . ." (p. 1a).

Although the American State Papers do not elaborate on the subjects of natural right and justice, we can nevertheless infer that they take the following positions. There *are* natural rights —the rights to life, liberty, and the pursuit of happiness are such rights. There may be others. The purpose of government is to secure these rights and to establish justice. In doing this, governments act justly as long as their actions are based on the consent of the governed.

What provisions does the Constitution contain to implement these theoretical positions? What, for example, does the Constitution do in order to safeguard the unalienable rights mentioned in the Declaration of Independence or any other natural rights?

Many of these rights are specifically mentioned in the Bill of Rights, *i.e.*, in the first ten amendments. The First Amendment, for example, establishes freedom of speech, of the press, of religion, of peaceable assembly, and of petition. The Fourth Amendment protects the people from unwarranted search and seizure; and the Fifth Amendment prevents a man's being placed in double jeopardy for the same crime or having to testify against himself in a criminal case.

We encounter some difficulty in deciding whether or not the rights to life and to the pursuit of happiness are guaranteed by the Constitution. The Eighth Amendment provides some protection for life. This amendment prohibits cruel and unusual punishments, thereby prohibiting the indiscriminate use of the death penalty for trivial offenses. The Fifth Amendment offers another protection of life: No person shall ". . . be deprived of life, liberty, or property, without due process of law . . ." (p. 17c).

We encounter more difficulty in finding passages in the Constitution that guarantee the right to pursue happiness. In fact, the word "happiness" does not occur in the Constitution; the closest expression to happiness that we do find is "general welfare." The preamble lists, among the ends for which the Constitution is established, justice, domestic tranquility, common defense, the promotion of the general welfare, and the blessings of liberty. Again, in Section 8 of Article One, we read that Congress shall have the power to lay and collect taxes ". . . to pay the debts and provide for the common defense and general welfare of the United States . . ." (p. 13a). But does "general welfare" really mean the same thing as "happiness"? If so, the Constitution seems to give the Federal Government almost unlimited powers, because it authorizes Congress to raise taxes to provide for the happiness of the people. (See Article One, Section 8, quoted above.)

However, even before the Constitution had been ratified, the question arose as to how the "general welfare" clause was to be interpreted. James Madison, writing in Federalist Paper Number 41, denies that this clause gives the government any powers beyond those that are specifically enumerated in the rest of Section 8. "It has been urged and echoed," he writes, "that the power 'to lay and collect taxes, duties, imposts, and excises, to pay the debts, and provide for the common defence and general welfare of the United States,' amounts to an unlimited commission to exercise every power which may be alleged to be necessary for the common defence or general welfare" (Vol. 43, p. 135c). Madison replies to this interpretation as follows:

> . . . what colour can the objection have when a specification of the objects alluded to by these general terms immediately follows, and is not even separated by a longer pause than a semicolon? . . . For what purpose could the enumeration of particular powers be inserted, if these and all others were meant to be included in the preceding general power? Nothing is more natural nor common than first to use a general phrase, and then to explain and qualify it by a recital of particulars. (Vol. 43, pp. 135d-136a)

Madison, at least, does not interpret the Constitution as giving Congress the right or duty to legislate for the happiness of the people. Perhaps in the twentieth century, a tendency has nevertheless arisen to interpret the Constitution as giving Congress a mandate to provide for the happiness of the people. Interestingly enough, the more the Federal Government concerns itself with happiness, the more the United States is said to approach being a "welfare state."

Let us leave the question of the correct interpretation of the Constitution and turn to a consideration of how the government set up by the Constitution derives its just powers from the consent of the governed. A large part of this document is devoted to assuring that the voice of the people can make itself heard in the election of the President and the Representatives in Congress. At the same time we must note that the Constitution does not attempt to refer every act of the government to the people; nor, indeed, can we overlook the fact that the election procedures are often so arranged that the will of the people—and hence their consent to governmental proposals—makes itself felt only slowly and indirectly. Though this is so, it is important to remember that, according to the Constitution, all power ultimately derives from the people and therefore from the consent of the governed. The makers of the Constitution did not completely trust the people and hence made various provisions to prevent the popular will from making itself felt either automatically or too quickly. In this way they hoped to prevent hasty and unwise action on the part of the people. The will of the people ultimately prevails, but the arrangements of the Constitution insure relative stability of the government of the United States even when the will of the people fluctuates drastically, as it tends to do in times of stress and crisis.

The devices to make the government less sensitive to changes of popular mood are numerous. The obvious ones are the election of the President by electors rather than by the people, and the provision (now superseded) that Senators were to be appointed by the state legislatures rather than elected by the people. The system of checks and balances, too, serves the purpose of preventing the popular will from making itself felt too quickly or too powerfully. The voice of the people is expressed indirectly in the House of Representatives; but it is unlikely that a precipitate action by the House will determine the course of government because the Senate must concur in any legislative action of the House, because the President has the power of the veto, and because the Supreme Court may make a judicial review of any law passed by the Congress.

However, the fact remains that the acts of the government of the United States are ultimately based on popular consent. There is a great deal of difference between preventing hasty and undeliberate execution of what the people desire and ignoring its wishes altogether. The former is government of the people by the people, even though the particular arrangements indicate a considerable distrust of the popular will; the latter, however, is despotism even if it is benevolent.

III

Both the Articles of Confederation and the Constitution of the United States are short documents. Both attempt to set up only the general outlines of government. Each contains a minimum of detailed provisions but creates machinery for making additional laws as the need arises. Since particular provisions are so few, those that we actually find are all the more significant. Obviously, the authors of the Articles of Confederation and of the Constitution thought these matters so important that they did not wish to leave them to future legislation but wanted to regulate them once for all themselves.

Here is what the United States is empowered to do by the Articles of Confederation. Note how limited the list is: to decide on peace or war, to send and receive ambassadors, to make treaties and alliances, to deal with pirates, and to determine on capture and prizes of ships. The United States was also given jurisdiction in disputes between two or more of the States. Furthermore, the United States had the right to mint coin, to regulate weights and measures, to deal with Indian affairs, to establish and run post offices, to appoint officers of the army and navy, and to direct the armed forces. The Congress also had the power to ascertain the money needs of the United States, to borrow on the credit of the United States, to build and equip a navy, and to requisition armed land forces from the various States. This about exhausts the list of rights and powers of the United States. With a few exceptions all the powers relate to war and foreign policy. Only the running of the post office, the minting of coin, and the regulation of weights and measures are primarily domestic activities.

Now let us look at the powers granted to the United States by the Constitution. This list is considerably longer than the previous one. Section 8 of Article One enumerates the powers of the Congress. Significantly, the first power named is one which the Congress did not possess under the Articles of Confederation:

> The Congress shall have power to lay and collect taxes, duties, imposts, and excises, to pay the debts and provide for the common defense and general welfare of the United States . . . (p. 13a)

The Articles of Confederation provided that the taxes necessary for paying the expenses authorized by the Congress should be raised by the legislatures of the several states. (See Article Eight.) This arrangement left the Congress nearly powerless since it did not control its own money.

Section 8 concludes with a paragraph which gives the Congress broad powers of legislation. The Congress shall have power

> To make all laws which shall be necessary and proper for carrying into execution the foregoing powers, and all other powers vested by this Constitution in the Government of the United States, or in any department or officer thereof. (p. 13c-d)

Thus the Congress is given wide scope in its legislative powers. Whereas the Congress set up by the Articles of Confederation could do almost nothing, the Congress set up by the Constitution is authorized to deal with nearly everything that bears on the "general welfare."

To complete our picture of the governmental machinery, we must mention that, according to the Constitution, "the executive power shall be vested in a President of the United States of America" (p. 14b). Under the Articles of Confederation the President had no executive power but merely presided over the "Committee of the States"; the Constitution makes him responsible for carrying out all laws passed by Congress. The Constitution for the first time gave the United States judicial power which is vested in the Supreme Court and inferior courts; nothing of the sort is mentioned in the Articles of Confederation.

IV

We must now consider a number of questions, many of them suggested by the obvious differences between the Articles of Confederation and the Constitution.

Is the power to lay and collect taxes the most important power of a legislative body?

This question is prompted by the fact that the power to raise taxes is the first power of Congress specifically mentioned in the Constitution. Is this order accidental or is it significant?

If we consider the matter abstractly, the power of taxation seems relatively unimportant. Other laws determine the kind of society a people have. Tax laws have no purpose beyond that of raising money whereas other laws determine what is right and wrong in conduct, what may or may not be done, what the offices of the state are, what the punishments for crimes are, and so forth. Such laws are directed toward definite ends; tax laws, however, are concerned only with means. Taxes are ways of raising money; and money itself is only a means for carrying out what other laws direct. The basic laws are those establishing policy and authorizing personnel to carry it out. The tax laws needed to implement those policies are secondary and relatively unimportant.

Although this view seems to be theoretically correct, matters do not turn out this way in practice. The power of taxation is crucial. With this power, governments implement what otherwise would remain empty gestures. For example, the Federal Insurance Contribution Act (Social Security) in the United States or the act that set up the British National Health Service would remain worthless pieces of paper unless the governments had the right and power to levy the taxes to pay for these programs. We can see that the power of taxation may be easily abused. Taxes may be so high or so wastefully employed that instead of contributing to the welfare of the country, they impoverish it or even lead to its ruin.

Under the legal machinery of the Articles of Confederation, the United States did not possess the power of taxation, and the government soon became ineffective. Men have always recognized that the power of taxation constitutes a primary governmental power. A major complaint of the colonists prior to the American Revolution was against "taxation without representation." In the Declaration of Independence, the King is accused of subjecting the American colonists to foreign legislation and of assenting to Parliament's ". . . imposing taxes on us without our consent . . ." (p. 2b).

The Constitution provides an important safeguard against discriminatory taxation. In Section 7, we read:

> All bills for raising revenue shall originate in the House of Representatives . . . (p. 12d)

Other kinds of bills may originate in either the House or the Senate, but bills having to do with taxation must originate in the chamber which, because of its proportional membership and the short term of its members, is most responsive to the will of the people. Though the Founding Fathers mistrusted the people in many respects, they insisted that the people should have close control over the raising of revenue lest they suffer from its abuse. Thirty years later the Chief Justice of the United States, John Marshall, affirmed this view of the importance of taxation in a famous remark:

> . . . that the power to tax involves the power to destroy; that the power to destroy may defeat and render useless the power to create . . . are propositions not to be denied. (*McCulloch* v. *Maryland*, 1819)

Since the people are presumably not so foolish as to destroy themselves, the power to tax is placed in their hands, or at least into the hands of those of their representatives who will be directly answerable to the people every two years. However, a new question now arises. Since taxation is always painful, what assurance does the Constitution provide that the necessary taxes will actually be voted? What is to prevent the House of Representatives from lapsing into fiscal irresponsibility in response to popular pressure? There would seem to be a definite danger that the House might simply not vote the necessary taxes should a popular outcry arise against them.

What does the history of the United States show on this score? On the one hand, we must note that the United States has a large national debt and often operates on an unbalanced, *i.e.*, deficit, budget. This indicates that taxes have not kept up with expenditures. On the other hand, we must also recognize that the House of Representatives has never indulged in complete fiscal irresponsibility. There have been no "tax rebellions" in the United States. Thus the good sense of the people and the devotion to duty of the Representatives have acted as real, if unwritten, safeguards where the Constitution itself failed to provide them.

Furthermore, there exist some provisions in the Constitution itself to prevent fiscal disaster. Though the Senate cannot initiate revenue-raising bills, it has the right to amend those proposed by the House. The Senate can therefore increase the amount of money to be raised if what the House proposes is insufficient. Moreover, tax bills do not have to be passed every year. The income tax, for instance, continues from year to year, and laws concerning it need not be initiated by the House unless the rates of the tax are to be changed.

In your opinion, is it correct to say that the power to tax carries with it the power to destroy? Is this an exaggeration stemming from eighteenth- and nineteenth-century prejudices against strong government? Could a defender of the welfare state maintain that taxation makes welfare government possible and hence that the power to tax involves the power to provide for human well-being?

Is the requirement that revenue bills must originate in the House of Representatives outdated because the Senate is now also elected by popular vote?

Does the graduated income tax clash with the provision that "No capitation or other direct tax shall be laid, unless in proportion to the census . . ." (p. 13d)?

In the United States there are two kinds of government and two sets of laws that operate in simultaneous and parallel fashion. Is this a good arrangement?

Each of the individual states has its own constitution, its own legislature, and its own set of laws. The resident of any state is therefore subject to two kinds of laws: those of the state in which he lives and the federal laws. Thus we have two parallel judicial systems: federal courts and state courts, federal grand juries and state (or county) grand juries, United States district attorneys and state (or county) district attorneys, etc. These two systems of laws and courts deal with different maters. The federal courts deal with federal laws; *i.e.*, those passed by Congress under the authority of the Constitution. The state courts deal with matters that fall under state laws which cover everything else.

Historically, this double system came into existence because the United States began as a federation of thirteen separate states. Before there was a Constitution, there were states with their own constitutions and their own laws. Is the system of double jurisdiction good in itself? Would it be the best system for the United States even if it had not begun as thirteen separate states? Would it be better if there were only one system of laws in the United States? This would mean that the several states would become merely administrative units. Is there any advantage to the federal system? Could the system be extended so that everyone would live under three systems of laws? For instance, if there were a federal world government, would it be feasible for a citizen of California to live under California laws, U.S. laws, and world laws?

What happens if there is a conflict between state and federal laws? Who decides if there is a real conflict? Who resolves it? Do the states have any rights which the Federal Government can never encroach upon? Is it possible for a federal law to be declared unconstitutional because it deals with a matter that legitimately belongs to state jurisdiction? Does the Constitution have any provision that calls for a review of laws from the point of view of their constitutionality?

SELF-TESTING QUESTIONS

The following questions are designed to help you test the thoroughness of your reading. Each question is to be answered by giving a page or pages of the reading assignment. Answers will be found on page 239 of this Reading Plan.

1 Where does the Constitution state that it is the supreme law of the land?

2 For what specific actions must the President seek the advice and consent of the Senate?

3 What is necessary in order to convict a person of treason against the United States?

4 How is the number of presidential electors determined?

5 Vacancies in the United States Senate may be temporarily filled by appointment by the governor of the state. Can a vacancy in the House of Representatives be similarly filled?

6 What provision do the Articles of Confederation make about Canada?

7 Do the Articles of Confederation have a provision for amending them? Does the Constitution have such a provision?

8 Would it be constitutional for one of the states not to have a republican form of government?

9 Which amendment of the Constitution abolished slavery?

10 Which amendment gave the vote to women?

Fourteenth Reading

HEGEL

Philosophy of Right

Third Part, Subsection II, B
(The Administration of Justice)

Vol. 46, pp. 69-75

According to an ancient myth, the goddess Athena sprang full grown from the head of Zeus. In an obvious interpretation, this fable indicates that wisdom, courage, and indeed virtue in general—the qualities traditionally symbolized by Athena—came into the world directly from the chief of the gods. Wisdom in this picture does not grow or decay; it remains unchanged throughout all time.

What is true of Athena or wisdom in general does not hold for particular human wisdom. It grows, slowly and painfully, both in a man's life and over the course of centuries, as men learn from the experience and wisdom of others.

Occasionally, however, a philosopher arises who tries, like Zeus, to bring forth wisdom full-grown. Georg Wilhelm Friedrich Hegel was such a philosopher. Out of his head, merely by the unfettered operation of reason, he attempted to bring forth the principles of knowledge in all departments of learning. In logic, in religion, in science, in philosophy, in history, and in law—in all these fields Hegel wrote extensive treatises.

It was not vanity that made Hegel write on all these subjects and treat them as capable of being explored by reason alone. On the contrary, it is one of his basic philosophical assumptions that "the real is the ideal"—that thought is the most basic and concrete thing there is in the world. Attention to the manifold materials of experience contributes nothing but confusion when we are looking for principles. It is thought alone which can get at the essence of things.

No wonder Hegel was scandalized by the unwritten British constitution, made up as it is of a maze of acts of Parliament, judicial decisions, precedents, and so on. It did not matter to Hegel that this constitution worked well from a pragmatic point of view. Hegel was interested in the philosophy of law and in the principles of right. He sought to derive the elements of law from the principles of reason. If he had any hesitancies or doubts about his conclusions, he did not show them. He liked his handiwork, just as Zeus favored Athena over his other children.

GUIDE TO

Fourteenth Reading

I

The *Philosophy of Right* obviously bears a close relationship to Kant's *Science of Right.* Hegel, like Kant, is interested in the principles of law and jurisprudence. Neither philosopher has much sympathy for the spirit of trial and error or for the concern with compromise and precedent that prevails in the common law of Great Britain and the United States. The aim of both Kant and Hegel is to establish a system of laws based on rational principles alone.

The *Philosophy of Right* is a highly structured book. Our reading assignment is in subsection II (entitled CIVIL SOCIETY) of the Third Part (ETHICAL LIFE). Let us briefly examine the Table of Contents on p. ix to see how the portion we read fits into the whole.

The book consists of an Introduction and three parts, of which the last one is by far the longest. The First Part is called ABSTRACT RIGHT, the Second Part, MORALITY, and the Third Part, ETHICAL LIFE. The Third Part itself contains three subsections. Subsection I is entitled THE FAMILY, subsection II (which contains our assignment), CIVIL SOCIETY, and subsection III, THE STATE. (This third subsection constitutes the Fourteenth Reading in *The Development of Political Theory and Government.*)

Hegel's Introduction explains how he arrives at his divisions and subdivisions. The first sentence tells us what the book is about:

> The subject-matter of the philosophical science of right is the Idea of right, i.e. the concept of right together with the actualization of that concept. (p. 9a)

The important word in this sentence is "Idea." Hegel contrasts

Ideas which are the concern of philosophy with "mere concepts." As long as we deal merely with empty concepts such as definitions we have not yet begun the philosophical task. Philosophy involves not only the concept of a thing but also the actualization of that concept. That is what an Idea is in Hegel's system—the unity of a concept and its actualization. In order to arrive at the philosophical knowledge of anything (including law or right), we must begin with the concept; we must then investigate the manner in which the concept is actualized or the kinds of objective existence which it has. We will find the Idea in the unity of the concept and its objective existence.

Hegel compares this unity to the unity of soul and body.

> The concept and its objective existence are two sides of the same thing, distinct and united, like soul and body . . . The unity of determinate existence and the concept, of body and soul, is the Idea. The unity is not a mere harmony, but rather a complete interpenetration. (Addition 2, p. 115d)[1]

The philosophic method consists in tracing the development of the Idea.

> The science of right is a section of philosophy. Consequently, its task is to develop the Idea—the Idea being the rational factor in any object of study—out of the concept, or, what is the same thing, to look on at the proper immanent development of the thing itself. (p. 9b)

The concept or form of an Idea is called its first moment. The second moment is the actualization of the concept in objective existence. The third moment consists in the synthesis of the first two moments. The divisions of the *Philosophy of Right* correspond to the three moments of the Idea of right. Abstract right, or the concept of right, is the first moment. Morality, or right as actually embodied, is the second moment. Ethical life is the third moment—the unity of the pure concept and the concept as actualized.

The pure concept of right is freedom of the will. The three

---

[1] Hegel made additions to many of the paragraphs in the course of his lectures. These additions were taken down in note form by Hegel's student, Edward Gans. They are appended to our edition of the *Philosophy of Right*, pp. 115-150. An [A] at the end of a paragraph in the main text indicates that there is an addition to it.

moments in the development of the Idea of right correspond, therefore, to three stages in the development of freedom. In paragraph 33, Hegel points out how he derives the three divisions of the book from these three stages. (See p. 20b-c.)

At the beginning of the Third Part, Hegel indicates how ethical life is the third moment of the Idea of right or freedom.

> . . . ethical life is the concept of freedom developed into the existing world and the nature of self-consciousness . . . this unity of the concept of the will with its embodiment—i.e. the particular will—is knowing . . . (p. 55a)

A little further on, Hegel explains the principle according to which the part dealing with ethical life is divided into three subsections.

> . . . in this identity of the universal will with the particular will, right and duty coalesce, and by being in the ethical order a man has rights in so far as he has duties, and duties in so far as he has rights . . .
>
> The ethical substance, as containing independent self-consciousness united with its concept, is the actual mind of a family and a nation. (p. 57c-d)

Family, civil society, and state are three ways in which the pure concept and its actualization are united through self-knowledge. These are successively higher levels of self-consciousness, the state being the supreme stage.

As we might expect, the subsection dealing with Civil Society is again divided into three parts. Civil Society, Hegel says, contains three moments: *The System of Needs, The Administration of Justice* (our assignment), and *The Police and the Corporation.* Such tripartite divisions are typical of Hegel's system and arise naturally out of his dialectical method in which the first moment (sometimes called the thesis) is opposed by the second moment (the antithesis); the two moments are then united in the third moment (the synthesis). Whether or not Hegel's method is suitable for philosophy need not concern us here. Nor, for that matter, need we investigate whether or not his triple divisions of the subject are illuminating and exhaustive. All we need to carry away with us from the special

Hegelian method is that it results in his treating law as one moment of civil society which is itself only one moment of ethical life, ethical life being the highest stage in the development of freedom.

II

Leaving the Hegelian machinery behind, let us look at the portion of text which deals with law. Paragraph 211 (p. 70a-c) is most important for our purposes.

Hegel begins by discussing the relationship between *right* and *law*. Right is a principle and as such is something abstract. When right acquires determinate and actual existence, it becomes law. What gives right this actual existence is thought; for right becomes determinate and particular by being thought about.

> To posit something as universal, i.e. to bring it before consciousness as universal, is, I need hardly say, to think . . . Thereby its content is reduced to its simplest form and so is given its final determinacy. In becoming law, what is right acquires for the first time not only the form proper to its universality, but also its true determinacy. (p. 70a)

Again we note the emphasis, characteristic of Hegel's philosophy, on the actual and the objective in its combination with the conceptual. Hegel concludes the paragraph from which we have just quoted by noting that the essence of lawmaking is not that it expresses a rule of behavior valid for everyone, but rather that the law be known "in its determinate universality."

Important consequences follow from this emphasis on the law as known and knowable. For instance, Hegel denies the common claim that customs are the best laws. Insofar as they are merely habitual ways of acting, customs are not laws at all. They have force as laws only because they are lawlike in being thoughts and being known. Since customs are known only in a subjective, accidental, and therefore less determinate way than positive laws, the universality of thought is less clearly seen in customs than in laws. As soon as possible, customs should be replaced by positive laws.

> When a nation begins to acquire even a little culture, its customary law

must soon come to be collected and put together. Such a collection is a legal code . . . (p. 70b)

A true legal code, however, is more than a collection of laws; it should display the principles of jurisprudence in their universality.

Hegel intensely disliked English law with its mixture of written and unwritten law. The fact that the unwritten law is unwritten does not bother him, since, he says, it ". . . is as good as written, and knowledge of it may, and indeed must, be acquired simply by reading the numerous quartos which it fills" (p. 70b). What Hegel objects to is the confusion—in his view—of legislative and judicial functions which necessarily occurs when cases are adjudicated by means of precedents, though the precedents are not totally binding.

The monstrous confusion, however, which prevails both in English law and its administration is graphically portrayed by those acquainted with the matter. In particular, they comment on the fact that, since this unwritten law is contained in court verdicts and judgements, the judges are continually legislators. The authority of precedent is binding on them, since their predecessors have done nothing but give expression to the unwritten law; and yet they are just as much exempt from its authority, because they are themselves repositories of the unwritten law and so have the right to criticize previous judgements and pronounce whether they accorded with the unwritten law or not. (p. 70b-c)

In the Addition to this paragraph, Hegel indicates that he is not at all impressed with the argument that a body of law constituted by cases and decisions is more "living" than a codified law, or that customary law is superior to a legal code because it retains more particularity and a reminiscence of history. (See p. 138a.) Codification of laws is an absolute necessity; it systematizes them and elevates them to the level of the universal. Hegel recognizes that in applying a law to cases there will be difficulties because of the law's universality; here is where the judge's discretion has its proper place. But, he adds,

. . . to go so far as to get rid of clashes altogether by leaving much to the judge's discretion is a far worse solution, because even the clash is intrinsic to thought, to conscious thinking and its dialectic, while the mere fiat of a judge would be arbitrary. (p. 138a)

Nevertheless, Hegel recognizes that there has to be a certain amount of arbitrariness in positive law. While the arbitrariness of a judge's fiat is completely inappropriate when it is a matter of determining what the law is, arbitrariness alone can decide how a law is to be applied to a particular case. Reason cannot decide whether the fine for some offense should be five dollars or four dollars and ninety-nine cents, or whether imprisonment for a crime should last one year or 364 days or 366 days. Yet a decision must be made.

> Here the only interest present is that something be actually done, that the matter be settled and decided somehow, no matter how (within a certain limit). (p. 71b-c)

These "ultimate decisions" (as Hegel calls them) are left to the judge's discretion.

Hegel has another objection to the uncodified condition of law which depends on previous cases and decisions. This kind of law makes it difficult, if not impossible, for the citizen to know what the law is.

> To hang the laws so high that no citizen could read them (as Dionysius the Tyrant did) is injustice of one and the same kind as to bury them in row upon row of learned tomes, collections of dissenting judgements and opinions, records of customs, &c., and in a dead language too, so that knowledge of the law of the land is accessible only to those who have made it their professional study. (p. 71c-d)

Consequently, those rulers—like the emperor Justinian—who formulated legal codes have been great benefactors of their people, for such codification enables the law to be known and hence to be obeyed.

Although Hegel admires codified law, he also realizes that every legal code is always in need of change and improvement. In part, this need results from changing conditions, but, in part, it results from what Hegel calls the "gradual intrusion of reason" (p. 72a). He means that the passage of time indicates more clearly what is right or wrong about certain institutions and that, accordingly, the laws need to be changed. For instance, certain Roman institutions (say, slavery) which had appeared to be rightful were later seen to be wrong. Similarly, some medieval institutions were later seen to be not in accord with right and hence in need of change. To refuse to change a legal code in the light of such better understanding of what is right and wrong betrays no deference for the law but merely stubbornness.

> It is misunderstanding which has given rise alike to the demand—a morbid craving of German scholars chiefly—that a legal code should be something absolutely complete, incapable of any fresh determination in detail, and also to the argument that because a code is incapable of such completion, therefore we ought not to produce something "incomplete," i.e. we ought not to produce a code at all. (p. 72a)

Next Hegel turns to a discussion of courts, trials, and punishments. When right takes the form of law, it loses its subjectivity and becomes something determinately universal. Its universality is displayed in its application to particular cases without subjective interest; this application occurs in the courts of justice.

The administration of justice in a court of law is different from an act of revenge. A court does not consider that some individual person has been injured and needs to be revenged; rather it considers that *right* itself, as a universal, has been injured. Right must, therefore, be restored to its proper balance. Revenge is

> . . . transformed into the genuine reconciliation of right with itself, i.e. into punishment. Objectively, this is the reconciliation of the law with itself; by the annulment of the crime, the law is restored and its authority is thereby actualized. Subjectively, it is the reconciliation of the criminal with himself, i.e. with the law known by him as his own and as valid for him and his protection; when this law is executed upon him, he himself finds in this process the satisfaction of justice and nothing save his own act. (p. 73b)

The last notion, that in punishment the criminal is reconciled with himself and that he finds satisfaction in this process, recalls the Kantian notion that punishment is something to which the criminal is entitled and that he is treated as less than a human person if the proper punishment is not meted out to him.

In discussing the procedures of a legal trial, Hegel arrives at some very familiar conclusions. Every accused person has a right to a trial; furthermore, he is entitled to have the proceedings held in full public view. Somewhat surprisingly—in view of Hegel's reputation as an authoritarian and antidemocrat—Hegel also believes in the value of trial by jury. First, he points out that no professional training is required in order to make a judgment of fact. "This is knowledge attainable by any educated man," he writes (p. 74b). He adds that

> . . . judgement on the facts lies in the last resort with subjective conviction and conscience . . . (*Ibid.*)

Secondly, every person has a right or rights arising from his own subjectivity and self-consciousness, *i.e.*, from his own subjective freedom. This right is preserved by a jury trial.

> . . . when a verdict is given on the particular, subjective, and external facts of the case . . . this right is satisfied by the confidence which the parties feel in the subjectivity of those who give the verdict. This confidence is based primarily on the similarity between them and the parties in respect of their particularity, *i.e.* their social position, &c. (p. 74d)

It is this second consideration, this right to subjective freedom, which is the real reason why trial by jury must be maintained, even if from some other point of view adjudication by professionally trained administrators seems superior to dependence on juries.

> It may be the case that if the administration of justice were entirely in the hands of professional lawyers, and there were no lay institutions like juries, it would in theory be managed just as well, if not better. It may be so, but even if this possibility rises by general consent to probability, or even certainty, it still does not matter, for on the other side there is always the right of self-consciousness, insisting on its claims and dissatisfied if laymen play no part. (p. 75a)

III

Is wrong-doing a more serious offense in civil society than under pre-societal conditions?

Hegel answers this question both affirmatively and negatively. In civil society, the principle of right becomes determinate as law. From being immediate and abstract, right passes into something that is embodied in "... the existent will and knowledge of everyone ..." (p. 72b). In civil society, everyone's personality becomes recognized as existing and possessing certain rights; property also achieves legal recognition. Under these circumstances

> ... wrongdoing now becomes an infringement, not merely of what is subjectively infinite, but of the universal thing which is existent with inherent stability and strength. Hence a new attitude arises: the action is seen as a danger to society and thereby the magnitude of the wrongdoing is increased. (p. 72c)

In other words, in civil society an injury done to one person is not confined to that person but rather is an injury to the entire society. This is signified by the fact that, in criminal cases in the United States, the prosecution is made on behalf of "the people"; in Great Britain, the "crown" is the prosecutor.

From the theoretical point of view, therefore, crime is a more serious matter in society than out of it, yet, as a practical matter, crime is not so important.

> ... the fact that society has become strong and sure of itself diminishes the external importance of the injury and so leads to a mitigation of its punishment. (p. 72c)

Before there is society and before right has become law, wrongdoing is punished by personal revenge. Each crime against a person is obviously of the greatest importance to him, since his very being as a man and person is threatened. As a result, personal revenge takes the extreme form, usually of killing. Furthermore, an act of revenge always implies another act of revenge, so that this becomes an endless process, unlike legal punishment.

Hegel contrasts revenge with legal punishment. Does this mean that Hegel thinks that punishment in society does not have a retributive aspect? Does Hegel believe that punishment is only remedial and deterrent in purpose? A little later on, Hegel writes as follows: In society

> ... the injured *universal* ... takes over the pursuit and the avenging of crime, and this pursuit consequently ceases to be the subjective and contingent retribution of revenge and is transformed into the genuine

reconciliation of . . . the law with itself; by the annulment of the crime, the law is restored and its authority is thereby actualized. (p. 73b)

What is the purpose of punishment according to this passage?

Is the philosophy of right a historical science?

As phrased, this question answers itself. Philosophy, according to Hegel, deals with Ideas and hence no branch of philosophy is a historical science. But let us ask the question not with respect to the philosophy of right, but rather with respect to the science of right or the science of law. This, Hegel admits, has a definite historical aspect. Under the conditions of law, the rightful and the legal are the same: ". . . it is the legal which is the source of our knowledge of what is right, or, more exactly, of our legal rights . . . . Thus the science of positive law is to that extent an historical science with authority as its guiding principle" (p. 70d). Furthermore, it is part of the science of positive law to study laws historically; *i.e.*, to study the laws of different countries, their historical change, their applications, their implications, and so on.

Although historical considerations play their part in the science of positive law, history is not to be confused with philosophy. At the end of paragraph 212, Hegel points out that all the historical investigation in the world cannot show why a particular law is rational. That question can be answered only by the philosophy of law, and in a philosophical manner.

Hegel is very willing to give history its due; but he does not want it confused with philosophy. He explains the different tasks of these two disciplines in his Introduction.

To consider particular laws as they appear and develop in time is a purely historical task. Like acquaintance with what can be logically deduced from a comparison of these laws with previously existing legal principles, this task is appreciated and rewarded in its own sphere and has no relation whatever to the philosophical study of the subject—unless of course the derivation of particular laws from historical events is confused with their derivation from the concept, and the historical explanation and justification is stretched to become an absolutely valid justification. This difference, which is very important and should be firmly adhered to, is also very obvious. A particular law may be shown to be wholly grounded in and consistent with the circumstances and with existing legally established institutions, and yet it may be wrong and irrational in its essential character . . . (p. 10c-d)

In the light of these remarks, what do you suppose Hegel's attitude would be toward Montesquieu's *Spirit of Laws*? Would you say that Hegel is more or less historically minded than Kant?

In Hegel's view, is morality a concern of the law?

In the theory of Aquinas, it will be remembered, one of the chief effects of law is to make men virtuous. Any theory of law will, of course, maintain that law is instituted for human welfare, even if it occasionally has unpleasant side effects (such as restraining a man from doing something he wants to do). So in Hegel's theory also, law has a good purpose. But this does not mean that law is instituted for the sake of morality.

In the *Philosophy of Right*, the term "morality" is used in a rather special sense. The Second Part of the book is called MORALITY. The Third Part, in which law is discussed, is called ETHICAL LIFE. These parts, we said earlier, each discuss one of the moments of right. The first moment is right in its purely conceptual form. This is abstract right (the title of the First Part). The second moment is right in its subjective form. This is what Hegel calls morality. The third moment is the unity of the first and the second moment. Ethical life, therefore, is the unity of the abstract and subjective forms of right. This unity is the concrete, determinate existence of right.

Law (which belongs to this third moment) is, therefore, one of the things which supersedes morality. Law cannot contribute to morality, because it replaces it. That is not to say that law denies morality; on the contrary, everything that is good about morality is carried along and concretized in a new way in ethical life.

Morality and moral commands concern the will on its most private, subjective, and particular side, and so cannot be a matter for positive legislation. (p. 71a)

Thus we see the reason why law is superior to morality. Law is objective; it goes far beyond the private and subjective concern of the individual person.

SELF-TESTING QUESTIONS

The following questions are designed to help you test the thoroughness of your reading. Each question is to be answered by giving a page or pages of the reading assignment. Answers will be found on page 239 of this Reading Plan.

1 What is Hegel's view of equity?

2 Does Hegel think knowledge of law and legal procedure should be common or should be restricted to a special professional class?

3 What is the reason for the ceremonies and formalities connected with the law?

4 Hegel is emphatic that trials must be public. Must the deliberations of the judges also be public?

5 What is the objective actuality of right?

6 What are the two aspects involved in a judgment of law?

7 Must the law be promulgated in order to be valid?

Fifteenth Reading

DOSTOEVSKY

The Brothers Karamazov

Book XII, "A Judicial Error"

Vol. 52, pp. 348-401

The reader may be surprised at the inclusion of Dostoevsky in a Reading Plan devoted to philosophy of law and jurisprudence. Dostoevsky is a novelist, not a lawyer. Yet *The Brothers Karamazov* is a better novel than it would otherwise have been because of its accurate portrayal of legal procedures, just as *Moby Dick* gains in interest because Melville was knowledgeable about whales.

Although Dostoevsky did not write a treatise on law, we can nevertheless discern a definite philosophy of law in his novels. Not only *The Brothers Karamazov* but also *Crime and Punishment* and *The Idiot* deal with the themes of human guilt, responsibility, and the need for punishment. Dostoevsky's views on the matter are somewhat paradoxical. He strongly believes that punishment has a salutary effect on the person punished: it brings the person face to face with the consequences of his action and at the same time cleanses him of his guilt. In this connection Dostoevsky does not seem to be greatly concerned with legal guilt and innocence or with legal right and wrong. He attaches greater importance to the person's own view of his guilt or innocence. Most of the characters in his novels have a profound sense of guilt and consequently welcome their punishment.

The attitude of Dostoevsky's characters toward legal penalties may in part reflect Dostoevsky's own experience. He himself, as a young man, was subjected to severe punishment for a crime of which he was not guilty. He was arrested because he belonged to a circle of young men who met to discuss literature as well as the events of the day. The members of the group were accused of treason and, after lengthy imprisonment, were tried, found guilty, and sentenced to be executed. The sentence was read to the young men on the field where they were to be shot; they were blindfolded, and only after all preparations had been completed were they told that the Czar had commuted the sentences. Dostoevsky was sent to Siberia for four years of hard labor. He describes many of his experiences in a work called *The House of the Dead.*

This experience profoundly influenced Dostoevsky. Instead of making him bitter and turning him into the radical he had never been, it increased his conservatism, his devotion to his country, to the Czar, and to Russian Christianity. Dostoevsky is himself the model for those characters in his novels who are purged and bettered by their punishment because it gives them an opportunity to serve humanity through their love. This is what Dostoevsky took to be the great task of the Russian people. At the unveiling of a memorial to Pushkin, Dostoevsky delivered an address which made him famous throughout Russia. Toward the end of it, he uttered the following words:

> Oh, the peoples of Europe have no idea how dear they are to us! And later—in this I believe—we, well, not we but the future Russians, to the last man, will comprehend that to become a genuine Russian means to seek finally to reconcile all European controversies, to show the solution of European anguish in our all-humanitarian and all-unifying Russian soul, to embrace in it with brotherly love all our brethren, and finally, perhaps, to utter the ultimate word of great, universal harmony, of the brotherly accord of all nations abiding by the law of Christ's Gospel![1]

[1] *The Diary of a Writer*, trans. by Boris Brasol. New York: 1954. George Braziller, pp. 979-980.

GUIDE TO

Fifteenth Reading

I

Our assignment comprises the last part (except for the Epilogue) of *The Brothers Karamazov*. It contains the climax of this turbulent novel which is probably Dostoevsky's greatest work. These climactic events take place in a courtroom.

In order to understand the events of the twelfth book, we must briefly outline parts of the entire novel. For a more detailed discussion, we refer the reader to the Seventh Reading in the Reading Plan on Imaginative Literature, Part II. Here we shall confine ourselves to the bare minimum necessary for an understanding of the significance of the trial.

The trial takes place in a Russian provincial town, Skotoprigonyevsk. Fyodor Karamazov, an old, rich, dissolute landowner, has been brutally murdered and robbed. His eldest son, Dmitri ("Mitya"), is accused of the crime. Dmitri has two half-brothers, sons of Fyodor from a second marriage. These brothers are Ivan and Alexey ("Alyosha"). The old man also had a personal servant, Smerdyakov, who was generally believed to be his illegitimate son. Smerdyakov commits suicide on the day before the trial begins.

Much of the trial is taken up with marshalling the evidence that points to Dmitri as his father's murderer. Dmitri appears to have ample motive. Father and son had been rivals for the favor of the voluptuous Agrafena Alexandrovna ("Grushenka"), described at one point as a "provincial hetaira." There is much evidence throughout the earlier part of the novel that Dmitri despises his father and that the father fears the son. Dmitri feels that Fyodor has cheated him out of part of the inheritance due him from his mother's estate. This is especially important because at the time of Fyodor's murder, Dmitri is in desperate need of money.

This need arose as follows: Dmitri is engaged to Katerina Ivanovna, a wealthy young woman. When Katerina and Dmitri first met, their circumstances were quite different. He was then a lieutenant in the regiment whose colonel was Katerina's father. Dmitri found that, because of personal difficulties, the colonel had misappropriated some of the regiment's funds; unless the colonel could restore 4,500 roubles immediately, he faced disgrace and dismissal from the army. Dmitri let it be known that if Katerina would come to him, he would give her the money to save her father. Katerina came to him, and Dmitri, overwhelmed by her noble sacrifice for her father, gave her the money without possessing her. Katerina, in turn, bowed down to the ground before him. A short time later she came into possession of much wealth through the death of her mother, so that at the time of the trial she is a well-to-do young woman. Meanwhile, she and Dmitri have become engaged.

The engagement is a stormy one. Dmitri is by no means ready to forego adventures with other women. His need for money at the time of the old man's murder arises precisely because of this. He has become interested in Grushenka, but his affair with her is handicapped by his lack of funds. Katerina gives Dmitri 3,000 roubles, asking him to send this sum to her sister in Moscow sometime within the next month or two. Instead, Dmitri uses the money to go on a spree with Grushenka.

Fyodor Karamazov, the father, also tries to win the favor of Grushenka. He lets it be known that he has put 3,000 roubles into an envelope, ready to be given to her if she will visit him. On the night of the murder, an old servant of Fyodor's, Grigory, hears a noise outside his master's window. When he investigates, he is set upon by Dmitri and receives a blow on the head with a brass pestle. Dmitri runs away and is next seen with Grushenka in the midst of a wild and drunken spree. Grigory's wife is awakened by moans from Smerdyakov, who is resting in an adjoining room recuperating from an attack of epilepsy. Grigory's wife realizes that her husband is not in bed, goes out to look for him, and finds Grigory, unconscious and bloody. She then runs up to Fyodor Karamazov's house and there discovers him dead. His skull has been crushed by a heavy object; the envelope that contained the money for Grushenka is found torn and empty on the floor near the old man.

II

When the police are called into the case, they at once arrest Dmitri for the murder of his father. All the signs point toward him as the criminal. This is brought out in detail in Book IX, entitled "The Preliminary Investigation" (pp. 235-271). Dmitri has been heard to call himself a murderer; there is blood on his hands and clothing. In vain Dmitri explains that he had thought himself guilty of killing the servant Grigory and that he is greatly relieved to find that Grigory is still alive. (The blood on Dmitri is, of course, Grigory's.) Other damning indications are Dmitri's presence near his father's house, as evidenced by his encounter with Grigory, and the fact that immediately after leaving Fyodor's house, he was again in possession of considerable money, evidently several thousand roubles. Another fact that turns out to be crucial is Grigory's testimony that just before Dmitri hit him, Grigory saw that the door into the Karamazov house was open. This testimony contradicts Dmitri's statement that the door was shut and that in fact Dmitri never entered the house. Dmitri claims merely to have observed his father through a window from the outside. He admits having desired his father's death, but he says his conscience or his better self intervened and stayed his hand.

In the light of the testimony, the jury finds Dmitri guilty. We must admit that the weight of the evidence against him is considerable. Nevertheless, there has been a judicial error. Dmitri did not kill his father. The deed was committed by Smerdyakov.

This fact is made known to the reader in Book XI, Chapter 8. Smerdyakov himself admits that he killed Fyodor Karamazov and tells Ivan how the murder was accomplished. Smerdyakov does not feel, however, that he is really responsible for the murder; he considers himself merely to have been the instrument of Ivan. It was Ivan who really desired his father's death, says Smerdyakov, and so it is Ivan who is guilty of parricide.

Chapters 6, 7, and especially 8, which is called "The Third and Last Interview with Smerdyakov," deal with the theme of Ivan's guilt and responsibility. Curiously enough, it is Smerdyakov, the self-confessed murderer, who plays the role of accuser. Smerdyakov talks very matter-of-factly about his own actions, but he torments Ivan with allusions and direct accusations of complicity. Accordingly, the interview results in such an increase of anxiety and fear for Ivan that he approaches a mental breakdown. He experiences a nightmare in which the Devil visits him. The dream is interrupted by Alyosha who brings the news of Smerdyakov's suicide: he has hanged himself.

Thus the stage is set for the judicial error. Dmitri is convicted of a crime he has not committed. The true murderer, however, cannot be brought to account since he has committed suicide. Nor can it be proved that Smerdyakov murdered Fyodor Karamazov. Smerdyakov had confessed to Ivan, and although Ivan repeats Smerdyakov's words from the witness stand (p. 365a-b), the jury does not believe him, for Ivan does not deliver his testimony as a healthy man would. He gives obvious signs of being highly distraught. Furthermore, Ivan incriminates himself in his testimony. The total effect is that of a man who hardly knows what he is saying, whether he is speaking of himself or of Smerdyakov. Ivan produces in court the 3,000 roubles that Smerdyakov had taken from Fyodor Karamazov.

"I got them from Smerdyakov, from the murderer, yesterday . . . I was with him just before he hanged himself. It was he, not my brother, killed our father. He murdered him and I incited him to do it . . . Who doesn't desire his father's death?"

"Are you in your right mind?" broke involuntarily from the President.

"I should think I am in my right mind . . . in the same nasty mind as all of you . . . as all these . . . ugly faces." . . .

. . . Alyosha jumped up and cried, "He is ill. Don't believe him: he has brain fever." . . .

"Don't disturb yourselves. I am not mad, I am only a murderer," Ivan began again. "You can't expect eloquence from a murderer," he added suddenly for some reason and laughed a queer laugh. (p. 365a-b)

This testimony of Ivan's throws the courtroom into confusion. Finally, the president of the court and Ivan exchange the following words:

> "Witness, your words are incomprehensible and impossible here. Calm yourself, if you can, and tell your story . . . if you really have something to tell. How can you confirm your statement . . . if indeed you are not delirious?"
>
> "That's just it. I have no proof. That cur Smerdyakov won't send you proofs from the other world . . . in an envelope. You think of nothing but envelopes—one is enough. I've no witnesses . . . except one, perhaps," he smiled thoughtfully.
>
> "Who is your witness?"
>
> "He has a tail, your excellency, and that would be irregular! *Le diable n'existe point! . . .*" (p. 365c)

Ivan continues in this manner, but the result is obvious. No one believes him; he is treated like a madman and forcibly removed from the courtroom.

Thus the one man who has heard Smerdyakov confess to the crime fails to make himself believed by the court. If Ivan's testimony accomplished anything, it served to acquit Smerdyakov in the eyes of all those who had heard rumors about him and who might have been inclined to put some stock in them; the rantings of Ivan clearly lack all credibility.

Ivan's failure to shift the burden of accusation from Dmitri to Smerdyakov is followed immediately by an even greater disaster. Now Katerina Ivanovna comes forth with testimony that unmistakably seems to point at Dmitri. In a manner almost as uncontrolled and irrational as Ivan's, she demands to be heard and cries out that she has documentary proof that Dmitri is the murderer of his father.

> The court usher took the document she held out to the President, and she, dropping into her chair, hiding her face in her hands, began convulsively and noiselessly sobbing, shaking all over, and stifling every sound for fear she should be ejected from the court. The document she had handed up was that letter Mitya had written at the Metropolis tavern, which Ivan had spoken of as a "mathematical proof." Alas! its mathematical conclusiveness was recognised, and had it not been for that letter, Mitya might have escaped his doom or, at least, that doom would have been less terrible. (p. 366a-b)

What did this letter contain? Ivan knew its contents, for Katerina Ivanovna had shown it to him when Ivan had come to her feeling distraught after the second visit with Smerdyakov. Smerdyakov's hints and insinuations had begun to take hold of Ivan, who had begun to hold himself responsible for his father's death. (At this time, however, Ivan did not yet know that it was Smerdyakov who had killed the old man.) Ivan paced the room like a madman, muttering self-accusations.

> At last he sat down, put his elbows on the table, leaned his head on his hands and pronounced this strange sentence: "If it's not Dmitri, but Smerdyakov who's the murderer, I share his guilt, for I put him up to it. Whether I did, I don't know yet. But if he is the murderer, and not Dmitri, then, of course, I am the murderer, too."
>
> When Katerina Ivanovna heard that, she got up from her seat without a word, went to her writing-table, opened a box standing on it, took out a sheet of paper and laid it before Ivan. This was the document of which Ivan spoke to Alyosha later on as a "conclusive proof" that Dmitri had killed his father. It was the letter written by Mitya to Katerina Ivanovna when he was drunk, on the very evening he met Alyosha . . . parting from Alyosha, Mitya had rushed to Grushenka. I don't know whether he saw her, but in the evening he was at the Metropolis, where he got thoroughly drunk. Then he asked for a pen and paper and wrote a document of weighty consequences to himself. It was a wordy, disconnected, frantic letter, a drunken letter, in fact. (pp. 327d-328a)

As the reader will remember, Dmitri had been entrusted with 3,000 roubles by Katerina Ivanovna, but had not sent them to her sister, as Katerina had requested. This letter, consequently, contains Dmitri's promise that he will return the 3,000 roubles, and his plans of how to obtain the money:

> FATAL KATYA: To-morrow I will get the money and repay your three thousand and farewell, woman of great wrath, but farewell, too, my love! Let us make an end! To-morrow I shall try and get it from everyone, and if I can't borrow it, I give you my word of honour I shall go to my father and break his skull and take the money from under the pillow, if only Ivan has gone. If I have to go to Siberia for it, I'll give you back your three thousand. And farewell. (p. 328b)

There is much more in the letter, but the sentences above are obviously sufficient to convict Dmitri. It was written two days before the crime was committed, and Katerina received it the day before the murder.

Dmitri confesses in open court that he wrote the letter; Katerina in turn explains why she came forth with this testimony which she had originally withheld. It becomes clear that her motivation is her feeling for Ivan with whom she is in love. She bursts into tears at the end of her testimony. Then Grushenka rushes up and throws her arms around Dmitri, while she wails and hurls accusations at Katerina. "Yes," Dostoevsky writes, "I think the ladies who came to see the spectacle must have been satisfied—the show had been a varied one" (p. 368c).

III

The Brothers Karamazov is a novel of many aspects and faces. It is a novel of passion, of love, of crime, and of lust. It is a detective story, a tract on Russia and its people, a glorification of the Russian monk and his religion. It is also an indictment of the prevailing Russian judicial system, employing the then new device of trial by jury.

The verdict which finds Dmitri guilty of his father's murder is erroneous on two levels. First of all, it is legally faulty, since the crime was committed by Smerdyakov, not by Dmitri. Secondly, it is morally faulty because the crime was desired and made possible by Ivan, not by Dmitri. In fact, Dmitri passed up an opportunity to kill his father. "Whether it was someone's tears, or my mother prayed to God, or a good angel kissed me at that instant, I don't know. But the devil was conquered" (p. 250c).

As a novelist, Dostoevsky is more interested in the second interpretation than in the first. The question that he asks more and more insistently as the novel sweeps toward its climactic end is whether Dmitri, the Russian, the "passionate heart," is really innocent in spite of all his excesses, while Ivan, the Europeanized Karamazov, the intellectual, is guilty of terrible crimes such as blasphemy and parricide.

We are also interested in what the novel reveals concerning the operation of the judicial system. There is reason to think that Dostoevsky was fairly knowledgeable on the subject of investigations and trials. Not only had he himself as a young man been arrested, tried, convicted, and sent to Siberia for treason, but in later years he paid close attention to famous trials. In his *The Diary of a Writer,* a literary journal which he edited and published toward the end of his life, he frequently refers to famous contemporary trials.

For instance, in the issue of February, 1876, Dostoevsky discusses at length the trial of a man named Kroneberg. This man was accused of flogging his seven-year-old daughter so severely and so long that it amounted to torture. This "punishment" was administered because the child had taken a prune that belonged to the woman with whom her father was then living. The child's cries attracted the attention of a stranger who called the police, and thus the case came to trial.

Kroneberg was acquitted. Dostoevsky comments with considerable passion on this verdict. At first, he reports himself as being outraged by it. After some reflection, however, he decides that this was the best verdict. To have found the father guilty, he points out, would have meant sending him to Siberia and leaving the child homeless and without her parent. Hence it is preferable that the father be found guiltless, although in fact Dostoevsky considers him to have acted brutally. At the same time, Dostoevsky comments on the skill of the defense attorney who managed to reshape the events that took place in such a fashion that the jury seemed to think it was the seven-year-old girl who was a criminal and a thief whereas the father was merely a misguided pedagogue.

In this case we see the same mixture of legal and moral principles as in *The Brothers Karamazov.* Dostoevsky apparently thinks that Kroneberg was legally and morally guilty but nevertheless applauds the decision which declares him legally innocent—for the sake of the child who was the victim of the crime. At the same time, Dostoevsky seems to be appalled by the power of the defense attorney to sway the jury by means of his persuasive skill. This power accidentally leads to a result that Dostoevsky considers praiseworthy.

In *The Brothers Karamazov,* the novelist uses his imagination to depict the failings of the judicial system in even more glaring colors. The verdict is legally wrong—Dmitri is innocent. The verdict is morally wrong—Ivan is guilty. Nor is there an ameliorating circumstance as in the actual Kroneberg case; no one is helped by this faulty verdict.

The two opposing attorneys, as they are drawn by Dostoevsky, rival each other in their display of legal talent and oratorical skill. It seems as if the jury will make its decision on the basis of the lawyers' speeches rather than on the evidence. Dmitri's lawyer, Fetyukovitch, speaks last, and here is how Dostoevsky describes the effect of his address:

> . . . Fetyukovitch concluded his speech, and the enthusiasm of the audience burst like an irresistible storm. It was out of the question to stop it: the women wept, many of the men wept too, even two important personages shed tears. The President submitted, and even postponed ringing his bell. The suppression of such an enthusiasm would be the suppression of something sacred, as the ladies cried afterwards. The orator himself was genuinely touched. (p. 398d)

While the jury is out of the courtroom deliberating, the audience discusses the case. They seem convinced that acquittal is inevitable.

> "It would be shameful, disgraceful, not to acquit him!" cried the official. "Suppose he did murder him—there are fathers and fathers! And, besides, he was in such a frenzy. . . . He really may have done nothing but swing the pestle in the air, and so knocked the old man down. But it was a pity they dragged the valet in. That was simply an absurd theory! If I'd been in Fetyukovitch's place, I should simply have said straight out: 'He murdered him; but he is not guilty, hang it all!' " (p. 400d)

Dostoevsky's intent seems to be to show the unreliability of the jury system. By his great oratorical skill, the defense lawyer manages to persuade the audience that Dmitri should be acquitted—even if he is guilty. It is a tribute to the jury, therefore, that they stand firm and find Dmitri guilty, as the evidence clearly indicates they should. The irony, however, lies in the fact that their decision, though in accordance with the facts presented, is faulty. It is dangerous to make sweeping generalizations about a writer as complex as Dostoevsky. Nevertheless, in *The Brothers Karamazov* he is trying to point out that questions of guilt or innocence, justice and responsibility, cannot be solved by such simple human devices as courts and juries.

IV

What are the crucial facts leading to Dmitri's conviction?

Although it was the weight of the total evidence that presumably persuaded the jury of Dmitri's guilt, there are two separate pieces of evidence that must have weighed heavily. One is the drunken letter that Dmitri wrote to Katerina Ivanovna, in which he promises to return the 3,000 roubles to her and swears that he will obtain the money somehow, even if it means murdering his father.

The second piece of evidence has to do with the door into Fyodor Karamazov's house. Dmitri testifies that when he was in the garden contemplating his father's murder, the door into the house was closed. Yet, when Fyodor's body was discovered, the door was found open, as the prosecutor tells Dmitri. (See pp. 250d-251b.) If Dmitri did not open it, somebody else must have done so. And, furthermore, whoever opened the door undoubtedly was the murderer, since the old Karamazov was killed inside the house. "The murder was committed in the room and *not through the window;* that is absolutely certain from the examination that has been made . . ." (p. 251a). In fact, we know that Smerdyakov opened that door. But Grigory, the old servant whom Dmitri had knocked down, steadfastly testified that when he saw Dmitri, he also saw that the door was open. When Smerdyakov discloses to Ivan that he killed Fyodor Karamazov, Ivan naturally asks about Grigory's testimony.

> "Stay," cried Ivan pondering. "What about the door? If he [Fyodor Karamazov] only opened the door to you, how could Grigory have seen it open before? For Grigory saw it before you went." . . .
>
> "As for that door and Grigory Vassilyevitch's having seen it open, that's only his fancy," said Smerdyakov, with a wry smile. "He is not a man, I assure you, but an obstinate mule. He didn't see it, but fancied he had seen it, and there's no shaking him. It's just our luck he took that

notion into his head, for they can't fail to convict Dmitri Fyodorovitch after that." (p. 334b-c)

Thus the two most damning pieces of evidence are brought into the novel almost accidentally by the author. There is no real explanation why Dmitri would write a letter outlining his intention to murder his father, except to say that it was a "drunken letter." And there is even less explanation of Grigory's crucial evidence concerning the open door. All we are told is that although Grigory was mistaken in his notion about it, he persisted in his testimony because of his obstinacy.

Does it seem likely that one judicial proceeding should be influenced by two such fortuitous items? Does this in any way invalidate Dostoevsky's point concerning the ability of courts and juries to arrive at an accurate verdict? Would it be beyond the "reasonable doubt" to which juries are entitled, to assume that Dmitri's letter was simply a piece of drunken bravado and that Grigory's testimony was simply mistaken?

Are the procedures of the Karamazov trial noticeably different from those employed in the courts of the United States and Great Britain?

The differences do not seem very great, but they do exist. We may note that the court consisted of three judges. (See p. 349a.) They are described as ". . . the President, one honorary justice of the peace, and one other" (p. 350c). There is a jury consisting of twelve men. Dmitri is addressed as "prisoner," not as "defendant," and he is not asked how he pleads, but rather "Prisoner, do you plead guilty?" (p. 351d). Both the mode of address and the form of the question would be considered prejudicial in a British or American court. We may perhaps infer that the Russian trial procedure as depicted by Dostoevsky does not start with the presumption of the innocence of the defendant.

Dmitri does not testify in his own behalf. While in English and American procedure the defendant cannot be forced to testify in a criminal action, he may do so and frequently does. In Dostoevsky's account of the trial, there is no indication that

Dmitri might have testified. However, we find that the president of the court asks Dmitri to comment on the testimony of the witnesses called by the prosecutor. This procedure may perhaps be thought to take the place of testimony by the defendant.

In general, does it seem as though the "civil rights" of the defendant are preserved by the court? In the preliminary investigation, statements by Dmitri are taken down. As far as Dostoevsky records it, no warnings are given to Dmitri that his testimony may be used against him, nor does he have the benefit of counsel. During the trial itself, are Dmitri's rights protected? Does the court force the verdict on the jury? Would you say that for its time (the 1870's) the trial was as fair as one which a defendant in the United States or Great Britain would have received?

Is justice served in The Brothers Karamazov?

Obviously not, if we have regard only to commission of a judicial error. But it is entirely probable that Dostoevsky intended to show us that justice had been done—although not through the legal machinery.

In Dostoevsky's view, at least three of the brothers bear various degrees of guilt. The unacknowledged brother, Smerdyakov, carries the most obvious guilt, for he actually killed Fyodor Karamazov. Yet justice is served in his case, for he commits suicide soon afterward. Smerdyakov waits just long enough to enlighten Ivan about the latter's degree of guilt in the crime. Ivan, who is the proud author of *The Grand Inquisitor,* a hymn to human freedom, and who has been heard to say that everything is lawful, now finds himself confronted with the consequences of his philosophical tenets. He admits to himself and to Smerdyakov that he, Ivan, desired his father's death, thereby becoming Smerdyakov's accomplice in the crime by not preventing it. This newly gained self-knowledge drives Ivan to madness—nightmarish encounters with the Devil —and perhaps to death. Dmitri also admits that he desired his father's death. The drunken letter which he wrote shows him capable of contemplating parricide and, in the garden outside his father's house, he still desires his death. But Dmitri is somehow saved—in ways that Dmitri himself does not understand. At the last moment, he does not do what he intended. Consequently, of the three brothers, he is the least guilty. Still, his criminal intent carries enough weight in Dostoevsky's eyes for him to consider it part of justice to condemn Dmitri to twenty years' imprisonment in Siberia. (The novel also contains hints that Dmitri will escape before serving the sentence.)

Of the four brothers, therefore, only Alyosha is innocent. And indeed, the last words of the novel, spoken about Alyosha, are:

"Hurrah for Karamazov!"

SELF-TESTING QUESTIONS

The following questions are designed to help you test the thoroughness of your reading. Each question is to be answered by giving a page or pages of the reading assignment. Answers will be found on page 239 of this Reading Plan.

1 Did the witnesses in the trial swear to tell the truth?

2 How does the defense counsel throw doubt on the validity of Grigory's testimony?

3 What are Dmitri's final words to the jury?

4 The prosecutor compares the course of Russia's history to a galloping troika. How does the attorney for the defense view this figure of speech?

5 Is the verdict accompanied by any recommendations of mercy?

6 According to the medical testimony, were Dmitri's mental faculties functioning normally at the time of the crime?

7 What fact favorable to Dmitri did Alyosha bring up?

8 What does Katerina Ivanovna give as her motive for first concealing and then revealing the "fatal letter" that Dmitri wrote?

9 Whom does Ivan accuse of the crime?

ANSWERS
to self-testing questions

First Reading

1. Cassandra 65a-d
2. 61d-62b
3. 67b
4. 72c
5. 78d-79b
6. 80c
7. 82a-83a
8. 81a, 83c
9. 90c-91b

Second Reading

1. 195b-196b
2. 193a-b
3. 198c-d
4. 643c
5. 683a-b
6. 684c-685a

Third Reading

1. 382b-c
2. 380b-c
3. 384a
4. 384a-385a; 386b-387a
5. 381a
6. 383a-b
7. 382a-b
8. 383d

Fourth Reading

1. Exodus 20:5; Deuteronomy 5:9
2. Exodus 20:19; Deuteronomy 5:22-28
3. Matthew 22:23
4. Romans 7:14-23
5. Romans 8:6-7
6. Exodus 20:24-26
7. Deuteronomy 6:6-9

Fifth Reading

1. Vol. 14, p. 70d
2. Vol. 9, p. 555c; Vol. 14, p. 73d
3. Vol. 9, p. 556c; Vol. 14, p. 71d
4. Vol. 9, pp. 558c-560c; Vol. 14, pp. 75c-76d
5. Vol. 9, p. 565b
6. The Oligarchy of the Thirty; Vol. 9, pp. 568c-570a
7. At Age 20; Vol. 9, p. 572b-d
8. Vol. 9, p. 578a-c
9. Vol. 9, pp. 581d-582b
10. Vol. 9, pp. 583b-584a, c

Sixth Reading

1. 207b
2. 208a
3. 222a-b
4. 225c
5. 224c
6. 207c
7. 206a-b

Seventh Reading

1. 229c-230b
2. 232c-d
3. 239a-b
4. 229a
5. 231c-232b
6. 237a-b

Eighth Reading

1. 95c-d
2. 90c-d
3. 89c
4. 92b-c
5. 137b-c
6. 139b-c
7. 132b-c
8. 133b-c
9. 148b

Ninth Reading

1. 410b-c
2. 416a-417a
3. 418b-c
4. 408a-b
5. 423a-b
6. 427a-b
7. 429d-430b

Tenth Reading

1. 111d
2. 117c-d
3. 1d
4. 102b-104a
5. 114c-115b
6. 120b-c
7. 124c-d

Eleventh Reading

1. 400a
2. 406a-d
3. 398c-d
4. 395d
5. 375c-d
6. 381c-382a
7. 377d
8. 380d-381a

Twelfth Reading

1. 403d
2. 416b-c
3. 414d-415a
4. 419c-420a
5. 424b
6. 423a-c
7. 429d-430a
8. 433b-c
9. 434b
10. 430a-431a

Thirteenth Reading

1. 16d
2. 15b
3. 16a
4. 14b
5. 11d
6. 9a
7. 9c; 16c
8. 16b
9. Amendment Thirteen 18c
10. Amendment Nineteen 19d

Fourteenth Reading

1. 73c-d
2. 75a-b
3. 72b-c
4. 73d
5. 69d-70a
6. 73d-74a
7. 71c-d

Fifteenth Reading

1. 352a
2. 353a-354b
3. 400a-b
4. 384c-d, 398c-d
5. 401c
6. 357b-358b
7. 360b-361b
8. 367b-c
9. 365a-d

ADDITIONAL READINGS

I. Works included in *Great Books of the Western World*

Vol. 5: SOPHOCLES, *Antigone*

7: PLATO, *The Republic*, Books IV and VIII; *Laws*, Books VI, IX-XII

9: ARISTOTLE, *Politics*, Books I, III, IV

12: MARCUS AURELIUS, *Meditations*, Book IV

14: PLUTARCH, *Lycurgus*

18: AUGUSTINE, *City of God*, Book XIX

20: AQUINAS, *Summa Theologica*, Part I-II, QQ. 91-93, 98-108

23: MACHIAVELLI, *The Prince*, Chapter XII

24: RABELAIS, *Gargantua and Pantagruel*, Book III, Chapters 39-44

25: MONTAIGNE, Essays, I. 22

32: MILTON, *Areopagitica*

33: PASCAL, *The Provincial Letters*, V-VIII

35: LOCKE, *A Letter Concerning Toleration; Concerning Civil Government,* Chapters II, VII, IX, XI, XIII, XIX

38: MONTESQUIEU, *The Spirit of the Laws,* Books II-XIII, XVIII, XXVIII, XXX-XXXI

ROUSSEAU, *On the Origin of Inequality; The Social Contract,* Books I, III, IV

42: KANT, *Fundamental Principles of the Metaphysics of Morals; General Introduction to the Metaphysic of Morals; The Science of Right,* Part II

43: HAMILTON, MADISON, and JAY, *The Federalist*
MILL, *On Liberty; Representative Government,* Chapters 5-7; *Utilitarianism,* Chapter 5

46: HEGEL, *The Philosophy of Right*

A. Other works by these authors

AQUINAS, *Summa Contra Gentiles,* Book III, Chapters 111-121, 128-130, 140-146. Translation, *On the Truth of the Catholic Faith.* Book III trans. by Vernon J. Bourke. Garden City, N.Y.: Doubleday and Co., 1956

HOBBES, *Philosophical Rudiments Concerning Government and Society.* In Vol. II, *English Works of Thomas Hobbes.* Ed. by Sir William Molesworth. 2 vols. London: J. Bohn, 1839-1845; *A Dialogue between a Philosopher and a Student of the Common Laws of England.* In Vol. VI, *ibid.; The Elements of Law, Natural and Political.* Ed. by F. Tönnies. Cambridge: Cambridge University Press, 1928

SPINOZA, *Tractatus Theologico-Politicus.* In *Political Works.* Ed. by A. G. Wernham. New York: Oxford University Press, 1958

HUME, *A Treatise of Human Nature.* Book III, Parts I and II. Ed. by L. A. Selby-Bigge, Oxford: The Clarendon Press, 1896

A. SMITH, *Lectures on Justice, Police, Revenue and Arms.* Ed. by E. Cannan. Oxford: The Clarendon Press, 1896

MELVILLE, *Billy Budd.* In *The Portable Melville.* Ed. by Jay Leyda. New York: The Viking Press, 1952

DOSTOEVSKY, *Crime and Punishment.* Trans. by Jessie Coulson. New York: Oxford University Press, 1953

FREUD, *Totem and Taboo.* New York: W. W. Norton & Co., 1952

II. Works by other authors

A. Philosophy of Law

ALLEN, C. K., *Law in the Making.* 6th ed. New York: Oxford University Press, 1958

AMOS, SHELDON, *The Science of Law.* London: Kegan Paul, Trench Trubner & Co., 1909

AUSTIN, JOHN, *Lectures on Jurisprudence or the Philosophy of Positive Law.* 2 vols., revised by Robert Campbell. London: John Murray, 1869

BENTHAM, JEREMY, *A Comment on the Commentaries: Criticism of William Blackstone's Commentaries on the Laws of England.* Ed. by Charles Warren Everett. Oxford: The Clarendon Press, 1928; *A Fragment on Government.* Ed. by F. C. Montague. London: Oxford University Press, 1931; *An Introduction to the Principles of Morals and Legislation.* Oxford: The Clarendon Press, 1907; *The Theory of Legislation.* Ed. by C. K. Ogden. New York: Harcourt, Brace & Co., 1931

BEROLZHEIMER, FRITZ, *The World's Legal Philosophies.* Trans. by R. S. Jastrow. New York: Macmillan Co., 1929

BLACKSTONE, WILLIAM, *Commentaries on the Laws of England*, from the 8th edition, 1778. 4 vols. Ed. by William Hammond. San Francisco: Bancroft-Whitney Co., 1890

BOORSTIN, DANIEL J., *Mysterious Science of the Law*. Boston: Beacon Press Pocketbooks, 1958

BROWN, BRENDAN F., *The Natural Law Reader*. New York: Oceana Publications Inc., 1960

BROWN, WILLIAM JETHRO, *The Austinian Theory of Law*. London: John Murray, 1926

BUCKLAND, WILLIAM WARWICK, *Some Reflections on Jurisprudence*. Cambridge: Cambridge University Press, 1945

CAHN, EDMOND N., *The Moral Decision; Right and Wrong in the Light of American Law*. Bloomington: Indiana University Press, 1955; *Sense of Injustice: An Anthropomorphic View of Law*. New York: New York University Press, 1949

CAIRNS, HUNTINGTON, *Legal Philosophy from Plato to Hegel*. Baltimore: Johns Hopkins Press, 1950

CARDOZO, BENJAMIN N., *The Growth of the Law*. New Haven: Yale University Press, 1924, *The Nature of the Judicial Process*. New Haven: Yale University Press, 1925; *The Paradoxes of Legal Science*. New York: Columbia University Press, 1928

CARPENTER, WILLIAM SEAL, *Foundations of Modern Jurisprudence*. New York: Appleton-Century-Crofts, Inc., 1958

CICERO, *De re publica, De legibus*. Trans. by Clinton Walker Keyes. Loeb Classical Library. New York: G. P. Putnam's Sons, 1928

COHEN, FELIX S., *Ethical Systems and Legal Ideals*. Paperback edition (Great Seal Books). Ithaca, N.Y.: Cornell University Press, 1959

COHEN, MORRIS R., *Law and the Social Order*, New York: Harcourt, Brace and Company, 1933; *Reason and Law*. Chicago: Free Press, 1950

COWAN, THOMAS A. (ed.), *The American Jurisprudence Reader*. The Docket Series. New York: Oceana Publications, Inc., 1960

DAVITT, THOMAS E., *The Nature of Law*. St. Louis: B. Herder Book Co., 1951

DENNING, ALFRED T., *Freedom under the Law*. London: Stevens and Sons, 1949

D'ENTREVES, ALEXANDER PASSERIN, *Natural Law: An Introduction to Legal Philosophy*. London: Hutchinson's University Library, 1951

DUGUIT, LÉON, *Law in the Modern State*. Trans. by F. and H. Laski. New York: B. W. Huebsch, 1919

FRANK, JEROME, *Law and the Modern Mind*. New York: Coward-McCann, 1949

FRIEDRICH, CARL J., *Philosophy of the Law in Historical Perspective*. Chicago: The University of Chicago Press, 1958

GIERKE, OTTO F., *Natural Law and the Theory of Society*. Boston: Beacon Press Pocketbook, 1957

GOODHART, ARTHUR LEHMAN, *English Law and the Moral Law*. London: Stevens & Sons, Ltd., 1953

GRAY, JOHN CHIPMAN, *The Nature and Sources of the Law*. New York: Macmillan Co., 1927

GROTIUS, HUGO, *De Jure Belli ac Pacis*. Classics of International Law Series, Carnegie Endowment for International Peace. Oxford: The Clarendon Press, 1913. Trans. by Francis Kelsey. Oxford: The Clarendon Press, 1925

HAINES, CHARLES GROVE, *The Revival of Natural Law Concepts*. Cambridge: Harvard University Press, 1930

HALL, JEROME, *Studies in Jurisprudence and Criminal Theory,* New York: Oceana Publications, Inc., 1958

HAND, LEARNED, *The Bill of Rights,* Cambridge: Harvard University Press, 1958

HARRISON, FREDERICK, *On Jurisprudence and the Conflict of Laws.* Oxford: The Clarendon Press, 1919

HOCKING, WILLIAM ERNEST, *Present Status of the Philosophy of Law and of Rights.* New Haven: Yale University Press, 1926

HOLMES, OLIVER WENDELL, *Collected Legal Papers.* New York: Harcourt, Brace & Co., 1920; *The Common Law.* Boston: Little, Brown & Co., 1881

HOOKER, RICHARD, *Of the Laws of Ecclesiastical Polity.* Everyman's Library. New York: E. P. Dutton, 1907

JACKSON, ROBERT H., *The Struggle for Judicial Supremacy.* New York: Alfred A. Knopf, 1941

JENNINGS, WILLIAM IVOR (ed.), *Modern Theories of Law.* London: Oxford University Press, 1933

KANTOROWICZ, HERMANN, *Definition of Law.* Cambridge: Cambridge University Press, 1958

KELSEN, HANS, *General Theory of Law and State.* Trans. by A. Wedberg. Cambridge: Harvard University Press, 1945; *What is Justice?* Berkeley: University of California Press, 1957

LAWSON, FREDERICK HENRY, *The Rational Strength of English Law.* London: Stevens & Sons, 1951

LORIMER, JAMES, *The Institutes of Law: A Treatise of the Principles of Jurisprudence as Determined by Nature.* Edinburgh: William Blackwood & Sons, 1880

MARITAIN, JACQUES, *The Rights of Man and Natural Law,* New York: Charles Scribner's Sons, 1943

O'SULLIVAN, RICHARD, *The Inheritance of the Common Law.* London: Stevens and Sons, 1950

POLLOCK, FREDERICK, *Essays in Jurisprudence and Ethics.* London: Macmillan Co., 1882; *Essays in the Law.* London: Macmillan Co., 1922; *The Expansion of the Common Law.* London: Stevens and Sons, 1904

POUND, ROSCOE, *Development of Constitutional Guarantees of Liberty.* New Haven: Yale University Press, 1957; *Introduction to the Philosophy of the Law.* Revised edition, 1954. Paperback edition, New Haven: Yale University Press, 1959; *The Spirit of the Common Law.* Francistown, N.H.: Marshall Jones Co., 1931; *Task of Law.* Lancaster, Pa.: Franklin and Marshall College, 1944

ROMMEN, HEINRICH A., *The Natural Law.* St. Louis: Herder Book Co., 1947

STAMMLER, RUDOLF, *The Theory of Justice.* Trans. by Isaac Husik. New York: Macmillan Co., 1925

SUAREZ, FRANCISCO, *A Treatise on Laws and God the Lawgiver.* Vol. II of *Selections from Three Works of Francis Suarez, S.J.* Ed. by J. B. Scott and trans. by G. L. Williams. Oxford: The Clarendon Press, 1944

TOURTOULON, PIERRE DE, *Philosophy in the Development of Law.* Trans. by Martha M. Read. New York: Macmillan Co., 1922

VECCHIO, GEORGIO DEL, *The Formal Bases of Law.* New York: Macmillan Co., 1921; *Justice: An Historical and Philosophical Essay.* Trans. by Lady Guthrie. New York: Philosophical Library, 1954; *Philosophy of Law.* Trans. by Thomas O. Martin from the 8th edition (1952). Washington: Catholic University of America Press, 1953

VINOGRADOFF, PAUL, *Common-Sense in Law.* New York: Henry Holt and Co., 1914; *Introduction to Historical Jurisprudence.* London: Oxford University Press, 1920

WRIGHT, BENJAMIN FLETCHER, JR., *American Interpretations of Natural Law.* Cambridge: Harvard University Press, 1931

WU, JOHN C., *Fountain of Justice.* New York: Sheed & Ward, 1955

B. Legal Systems and Procedures

BRADY, JOSEPH H., *Confusion Twice Confounded: The First Amendment and the Supreme Court; An Historical Study.* South Orange, N.J.: Seton Hall University Press, 1954

CAHN, EDMOND NATHANIEL (ed.), *Supreme Court and Supreme Law.* Bloomington: Indiana University Press, 1954

DEVLIN, PATRICK, *Trial by Jury.* London: Stevens & Sons, 1956

DICEY, ALBERT VENN, *Law and the Public Opinion in England.* London: Macmillan Co., 1905

DICKINSON, JOHN, *Administrative Justice and the Supremacy of Law in the United States.* Cambridge: Harvard University Press, 1927

ELLIOTT, SHELDEN D., *Improving Our Courts.* New York: Oceana Publications, Inc., 1959

Equal Justice for the Accused. By a Special Committee to study the Defender System of the Association of the Bar of the City of New York and the National Legal Aid and Defender Association. Garden City: Doubleday & Co., Inc., 1959

FRAENKEL, OSMOND K., *The Supreme Court and Civil Liberties.* New York: Oceana Publications, Inc., 1960

FRANK, JEROME, *The Courts on Trial.* Princeton: Princeton University Press, 1949

FREUND, ERNST, *Legislative Regulation.* New York: The Commonwealth Fund, 1932; *Standards of American Legislation.* Chicago: The University of Chicago Press, 1917

GAIUS, *Elements of Roman Law.* Translation and commentary by Edward Poste. Oxford: The Clarendon Press, 1890

HALL, JEROME, *Living Law of Democratic Society*. Indianapolis: Bobbs-Merrill Co., 1949

HOHFELD, WESLEY NEWCOMB, *Fundamental Legal Conceptions*. Ed. by Walter Wheeler Cook. New Haven: Yale University Press, 1932

JUSTINIAN, *The Institutes of Justinian* in *Imperatoris Iustiniani Institutiones*. 2 vols. Translation and commentary by J. B. Moyle. Oxford: The Clarendon Press, 1883

LANDMAN, JACOB HENRY, *The Case Method of Studying Law. A Critique*. New York: G. A. Jennings, 1930

MAGUIRE, JOHN M., *Evidence of Guilt*. Boston: Little, Brown & Co., 1959

MAYERS, LEWIS, *The American Legal System*. New York: Harper & Bros., 1955

MENDELSON, WALLACE, *Justices Black and Frankfurter: Conflict in the Court*. Chicago: The University of Chicago Press, 1961

ST. JOHN-STEVAS, NORMAN, *Life, Death and the Law*. Bloomington: Indiana University Press, 1961

VANDERBILT, ARTHUR T., *Men and Measures in the Law*. New York: Alfred A. Knopf, 1949

WIGMORE, JOHN HENRY, *A Panorama of the World's Legal Systems*. 3 vols. Saint Paul: West Publishing Co., 1928

WILLIAMS, GLANVILLE, *The Proof of Guilt: A Study of the English Criminal Trial*. 2nd edition. London: Stevens & Sons, 1958

C. The History of Law

AMES, JAMES BARR, *Lectures on Legal History*. Cambridge: Harvard University Press, 1913

BONNER, ROBERT J., *Lawyers and Litigants in Ancient Athens*. Chicago: The University of Chicago Press, 1927

CAM, HELEN M. (ed.), *Selected Historical Essays of F. W. Maitland.* Cambridge: Cambridge University Press, 1957

CARTER, JAMES COOLIDGE, *Law: Its Origin, Growth and Function.* New York: G. P. Putnam's Sons, 1907

DIAMOND, ARTHUR S., *Evolution of Law and Order.* New York: Humanities Press, Inc., 1951

HAMBURGER, MAX, *Awakening of Western Legal Thought.* New York: Humanities Press, Inc., 1942

HENSON, RAY D. (ed.), *Landmarks of Law.* New York: Harper & Bros., 1960

HOLDSWORTH, WILLIAM SEARLE, *A History of English Law.* 9 vols. Boston: Little, Brown & Co., 1926

JENKS, EDWARD, *The Book of English Law.* London: John Murray, 1928; *Law and Politics in the Middle Ages.* London: John Murray, 1919

MAINE, HENRY JAMES SUMNER, *Ancient Law: Its Connection with the Early History of Society and Its Relation to Modern Ideas.* New edition. New York: Oxford University Press, 1931

SMITH, MUNROE, *The Development of European Law.* New York: Columbia University Press, 1928

VINOGRADOFF, PAUL, *Roman Law in Medieval Europe.* Oxford: The Clarendon Press, 1929

WARREN, CHARLES, *The Supreme Court in United States History.* 2 vols. Boston: Little, Brown & Co., 1926

D. Great Figures of the Law

ATKINSON, CHARLES M., *Jeremy Bentham, His Life and Work.* London: Methuen, 1905

BEVERIDGE, ALBERT J., *The Life of John Marshall.* 4 vols. Boston: Houghton Mifflin and Co., 1916-1919

Bowen, Catherine D., *The Lion and the Throne; The Life and Times of Sir Edward Coke (1552-1634).* Boston: Little, Brown & Co., 1957; *Yankee from Olympus: Justice Holmes and his Family.* Boston: Little, Brown & Co., 1944

Duff, John J., *A. Lincoln—Prairie Lawyer.* New York: Rinehart & Co., 1960

Howe, Mark de Wolfe (ed.), *The Holmes-Laski Letters.* The correspondence of Mr. Justice Holmes and Harold J. Laski, 1916-1935. Cambridge: Harvard University Press, 1953; *The Holmes-Pollock Letters.* The correspondence of Mr. Justice Holmes and Sir Frederick Pollock. Cambridge: Harvard University Press, 1941

Howe, Mark de Wolfe, *Justice Oliver Wendell Holmes: The Shaping Years, 1841-1870.* Cambridge: Harvard University Press, 1957

Levy, Beryl Harold, *Cardozo and the Frontiers of Legal Thinking.* New York: Oxford University Press, 1938

Lyon, Hastings and Block, Herman, *Edward Coke, Oracle of the Law.* Boston: Houghton Mifflin Co., 1929

Ogden, C. K., *Jeremy Bentham, (1832-2032).* London. Kegan Paul, Trench Teubner & Co., 1932

Seagle, William, *Men of Law: From Hammurabi to Holmes.* New York: Macmillan Co., 1947

Stone, Irving, *Clarence Darrow for the Defense.* Garden City, N.Y.: Doubleday and Co., 1941

Wilkin, Robert N., *Eternal Lawyer: A Legal Biography of Cicero.* New York: Macmillan Co., 1947

E. The Law in Literature

Balzac, Honoré de, *Eugénie Grandet.* Ed. by G. Saintsbury. Trans. by E. Marriage. Everyman's Library. New York: E. P. Dutton, 1907

BOK, CURTIS, *I too, Nicodemus.* New York: Alfred A. Knopf, 1946; *Star Wormwood.* New York: Alfred A. Knopf, 1959

BOTEIN, BERNARD, *The Prosecutor.* New York: Simon & Schuster, 1956

CLARK, WALTER VAN TILBURG, *The Ox-Bow Incident.* New York: Random House, 1940

COZZENS, JAMES G., *The Just and the Unjust.* New York: Harcourt, Brace & Co., 1942

DICKENS, CHARLES, *Bleak House.* Everyman's Library. New York: E. P. Dutton, 1948; *The Posthumous Papers of the Pickwick Club.* Everyman's Library. New York: E. P. Dutton, 1934

HOLDSWORTH, WILLIAM SEARLE, *Charles Dickens as a Legal Historian.* New Haven: Yale University Press, 1928

KAFKA, FRANZ, *The Trial.* Trans. by Edwin & Willa Muir. New York: Alfred A. Knopf, 1937

LONDON, EPHRAIM (ed.), *The World of Law.* 2 vols. New York: Simon & Schuster, 1960

MANKIEWICZ, DON M., *Trial.* New York: Harper & Brothers, 1955

PATRIDGE, BELLAMY, *Country Lawyer.* New York: McGraw-Hill, 1939

RATTIGAN, TERENCE M., *The Winslow Boy.* London: Pan Books, 1950

SHAW, GEORGE BERNARD, *St. Joan.* Baltimore: Penguin Books, Inc., 1960

WARREN, ROBERT PENN, *All the King's Men.* New York: Bantam Books, Inc., 1946